The publisher gratefully acknowledges the generous contribution to this book provided by the Ahmanson Foundation Humanities Endowment Fund of the University of California Press Foundation.

The Magna Carta Manifesto

Four figures, bicycle, and estovers in the garden of the tomb of Humayun, New Delhi. Photo by the author.

The Magna Carta Manifesto

Liberties and Commons for All

Peter Linebaugh

⊞

UNIVERSITY OF CALIFORNIA PRESS

Berkeley   Los Angeles   London

University of California Press, one of the most distinguished
university presses in the United States, enriches lives around the
world by advancing scholarship in the humanities, social sciences,
and natural sciences. Its activities are supported by the UC Press
Foundation and by philanthropic contributions from individuals
and institutions. For more information, visit www.ucpress.edu.

University of California Press
Berkeley and Los Angeles, California

University of California Press, Ltd.
London, England

Library of Congress Cataloging-in-Publication Data

Linebaugh, Peter.
   The Magna Carta manifesto : liberties and commons for all /
   Peter Linebaugh.
      p.   cm.
   Includes bibliographical references and index.
   ISBN 978-0-520-24726-0 (cloth : alk. paper)
      1. Magna Carta.   2. Civil rights.   3. Constitutional history—
United States.   I. Title.

JN147.L56   2008
323.44—dc22   2007025516

Manufactured in the United States of America

16   15   14   13   12   11   10   09   08   07
10   9   8   7   6   5   4   3   2   1

This book is printed on New Leaf EcoBook 50, a 100% recycled
fiber of which 50% is de-inked post-consumer waste, processed
chlorine-free. EcoBook 50 is acid-free and meets the minimum
requirements of ANSI/ASTM D5634–01 (Permanence of Paper).

Michaela Brennan, Amjad Domani, Mike Ferner,
Al Hart, Terry Lodge,

gallant and true

"and she shall have in the meantime her reasonable estovers in the common."

Chap. 7, Magna Carta *(1217)*

Arthur. I am Arthur, King of the Britons.
Woman. King of the who?
Arthur. The Britons.
Woman. Who are the Britons?
Arthur. We all are. We are all Britons. I am your king.
Woman. I didn't know we had a king. I thought we were an
    autonomous collective.

John Cleese, Graham Chapman, Terry Gilliam,
Eric Idle, Terry Jones, and Michael Palin,
Monty Python and the Holy Grail *(1975)*

CONTENTS

ILLUSTRATIONS

PREFACE

Communism was certainly the bugaboo of my cold war childhood when the FBI came knocking at the door and went snooping around the neighborhood. Nevertheless, as I think about it in light of the "fall of Communism" on the one hand and the planetary movement to "reclaim the commons" on the other, elements of the commons have never been far.

As a child in postwar London I explored bombed-out buildings, taking what I pleased with disregard of danger and private property alike. A year or two later on Hampstead Heath I freely collected horse chestnuts in season to marinate for the game of conkers. Once two older boys, Cockneys, took away from me an air pistol I had taken myself from the rubble of a bombed-out building ("finders keepers"). "All right, mate, you want to fight?" Quickly I discovered the philosophy of "easy come easy go," and saved myself a bruising. Such were childhood lessons in the ambiguity of English commoning.

As an American I was "common," which meant I was not part

of the upper branches of the class structure where posh accents, expensive schools, and privilege were the rule. My great aunt Ruth had marched in parades with Civil War veterans: I belonged to a republic that had freed the slaves. Moreover, while I had always known that my paternal grandfather was an Indian lawyer who spoke the languages of the Five Civilized Tribes of Okalahoma, only recently have I learned that he was orphaned at the time when the communal lands of the Oklahoma Indians were privatized and relinquished to white guardians. Later in life when I crossed paths in the Boston Fenway with Governor Michael Dukakis out for his morning "power walk" he turned a neighborly blind eye to my gathering windfalls for my fireplace.

This book began as a pamphlet prepared as a gift to friends from Paris, Chiapas, and Boston in 2002 who were gathered during a winter storm at Christmas dinner in Brooklyn. The Honorable Elizabeth Benjamin sprang to its aid. It was immediately nurtured by Deborah Chasman of *The Boston Review*. Much later it received a respectful hearing at the centennial meeting in Chicago of the Industrial Workers of the World. The Bristol Radical History group (U.K.) provided an Atlantic setting for a discussion of these ideas.

I tried out these ideas at seminars at the University of Puerto Rico, San Juan, at the University of the Witwatersrand in Johannesburg, and at a conference at Sarai, in New Delhi. Micky West and the Braudel Center of SUNY Binghamton, Dave Roediger and Carl Estabrook at a seminar at the University of Illinois at Urbana-Champaign, and Bryan Palmer at the Canadian Historical Association were invaluable interlocutors. My ruminations after these trips were always welcomed by Alexander Cockburn and Jeffrey St. Clair of *CounterPunch*. The esteemed

Gustavo Esteva of the Universidad de la Tierra, Oaxaca, encouraged this work by putting it to use. I thank Jeff Lustig for inviting me to speak on the subject to an exhilarating conference of the California Studies Association.

Manuel Yang and John Little, students at the University of Toledo, accompanied me on road trips in the Midwest searching hither and yon for signs of Magna Carta and commoning. Kate Linebaugh gave steadfast support; Riley Ann Linebaugh provided decisive interpretations of Monty Python. The book owes much to generous conversations with Iain Boal over several years and to his colleagues of Retort. I thank colleagues at Toledo, Stephanie Gilmore and Timothy Messer-Kruse. I thank Staughton Lynd, Vijay Prashad, and Rebecca Solnit for reading and commenting on a complete draft. I was privileged to meet Maria Mies on her way to Seattle in 1999. She, together with George Caffentzis and Silvia Federici, blazed paths I have tried to follow. Massimo de Angelis, Terisa Turner, and Leigh Brownhill have written inspiring works on the same theme.

For answers to queries and helpful comments I thank Anthony Arnove, Antoinette Burton, Tom Chisholm, Steve Colatrella, Harry Cleaver, Brenda Coughlin, Roxanne Dunbar-Ortiz, Nicholas Faraclas, Geoff Field, Jim Fleming, Eric Foner, Paul Gilroy, Dee Dee Halleck, Doug Hay, Ruth Herndon, Steve Hindle, Wythe Holt, Winston James, Peter Jaszi, Lewanne Jones, Chitra Joshi, Joel Kovel, Terry Lodge, Doug Lummis, Mukul Mangalik, David Montgomery, Prabhu Mohapatra, Jeanette Neeson, Michael Ratner, Dave Riker, John Roosa, Sumit Sarkar, Deborah Valenze, Richard Walker, Ken Wark, Kevin Whelan, Bruce Tyler Wick, Peter Lamborn Wilson, and JoAnn Wypijewski. Thanks to James Landman of the American Bar Association and to *MetaMute* magazine. I thank Phoebe Ballard of the University of Toledo for the graphic in chapter nine, and I thank Mark Horan of the Toledo Carlson Library for help with Lexis-Nexis. I thank my editors at the University of California Press: Niels Hooper for unflagging encouragement, Edith Gladstone for peerless copyediting, Rachel Lockman for patience, and Kate Warne for keeping everything on track.

Commoners, all.

CHAPTER ONE

Introduction

[The bourgeoisie] has resolved personal worth into exchange value,
and in place of the numberless indefeasible chartered freedoms,
has set up that single, unconscionable freedom—Free Trade.
    Karl Marx, The Communist Manifesto *(1848)*

In a communiqué from the Lancandan jungle of Central
America Subcomandante Marcos, the spokesman of the revolt of
indigenous people that burst upon the world in 1994, referred to
Magna Carta. The brilliant postmodern revolt of Mexico cited a
tedious premodern source of England in 1215. That reference
prompted this book. To be sure its overall genesis lay within the
emergency posed by the autocratic aggressions of the Bush regime
but what actually prodded me to put pen to paper on this subject
was a mistake in translation, or rather an absence of translation altogether, because in Mexico it so happens everybody calls the constitution the *magna carta.* The semantic error revealed a deeper
truth: indeed, the clue to Magna Carta lay upon the two winds
Marcos described, the wind from above (these are the forces of the

rulers) and the wind from below (these are the forces of the indigenous, the campesinos, and the workers). Marcos explains how the wind from above daily sucks out 92,000 barrels of oil, leaving behind "ecological destruction, agricultural plunder, hyperinflation, alcoholism, prostitution, and poverty," while the wind from below causes the campesinos in Ococingo to cut wood to survive.[1] The *ejido,* or village commons, was destroyed, and its legal protection, Article 27 of the Mexican Constitution, repealed.

The story is repeated around the world.

Nigeria: in the summer of 2003 hundreds of women seized the Chevron Escravos Oil Terminal (*escravos* means slavery in Portuguese). The Americans plan to obtain 25 percent of their oil soon from Africa. Chevron's engineers have widened Escravos River in the Bight of Benin, and this act is destroying the mangrove forest and the village of Ugborodo. Women can no longer hew wood for fuel or draw water for drink. Prostitution is the only "decent-paying job for a woman."[2] Woods, forests, and mangrove are destroyed while propane, gasoline, kerosene are substituted. As a result of this "advance," the people are expropriated.

Vietnam: in the upland hamlets women collect firewood, bamboo shoots, medicinal plants, and vegetables from forest areas. Some of these products are sold locally, most are used directly. Broom

1. "The Demands Submitted by the Zapatistas during the February 1994 Dialogue" refer to Magna Carta. The document is easily accessible on the Internet where Marcos's great speech, "The Southeast in Two Winds: A Storm and a Prophecy," is also found. But see *Zapatistas! Documents of the New Mexican Revolution* (New York: Autonomedia Press, 1994).

2. Norimitsu Onishi, "As Oil Riches Flow, a Poor Village Rises Up," *New York Times,* 22 December 2002.

grass makes charcoal in Trang Tri. Rice and cassava are food staples and both are obtained by *swidden* farming (a Yorkshire dialect term for land that has been cleared by slashing and burning the vegetation cover). Free-range domesticated animals provide sources of protein. The forest reserves have recently been enclosed by metal fence. The women of the hamlets suffer especially.[3]

New York: to the communities of Iroquois Indians and French Canadians in the Adirondacks, the conservation movement of the 1880s meant "the transformation of previously acceptable practices into illegal acts: hunting or fishing redefined as poaching, foraging as trespassing, the setting of fires as arson, and the cutting of trees as timber theft." These inhabitants were charged by state officials with looking upon the forests as "a piece of commons," or as "a public crib where all may feed who choose." The Forest Commission "endeavored to strike terror, as it was, into the people who trespassed in that way."[4]

Ireland: following the despoliations of the plantations and the demographic and settlement history of conquest in the seventeenth century, which destroyed the Gaelic order and denuded the landscape, the Irish lamented,[5]

---

3. Tuong Vi Pham, "Gender and the Management of Nature Reserves in Vietnam," *Kyoto Review of Southeast Asia* (October 2002).

4. Karl Jacoby, *Crimes Against Nature: Squatters, Poachers, Thieves, and the Hidden History of American Conservatism* (Berkeley: University of California Press, 2001), 2, 50.

5. Roy Tomlinson, "Forests and Woodlands" in *Atlas of the Irish Rural Landscape,* ed. F. H. A. Aalen, Kevin Whelan, and Matthew Stout (Cork: Cork University Press, 1997), 122.

> What shall we do without timber
> The last of our woods is gone?

The woods were the location of visions, or the *aisling,* and of the *fiana,* or the defenders of Ireland. Hence the conquerors cut them down. It is a lament of early modern history, partially answered in modern times by the coal mine, then the oil pump, for these were truly the three ages of history, at least if you divide it up according to hydrocarbon energy sources—wood, coal, and oil.

India: Akbar the Great accounted the cutting down of forests a major achievement of his advance into Kashmir. The colonial government of Britain just took over the *dharma khandams,* or community common lands, and asserted its control over collection of fuel, leaf manures for composting, and wood for agricultural implements.[6] A huge rise in wood thefts preceded the national upsurge of 1919–20. A nationalist song from the time asks,

> Three hundred years back
> Company man descended
> You have kept quiet
> He robbed the whole nation
> He claims all forests are his
> Did his father come and plant?

6. Atluri Murali, "Whose Trees? Forest Practices and Local Communities in Andhra, 1600–1922," in *Nature, Culture, Imperialism: Essays on the Environmental History of South Asia,* ed. David Arnold and Ramachandra Guha (Delhi: Oxford University Press, 1995), 97. See also Ramachandra Guha, *The Unquiet Woods: Ecological Change and Peasant Resistance in the Himalaya* (Berkeley: University of California Press, 1989).

The Amazon: from the sixties until today the entire region has been convulsed by an enormous enclosure movement. The bulldozer and the chain saw led the attack. The workers and Indians fought back. In 1976 they came up with the *empate,* or "standoff."[7] The struggle is old. The teacher of young Chico Mendes of the rubber tappers' union worked with Carlos Prestes, the revolutionary of the 1920s and 1930s. It is old and it is transatlantic: the Forest People's Manifesto of 1985 has been compared to Winstanley and the Diggers, whose defense of the English forest commons we discuss in chapter four.

From such stories three tendencies emerge. First, as an aspect of the recent enclosures, planetary woodlands are being destroyed in favor of commercial profit.[8] Second, petroleum products are substituted as the base commodity of human reproduction and world economic development. Third, indigenous people worldwide—commoners all—are expropriated. Michael Watts has dubbed "petro-violence" the terror, dislocation, separation, poverty, and pollution associated with petroleum extraction.[9] War intensifies these tendencies. In Iraq the petroviolence of the Basra oil field has exterminated the commoning ecology of "the people of the reeds," the so-called Marsh Arabs.

7. Susanna Hecht and Alexander Cockburn, *The Fate of the Forest: Developers, Destroyers and Defenders of the Amazon* (London: Verso, 1989).

8. See particularly Midnight Notes, *Midnight Oil, Work, Energy, War, 1973–1992* (New York: Autonomedia, 1992), 303–33.

9. Michael Watts, "Petro-Violence: Community, Extraction, and Political Ecology of a Mythic Commodity," in *Violent Environments,* ed. Michael Watts and Nancy Peluso (Ithaca: Cornell University Press, 2001), 189–212.

The indigenous voice from the Lancandan rainforest suggests that Magna Carta concerns both juridical rights of the accused and the extraction of hydrocarbon energy resources. How can this be? Marcos is right. There were two charters forced on King John at Runnymede. Beside the great charter with which we are all vaguely familiar, there was a second charter known as the Charter of the Forest. Whereas the first charter concerned, for the most part, political and juridical rights, the second charter dealt with economic survival. Historians have always known the Charter of the Forest existed but many of its terms—for example, *estovers*,[10] or subsistence wood products—seem strange and archaic, and have prevented the general public from recognizing its existence and understanding its importance. The message of the two charters and the message of this book is plain: political and legal rights can exist only on an economic foundation. To be free citizens we must also be equal producers and consumers. What I shall call the *commons*—the theory that vests all property in the community and organizes labor for the common benefit of all— must exist in both juridical forms and day-to-day material reality.

In the pages that follow I employ four kinds of interpretation of Magna Carta, documentary, legal, cultural, and constitutional. First, the *documentary* interpretation introduces significant emendations to the charter of 1215, such as "widow's estovers," along with the entire Charter of the Forest. They lead to the concept of the commons, which is grasped as an anchor of hope in the storm. The recovered charter and its addition was confirmed on 11 September in the year 1217, as chapter two shows.

---

10. Italicized archaic or technical terms are explained in the glossary.

Second, I trace the *legal* interpretation largely in chapter eight, in the history of the United States via the interpretations of chapter 39 and habeas corpus, trial by jury, prohibition of torture, and due process of law, which all are derived from it.

The third type of interpretation is *cultural*. It takes as its evidence music, murals, theater, painting, architecture, and sculpture. Sometimes these representations can be iconic or quasi-sacral. They have easily led to chauvinism and to barely concealed notions of racial superiority whose origins are described in chapters four and five.

Fourth, Magna Carta has a *constitutional* history, arising from its character as an armistice between belligerent powers, and as a treaty concluding rebellion. Magna Carta expressed a deal between church and state, barons and king, city merchants and royalty, wives and husbands, commoners and nobles. It was the proud product of rebellion. The U.S. Declaration of Independence of 1776 was the result of Tom Paine's suggestion for an American magna carta. In May 2006 the British people, when polled, preferred that a Magna Carta day become the national day.[11] Chapters eleven and twelve attempt to renew this interpretation.

If Magna Carta is to be recovered in its fullness, we must bring with it all that can be obtained from these interpretations. The first one calls for the abolition of the commodity form of wealth that blocks the way to commoning. The second one gives us protection from intrusions by privatizers, autocrats, and militarists. The third one warns us against false idols. The fourth renews the right of resistance. In the 1620s Edward Coke, Speaker of the House of

11. "Magna Carta Date Tops Poll as Best Choice for a National Day," *The Guardian,* 30 May 2006.

Commons and attorney general, provided the interpretations of these charters that paved the way for the English revolution of the 1640s. In 1759 William Blackstone, the magisterial Oxford professor of law, provided the scholarship of Magna Carta that helped prepare the mind for the American revolution of the 1770s. To them the "Great Charters of the Liberties of England" formed a unified instrument of law. This book explores that unity. The first three chapters present a problem, the middle six chapters tell the history, and the last three chapters indicate materials for a solution.

Rather than the separation of economic or social rights and civil or political rights that is familiar to us from the United Nations' Declaration of Human Rights (1948) and its Covenant on Economic, Social and Cultural Rights (1966), in the two charters political rights in restricting autocratic behavior paralleled common rights in restoring subsistence usufructs (goods or usages required for well-being). Thus the charters limited expropriations, as with honey, the common sweetener.[12] The 13th chapter

---

12. The Elizabethan exchequer decreed against usurped customs and loss of "windfall wood, rootfall trees, and inbowes," where these latter were defined "also only to so much thereof as the bees do light on, and the honey that shall be found in the tree, but not to cut any main bough or tree itself by color thereof." Percival Lewis, *Historical Inquiries concerning Forests and Forest Laws with Topographical Remarks upon the Ancient and Modern State of New Forest* (London: T. Payne, 1811), 186. See also Clarence J. Glacken, *Traces on the Rhodian Shore: Nature and Culture in Western Thought from Ancient Times to the End of the Eighteenth Century* (Berkeley: University of California Press, 1967), 322.

The complete text of both Magna Carta and Charter of the Forest may be found in the appendix. Over the centuries there have been many English translations from the Latin, and so readers will find slight inconsistencies of spelling and wording.

of the Charter of the Forest states, "Every freeman may in his own woods have eyries of hawks, sparrow hawks, falcons, eagles, and herons; and he may also have honey that is found in his woods."

That was the thirteenth century. In the nineteenth century the Forest Bill of India (1878) was objected to because "the powers proposed to be given to the police are arbitrary and dangerous, arrest without warrant of any person suspected of having been concerned at some unknown time of being concerned in a forest offence (taking some wild bee's honey from a tree or skin of any dead animal)."[13] In twentieth-century Kenya, Karai Njama, a peasant in the independence struggles, remembered family expropriations. "One day I was sitting down on our homestead lawn when my grandfather pointed to a small hill in the middle of the forest just above the juncture of the Gura River and the Charangatha River and asked me, 'My grandson, do you see that hill?' 'Yes, grandfather,' I replied. 'That is where I used to hunt before the arrival of the *Chomba*—the European. That hill is still called Karari's Hill. If you went there, you could see my cooking pots in my cave. I have many beehives on that hill which would yield a lot of honey.... Oh! My beloved beehives will rot there.'"

In the cries of Njama's grandfather we do not hear "the tragedy of the commons," as the title of an influential essay by the American sociobiologist Garrett Hardin (1915–2003) puts it. His biological and mathematical arguments concluded, "Freedom in a commons brings ruin to all" and "injustice is preferable to total ruin." Hardin's premise depends on absolute egoism and denies several millennia of experience in the mutuality and negotiation

13. D. Brandis, *Memorandum on the Demarcation of the Public Forests in the Madras Presidency* (Simla, 1878).

of commoning.[14] If anything, we hear the cries of the victim of theft.

In 2004 the Nobel Peace Prize was awarded to Wangari Maathai of Kenya, who led the grassroots Green Belt Movement to plant thirty million trees for subsistence—wood fuel, fencing, and building—to restore a forest ecology, to prevent Kenya from becoming a dried-out desert. The spirit was expressed in the word *harambee,* meaning "let us all pull together!" At each tree planting the community committed itself to preserving for future generations "the bounty which is the birthright and property of all."[15]

The robbery of the honey and the robbery of our safety, the robbery of commoning and the taking of liberties, have gone hand in hand. How are subsistence rights related to civil rights that protect us against detention without trial?

Subcomandante Marcos asked us to remember the *ejido* of the Mexican Constitution in the struggle against neoliberalism. This voice from the Lancandan rainforest in Chiapas caused me to ask: what does the Magna Carta actually say? While I was thinking this over in the summer of 2001, the movements summed up by the slogans "The world is not for sale" and "Reparations!" were checked by the police murder of Carlos Giuliani among the demonstrators in Genoa, Italy, and by the withdrawal of the United States from the UN conference on racism convened in Durban, South Africa. A week later hijacked airplanes were flown into the twin towers of the World Trade Center and the

14. Garrett Hardin, "The Tragedy of the Commons," *Science* 162 (1968): 1243–48.

15. Wangari Maathai, *The Green Belt Movement: Sharing the Approach and the Experience* (New York Lantern Books, 2004), 20–21.

Pentagon. President Bush then announced the endless "war on terror," which he compared to the Second World War, though in summarizing its goals (the four freedoms) he failed to mention freedom from want and freedom from fear.

With the assault on Mesopotamia in 2003 came the imposition of neoliberalism—free trade, unrestricted profiteering, and the infamous Order no. 39 privatizing the public enterprises of Iraq. Parallel to this infamy were the losses of liberties derived from Magna Carta's forgotten chapter 39: habeas corpus has suffered particularly, trial by jury has suffered attack, the prohibition against torture wilts, due process of law is lost in Guantánamo.

President Bush is not the only one who has forgotten his history lessons. We British historians have not done our job. Both neoconservative historians as well as feminists, critical legal theorists, social and economic historians have been derelict, ignoring Magna Carta and thus laying the groundwork of forgetting. As for the commoning provisions in the Charters of Liberties, they have been ignored as out-of-date feudal relics. The argument of this book says their time has come.

Neoliberalism is an economic doctrine of globalization and privatization that depends on police regimes of security and privatization. It came into being as Margaret Thatcher and Ronald Reagan came to power, in 1979 and 1980. Accompanying the privatization and marketeering of neoliberalism was its historically inseparable sidekick, neoconservativism, which provided the police and the military. Postmodernism is an aesthetic and cultural style characterized by irony, eclecticism, high speeds, epistemological subjectivity (hence its compatibility with "identity politics"), and the refusal to accept a unity in history. Excluded from both the economic policies of neoliberalism and the cultural politics of postmodernism were the actual planetary shifts of the 1990s—the planetary migrations, the new enclosures, the feminization of poverty, the development of precarious labor, and neoslavery. Margaret Thatcher had said "there is no alternative." Magna Carta seemed nothing more than an archaic element in an obsolete "grand narrative." In 1999 it seemed that postmodernism and neoliberalism reached a turning point in Seattle, where diverse movements challenged the "intellectual property" discussions of the World Trade Organization.

This was the context of the Stansky report, named after the chair of the committee that drafted the "Report on the State and Future of British Studies in North America." The report was issued in 1999 and its recommendations and its omissions bear the marks of neoliberalism and postmodernism. On the one hand, it is a guild document defending British history as an old but disappearing part of the American university curriculum. On the other hand, it must explain the fashionable anglotude of the Anglo-American relationship. After all, English glamour dusts the high seats of power with its charms and fairy crystals: a president who was knighted at Buckingham Palace, another president an Oxford student and surrounded by Rhodes scholars, an American republic that adores an English princess, and two leaders who really resemble running dogs of imperialism, pit bull and poodle. "We need to demonstrate that the history of Britain is not merely an 'island story,' but indeed a world story," the report continues. "British history used to flourish because it was consistent with what a lot of undergraduates and/or their parents wanted from a college education, a familiarity with the Western tradition but also helping their child succeed in later life. The decline of those particular values has hurt the popularity of British studies."[16]

The concept here of "Western tradition" is unthought out and carries crusading overtones that are sinister or stupid.[17] As for "particular values," these are completely unmentioned. The birthplace of democracy? The home of liberty? The rule of law? The free press? Habeas corpus? Trial by jury? Religious toleration? The commonwealth? Yes, we have known these as the politician's sham, and when we heard them we have suspected guff, humbug, or "bourgeois rights," but that is not reason to discard them. Let us look again. While the decline of habeas corpus, the cooperative values of the commons, the erosion of trial by jury *may have* hurt the popularity of British studies, they have *certainly* hurt the people of the planet.

There have been several moments when these "particular values" have had to be particularized, such as during the 1790s when the American Bill of Rights was drawn, or the Putney debates during the English Revolution, another such time of particularizing, or in 1940 when England stood alone against Nazi imperialism. Certainly 1215 was also a time when such values were particularized. Had we been in the habit of particularizing

---

16. See www.nacbs.org/report.html. See also Antoinette Burton, "When Was Britain? Nostalgia for the Nation at the End of the 'American Century,'" *Journal of Modern History* 75 (June 2003). The journals in England of social history, *History Workshop* or *Past and Present,* have published little on the Charters of Liberties.

17. Silvia Federici, ed., Enduring Western Civilization: The Construction of the Concept of Western Civilization and Its "Others" (Westport: Praeger, 1995).

these values we would not be detaining people without trial, starving them to make them talk, invigilating their expressions of worship, "abusing" them in torture chambers, or looking for "our" oil under "their" soil by bombing the daylights out of them.

The reason given for the decline is this. The collapse of the Soviet Union and the apparent defeat of Communism in 1990 pulled the rug of relevancy out from under all disciplines that had depended for their rhetorical thrust on proving or disproving Marxist paradigms. Marx was a British social historian whose study of the length of the working day in Britain and Ireland, whose analysis of the *division of labor,* whose account of the mechanization of work, whose studies of the recomposition of the proletariat, and whose understanding of expropriation from the commons form the basis of the analysis of capitalism. These provide five gateways to the continuing relevance of his ideas. They open on to themes such as the charter's call for "widow's estovers" or the charter's provision for subsistence in the commons.[18]

The failure to preserve the memory of Magna Carta's liberties became clear to me in an unexpected way in the case of Maher Arar, a Canadian software engineer and father of two, who on returning from holiday via a U.S. airport was detained in September 2002 by U.S. authorities who shackled, chained, and blindfolded him, placed him in a cell with no bed but with permanent lighting, and prevented him from contacting family or lawyer before secretly "rendering" him to Syria where he was imprisoned for twelve months in a cell measuring three feet by

---

18. Maria Mies and Veronika Bennholdt-Thomsen, *The Subsistence Perspective: Beyond the Globalised Economy,* trans. Patrick Camiller, Marie Mies and Gerd Wieh (New York: Zed Books, 1999).

six feet by seven and repeatedly beaten by a length of shredded electrical cable. His was the first civil suit against the practice of "extraordinary rendition." In 2005 the U.S. government defended the practice by asserting the privilege of "state secrets." The senior trial lawyer for the government was known to me as a child thirty-four years earlier when I worked with her parents in hopeful causes such as the reform of prisons in the aftermath of the massacre at Attica, such as bringing the troops home from war in Vietnam, or the cause of democracy in the coal miners' union of eastern Kentucky.

Although we in the prison movement, the peace movement, and the workers' movement struggled against racial oppression and class exploitation, we never did so based on Magna Carta. Nor did we pass on knowledge of the 1679 Habeas Corpus Act whose full title, "An Act for the better securing the liberty of the subject, and for the prevention of imprisonments beyond the seas," applies directly to the shameful practices known euphemistically as "extraordinary rendition." Nor were we familiar with America's magna carta, the 1776 Declaration of Independence, which enumerates twenty-seven reasons for declaring independence from England, one of which castigates King George III for permitting legislation to be passed "for transporting us beyond the seas to be tried for pretended offences." We did not pass on this knowledge, as we did not have it ourselves, hence the apple fell far from the tree. Nevertheless, it is immoral to leave such errors against Maher Arar unrefuted.

Three champions from both sides of the Atlantic have carried the standard of Magna Carta into the lists of the powerful. The first is Ian Macdonald, QC, who in December 2004 resigned from the U.K.'s Special Immigration Appeals Commission. "You lock people up indefinitely, and that's such a dangerous inroad into part of the cultural tradition of the UK. It goes back to Magna Carta."[19] The *cultural* tradition of the Charters of Liberties have been perverted, as I show in chapters nine and ten.

The second champion spoke up in England's Parliament, which on 16 December 2004 ruled that Prime Minister Blair's detention of terrorism suspects without trial under the Anti-terrorism, Crime and Security Act of 2001 (the English equivalent to the U.S. Patriot Act), was incompatible with the human rights stated in the European Convention on Human Rights, and thus illegal.[20] The detained suspects were freed. In the House of Lords Lord Hoffman explained that this was the most important case Parliament had faced in years. "It calls into question the very existence of an ancient liberty of which this country has until now been very proud: freedom from arbitrary arrest and detention." He concluded, "the real threat to the life of the nation . . . comes not from terrorism but from laws such as these." In his argument we hear echoes of Col. Rainborough at a turning point in the English Revolution in October 1647—"I should doubt whether he was an Englishman or no, that should doubt of these things"—who continued wondering whether the poorest he or she had a life to live as the greatest he or she and whether consent was a condition of government, and if not, whether obedience to government was binding. The social contract has been violated.

The third champion of Magna Carta is Michael Ratner, president of the Center for Constitutional Rights (CCR), which initi-

---

19. "QC for Detainees Quits over Terror Law," *The Guardian,* 20 December 2004.

20. *Parliamentary Debates,* Lords, 5th ser., vol. 56 (2004).

ated the litigation since 2001 against the draconian actions of the U.S. government. The CCR took the Guantánamo cases that challenged indefinite detentions, torture, and disappearances, or renditions. The CCR obtained victory in the Supreme Court in June 2004 in *Rasul v. Bush,* in which Justice Stevens, writing for the majority of the Court, stated: "Executive imprisonment has been considered oppressive and lawless since John, at Runnymede, pledged that no free man should be imprisoned, dispossessed, outlawed, or exiled save by the judgment of his peers or by the law of the land (*Shaughnessy v. United States,* 1953)." By coincidence, at the time of this court decision I was in Runnymede inspecting the lovely field (only a bus ride from Heathrow Airport), where I found a peculiar distortion in the meaning of Magna Carta (I discuss it in chapter 9). On a little granite plinth in a star-studded columned rotunda were carved the words FREEDOM UNDER LAW. Ratner again, "We must continue fighting for core values, for human rights and for *authority under law.* This is about Magna Carta."[21]

Ratner said that when he joined the CCR in 1972, he looked at law as an agent for social change, and that to defend "basic constitutional law and very basic, fundamental human rights" as he was doing thirty-four years later has been "a big shift." As Macdonald remarked in the *Guardian* interview, "If anyone had told me 20 years ago that fighting for the rights in Magna Carta or the rule of law would be seen as revolutionary behavior, I would have laughed." The big shift can lead back to the

---

21. Michael Ratner, "From Magna Carta to Abu Ghraib: Detention, Summary Trial, Disappearances and Torture in America," the Clara Boudin Lecture, City College of New York, spring 2005.

beginning, because the Charters of Liberties sought to preserve social and economic rights. Likewise, the revolutionary behavior that Macdonald referred to also belongs to Magna Carta, which was the result of rebellion and civil war. Not only have apples fallen far from the tree, the orchard has been infiltrated by multiple pests.

Both Macdonald and Ratner had their legal baptism in the struggle of people of color to participate equally in British and American society without police brutality. In the case of Macdonald the issue was immigration from the anglophone Caribbean; in the case of Ratner it concerned the civil rights movement. The history of Magna Carta is intertwined with the struggle against slavery, and in the history of the Western Hemisphere the question of slavery is inseparable from the continent of Africa, as I show in chapter six. Magna Carta has been essential to the black freedom struggle.

Most of the appellants to the House of Lords case where Lord Hoffman waxed eloquent about the English nation were non-nationals from North Africa. His colleague Lord Bingham continued, "Habeas corpus protection is often expressed as limited to 'British subjects.' Is it really limited to British nationals? Suffice it to say that the case law has given an emphatic 'no' to the question." He then cited Lord Mansfield's decision in the Somerset case (1772) to establish the principle that "every person within the jurisdiction enjoys equal protection of our laws." We see this in a curious way in English heraldry. St. George, the patron saint of England, was from Palestine. His legendary slaying of the dragon was said to have taken place in Libya. The English flag, the Union Jack, is based on the red cross of St. George. In 1222

St. George's Day was set as 23 April. The symbols of the English nation go back to Magna Carta and North Africa.[22]

Does history advance? It may, but we know it also goes backward. The age of the law enhances its importance, but the antiquity of a tradition suggests that it is out of date. The appeal of the modern pulls against the veneration of the old. We tend to think that ideas, like law or religion, depend on the mode of production of a given society; we are not used to considering them as invariables in the midst of technological changes and massive material production. We need a philosophy of history. Neither neoliberalism nor postmodernism can provide it, as they are so attached to the new with its attendant forgetting.

The American sociologist C. Wright Mills advised making "trans-historical constructions." He continued, "Examine in detail little facts and their relations, and big unique events as well. But do not be fanatic: relate all such work, continuously and closely, to the level of historical reality. Do not assume that somebody else will do this for you, sometime, somewhere. Take as your task the defining of this reality; formulate your problems in its terms; on its level try to solve these problems and thus resolve the issues and the troubles they incorporate."[23] What is the "level of historical reality" if not the suppressed praxis of the commons in its manifold particularities, despite a millennium of privatization, enclosure, and utilitarianism?

22. Hippolyte Delehaye, *The Legends of the Saints,* trans. V. M. Crawford (New York: Longmans, Green, 1907), 190, 212.

23. C. Wright Mills, *The Sociological Imagination* (New York: Oxford University Press, 1959).

One aim of this book is to put the commons back on the agenda of the political constitution. As an economic issue, the commons seems pie-in-the-sky, but scholarly scrutiny shows that on the contrary it is down-to-earth. Another aim is addressed to the world's commoners to say that we must begin to think constitutionally, as already is the case in Venezuela, Bolivia, and Mexico. Magna Carta is radical, near the root of the constitution, yet the root of Magna Carta presupposes the commons. In October 2006 Maher Arar accepted the Letelier-Moffitt Human Rights Award from the Institute of Policy Studies, concluding that what keeps him going is "the hope that one day our planet Earth will be free of tyranny, torture, and injustice."

CHAPTER TWO

Two Charters

What are thou Freedom?

Thou are not, as imposters say,
A shadow soon to pass away,
A superstition, and a name
Echoing from the cave of Fame.

For the labourer thou art bread,
And a comely table spread.
From his daily labour come
To a neat and happy home.

Thou art clothes, and fire, and food
P. B. Shelley,
The Masque of Anarchy (1819)

For eight centuries Magna Carta has been venerated. "It was born with a grey Beard," Samuel Johnson said. The Massachusetts Body of Liberties (1641), the Virginia Bill of Rights (1776), the Fifth and Fourteenth Amendments to the U.S. Constitution quote its language.[1] The story of the political and legal rights is known. Indeed it is too well known, inasmuch as it is remembered largely as myth and as icon, as part of the foundation of Western civilization. In 1956 Winston Churchill published the first volume of his *History of the English-Speaking Peoples* in which he glorified Anglo-American "brotherhood," "destiny," and empire by reverent references to childhood memories of Magna Carta.[2]

Magna Carta puts an emergency brake on accelerating state despotism. The handle for the brake is chapter 39. The British human rights barrister Geoffrey Robertson writes, "The appearance of 'rights' as a set of popular propositions limiting the sovereign is usually traced to Magna Carta in 1215, although that document had nothing to do with the liberty of individual citizens: it was signed by a feudal king who was feuding with thuggish barons, and was forced to accede to their demands."[3] There is no evidence that King John could write. Besides, we must ask *who* traces rights to Magna Carta? There is a conservative interpretation restricting it to the elite, and there is a popular interpretation that includes free people and commoners.

Robertson continues, Magna Carta "contained some felicitous phrases which gradually entered the common law and worked

---

1. On Magna Carta's influence see Alan Harding, *A Social History of English Law* (Baltimore: Penguin Books, 1966), 55.

2. Winston Churchill, *The Birth of Britain,* vol. 1 of *A History of the English-Speaking Peoples* (New York: Dodd, Mead, 1956), vii, xvi.

3. Geoffrey Robertson, *Crimes Against Humanity: The Struggle for Global Justice* (New York: New Press, 1999), 2–3. See also Anne Pallister, *Magna Carta: The Heritage of Liberty* (Oxford: Clarendon Press, 1971).

their rhetorical magic down the centuries." To call "the felicitous phrases" magic is to overlook the struggle in the streets and fields, the struggle in the prisons, the struggle in the slave ships, the struggle in the press, the struggle in parliament. The historian Simon Schama blithely waves a magic wand, "But for once, England didn't want an Arthur. It had Magna Carta instead. And that, it was hoped, would be Excalibur enough." Monty Python explains.

ARTHUR: I am your king.

WOMAN: I didn't know we had a king. I didn't vote for you.

ARTHUR: People don't vote for king.

WOMAN: How did you become king?

ARTHUR: The Lady of the Lake. Her arms clad in the purest shimmering samite held aloft Excalibur from the bosom of the water signifying by divine authority that I, Arthur, was to carry Excalibur. That is why I am your king.

MAN: Listen. Strange women lying in ponds distributing swords is no basis for a system of government. Supreme executive power derives from a mandate from the masses, not from a farcical aquatic ceremony.

ARTHUR: Be quiet.

MAN: You can't expect to wield supreme executive power just because some watery tart threw a sword at you.

ARTHUR: Shut up.[4]

In the middle of June 1215, on a meadow, Runnymede, along the river Thames the rebellious barons and King John promised

---

4. Simon Schama, *A History of Britain: At the Edge of the World* (New York: Hyperion, 2000), 65. John Cleese et al., *Monty Python and the Holy Grail* (1975).

on oath to be faithful to one another along the lines of the sixty-three chapters of Magna Carta. Behind the event lay powerful forces of pope and emperor, dynastic intrigues of France and England, wicked deeds of pogrom and bigotry in the name of God Almighty, the disintegrating effects of the money economy, and the multifaceted popular defense of the commons.

As we assess the experience of the long twelfth century (culminating in 1215), what strikes us is the similarity of global debates with our own in the twenty-first century. In the summer of 2001 it was the call for reparations for the racist exploitation of Africa and the insistence at a mass gathering in Genoa that "another world is possible," which preceded the "war on terror" so often compared to a modern crusade. Islam replaced Communism as the demonized Other in the ideology of the ruling class. The genesis of capitalist society has been pushed back to the Middle Ages, when communistic heretical movements and Islam were the main threats to church and king.[5]

The Crusades were military diversions from the social and economic conflicts within Europe. Pope Urban II made this clear in his Clermont speech in 1095 when he declared the *bellum sacrum*, or the First Crusade, saying "let those who have been robbers for a long time now become knights." In the same speech he demonized the Arab and Turkish Muslims: they worship Satan, they torture, they're filthy, they're rapists, and, in one of the first racist and genocidal programs of European history, he called on the Christians "to destroy that vile race." During the Crusades of the next century recruiters attempted to drum up

---

5. Silvia Federici, *Caliban and the Witch: Women, The Body, and Primitive Accumulation* (New York: Autonomedia, 2004).

support with visions of a land of milk and honey, and the realization on earth of a harmonious peaceable kingdom.[6] It was a combination of utopian thinking and genocidal reality that would recur in European and American history.

The forces that caused the violence within Europe during the twelfth century—increased pauperization, intensification of expropriation of serfs, growth of towns, and the emergence of monetary and commercial relations—led, on the one hand, to competing claims of order between centralizing monarchies and the expanding papacy, and on the other hand, to a wide variety of movements from below deemed to be heretical. These movements have been likened to a proto–First International to stress their proletarian character. Cathars, Waldensians, followers of the French pantheist Amalric of Bena, the Fraticelli, the flagellants, the Brethren of the Free Spirit, and followers of Joachim of Fiore had a diverse theological and social program, but all were regarded as threatening by the feudal and church hierarchy. Joachim prophesized a new age, the age of the spirit, when church hierarchy would be unnecessary and when Christians would unite with infidels.

Prophets and messiahs preached the doctrine of having all things in common, which made sense to peasants who resolutely defended their customs and communal routine against the encroachments of feudal landlords and grasping clergy. The notion of having all things common was made plausible by the network of customary rights and practice on common lands, which

6. Norman Cohn, *The Pursuit of the Millennium: Revolutionary Millenarians and Mystical Anarchists of the Middle Ages,* rev. ed. (New York: Oxford University Press, 1970), 66–71.

already by the thirteenth century was both old and endangered. On the one hand the shortage of arable land led to *assarts* (arable clearings made by grubbing up the trees) in wastes and woodlands, and on the other hand, the intensified pressure in the face of rising prices by the lords on the impoverished peasantry threatened forms of commoning that were essential to smallholders in the thirteenth century.

If crusades against Islam were bids to control the commercial economy of the East, then crusades against heretics were means of terrorizing the landless population of the West. In 1208 the pope launched an exterminating crusade upon the heretics of Albi, in the south of France. Believing that the world around them was diabolical, they opposed procreation as an unkindness. The children of the Children's Crusade of 1212 were sold into slavery. Meanwhile in England, against John's will, the pope appointed Stephen Langton archbishop of Canterbury. In 1208 the pope placed King John under interdict and in the following year excommunicated him and his kingdom. The church bells were removed from the steeples, statues of the saints were laid on the ground. King John made up by surrendering his kingdom as a feudal fief to the pope.

In 1214 John's ambitions in France were dashed at the battle of Bouvines. He lost Normandy, the ancestral homeland of the ruling class of England since the Norman invasion of 1066. Philip of France now looked at England with acquisitive eyes. In February 1215 King John responded by making a vow to lead a crusade to the holy land to take it from the Muslim infidels. Becoming "a warrior of God," he enjoyed immunities protecting him from the barons. Raising money to recover Normandy and to join the crusade, King John oppressed the barons with *scutage* (a tax paid by a knight in lieu of military service), by stealing forests, by taking children hostage for ransom (he slaughtered the twenty-eight sons of Welsh hostages), and by selling women. He made a regular traffic in the sale of wards, maids of fourteen and widows alike. In 1214 he sold his first wife, Isabella of Gloucester, to Geoffrey de Mandeville for the sum of 20,000 marks.[7] These oppressions were the direct result of his plans to fight the infidels.

The Fifth Crusade set out in 1215; its principal ideological recruiter was Philip of Oxford. His general argument for "taking up the cross" is that crusading is an exalted vocation imitating Christ. His way of saying so is confused because he uses figures of speech that directly refer to the expropriations of European forest dwellers. "In the beautiful wood of paradise death was hidden under the mantle of life, so, on the contrary, in the deformed and horrible wood life was hidden under the mantle of death, just as life is concealed, in the case of the crusaders, under the mantle of a labor, which is like death."[8] Are the woods beautiful or horrible? Are the woods paradise or death? The answer depended on whether you were a baron or a commoner. Crusading was thus a murderous device to resolve a contradiction by bringing baron and commoner together in the cauldron of religious war.

Magna Carta was a document of Christian Europe—its first chapter concerned the freedom of the Christian Church from the

---

7. Frances Gies and Joseph Gies, *Women in the Middle Ages* (New York: Crowell, 1978), 28.

8. Reinhold Röricht, "Ordinacio de predicatione S. Crucis, in Anglia," in *Quinti belli sacri scriptores* (Geneva, 1879); quoted in James M. Powell, *Anatomy of a Crusade, 1213–1221* (Philadelphia: University of Pennsylvania, 1986), 52.

secular authority of king. Events in the church and in England ran parallel. The pontificate of Innocent III (1198–1216) corresponded to the reign of John (1199–1216). King John agreed to a five-year truce with al-Adil in 1211, the great Saladin's brother and his successor as sultan of Egypt. The pope meanwhile in 1215 opened the fourth Lateran Council, which established the church doctrine of transubstantiation, annual confession, and Easter communion, and which defined heresy. Jews were required to wear identifying badges. It is not a coincidence that the Lateran Council and Magna Carta occurred in the same year. The Lateran Council condemned Joachim of Fiore as a heretic in its second canon and prepared the groundwork of the ruthless Inquisition, a poisonous fungus whose deadly work in an underground, unseen mycelium has spawned racist results for centuries afterward.

In May 1215 the barons took London and withdrew their homage and fealty. In June King John and the barons faced each other in armed camps at Runnymede. The parchment charter of sixty-three chapters of liberties to the "freemen of England" was sealed, and homage renewed viva voce. The charter protected the interests of the church, the feudal aristocracy, the merchants, the Jews, *and* it acknowledged commoners. It assumed a commons. Here we pause in our story in order to summarize some of the leading chapters of the charter.

Its provisions revealed the oppression of women, the aspirations of the bourgeoisie, the mixture of greed and power in the tyranny, an independent ecology of the commons, and the famous chapter 39 from which habeas corpus, prohibition of torture, trial by jury, and the rule of law are derived. "No freeman shall be arrested or imprisoned or dispossessed or outlawed or exiled or any way victimized, neither will we attack him or send anyone to attack him, except by the lawful judgment of his peers or by the law of the land." The next chapter simply stated, "To no one will we sell, to no one will we refuse or delay right or justice."

The value of the individual provisions in the eyes of the only contemporary chronicler (a minstrel attached to Robert of Béthune) put first those treating the disparagement of women and the loss of life or member for killing beasts in the forest.[9]

Chapters 7 and 8 said simply, "A widow shall have her marriage portion and inheritance forthwith and without difficulty after the death of her husband." No widow shall be forced to marry so long as she wishes to live without a husband. We can truly say that "one of the first great stages in the emancipation of women is to be traced" to Magna Carta.[10] These provisions arose from a grassroots women's movement that contributed to the construction of alternative models of communal life.[11]

Magna Carta acknowledged the interests of the urban bourgeoisie. The London commune was established in 1191, and its oath was sworn, unlike the oath of homage, among equals. John was the first king to give a charter to the City of London, with annual election for mayor. The eighteenth-century Scottish philosopher and historian David Hume says that during John's reign

---

9. The minstrel Sarrazin's *Histoire des ducs de Normandie et des rois d'Angleterre,* though composed in 1220, was not published until 1840. The four types of disparaged husbands were lunatics, villeins, cripples, and the impotent.

10. J. C. Holt, *Magna Carta,* 2nd ed. (Cambridge: Cambridge University Press, 1992), 46.

11. Federici, *Caliban and the Witch,* see chap. 1. See also Terisa E. Turner and Leigh S. Brownhill, eds., "Gender, Feminism and the Civil Commons," *Canadian Journal of Development Studies* 22 (2001), a significant collection of articles.

London Bridge was finished in stone. Magna Carta established the freedom of travel for merchants. Chapter 41 stated, "All merchants shall be able to go out of and return to England safely and securely and stay and travel throughout England, as well by land as by water." It set weights and measures, the basis of the commodity form. Never far from Coke's thoughts, as he wrote, were "those two great pronouns, *meum* and *tuum,*" possessive pronouns that referred to possessions. As a practical matter, possessions required measurement and thus depended on chapter 35: "Let there be one measure for wine throughout our kingdom, and one measure for ale, and one measure for corn, namely 'the London quarter'; and one width for cloths whether dyed, russet or halberget, namely two ells within the selvedges. Let it be the same with weights and measures." The provisions both fleeced and protected the Jews, who had been disarmed and then massacred at the coronation of Richard I, John's elder brother and predecessor on the throne. As chapter 10 stipulated, "If one who has borrowed from the Jews any sum, great or small, die before that loan be repaid, the debt shall not bear interest while the heir is under age, of whomsoever he may hold; and if the debt fall into our hands, we will not take anything except the principal sum contained in the bond."

Chapters 28, 30, and 31 put a stop to the robberies of petty tyrants. "No constable or other bailiff of ours shall take anyone's corn or other chattels unless he pays on the spot in cash for them." The etymology of the word *chattels* recapitulates the evolution of the commodity and in this case suggests the change from a pastoral to an agrarian economy. "No sheriff, or bailiff of ours, or anyone else shall take the horses or carts of any freeman for transport work save with the agreement of that freeman." "Neither we nor our bailiffs will take, for castle or other works of ours, timber which is not ours, except with the agreement of him whose timber it is."

Other chapters have to be understood in terms of the energy ecology, which was based not on coal or oil but on wood. Chapter 47 said, "All forests that have been made forest in our time shall be immediately disafforested; and so be it done with riverbanks that have been made preserves by us in our time." To *disafforest* meant to remove from royal jurisdiction; it did not mean to clear-cut timber or destroy the trees. Chapter 48 said, "All evil customs connected with forests and warrens, foresters and warreners, sheriffs and their officials, riverbanks and their wardens shall immediately be inquired into in each county by twelve sworn knights of the same county who are to be chosen by good men of the same county and within forty days of the completion of the inquiry shall be utterly abolished by them so as never to be restored." It refers to the common rights of the *forest*. The physical forest was woodlands; the legal forest was a royal domain under forest law where the king kept deer. Both the word and the law came to England with William the Conqueror.

If noticed at all as part of Magna Carta, chapters 47 and 48 are often discarded as feudal relics, English peculiarities, or irrelevancies of the heritage industry. Yet if we see woodlands as a hydrocarbon energy reserve, we may be willing to give the subject more than a condescending dismissal. We need to adopt a "subsistence perspective."[12] "In an age when the primeval

12. Maria Mies and Veronika Bennholdt-Thomsen, *The Subsistence Perspective: Beyond the Globalised Economy,* trans. Patrick Camiller, Maria Mies, and Gerd Wieh (New York: Zed, 1999).

instinct of foraging was nearer to the surface than it is today,"
wrote Marc Bloch, the great scholar of the Middle Ages, "the
forest had greater riches to offer than we perhaps appreciate.
People naturally went there for wood, a far greater necessity of
life than in this age of oil, petrol, and metal; wood was used for
heating and lighting (in torches), for building material (roof
slats, castle palisades), for footwear (sabots), for plough handles
and various other implements, and as faggots for strengthening
roadways."[13]

"Grey, gnarled, low-browed, knock-kneed, bowed, bent,
huge, strange, long-armed, deformed, hunchbacked, misshapen
oakmen." This is a personification of the massive trunks and
small crowns of the ancient oaks of Staverton. The English oak
remains where millennia of cattle, goat, and deer ate its more ed-
ible competitors. The grazing determines what species thrive.
Old trees are the result not of the wildwood (of the Ice Age thirteen millennia earlier) but of wooded pasture. The wooded pasture is a human creation, through centuries of accumulated
woodsmanship, whose attributes include the *coppice* (which
grows again from the stump)—ash and elm provide indefinite
succession of crops of poles (for making rakes, scythe handles,
surplus used for stakes and firewood); the sucker (which grows
again from the root system)—aspen, cherry forming a patch of
genetically identical trees called a clone; and the *pollard*—these
are cut six to fifteen feet above the ground, leaving a permanent

---

13. Marc Bloch, *French Rural History,* trans. Janet Sondheimer (Berkeley:
University of California Press, 1966), 6.

Figure 1. A multi-use enclosure at Runnymede showing cattle grazing and tree pollards. Photo by the author.

trunk called a bolling with sprouts like coppice but out of reach of the livestock.[14]

Wooded pasture: same land for trees and grazing animals. Wooded commons: owned by one person, but used by others, the commoners. Usually the soil belonged to the lord while grazing belonged to the commoners, and the trees to either—timber to the lord, and wood to commoners. Whole towns were timber-framed: the strut and beam of cottages, the curved wooden rafters, the oak benches of worship. Then wheels, handles, bowls, tables, stools, spoons, toys, and other implements were all made of wood. Wood was the source of energy.

14. Oliver Rackham, *The History of the Countryside* (London: J. M. Dent, 1986), 66.

The growth of state power, the ability to make war, and complaints against the monarchy arose from its power to *afforest,* or place under royal law.[15] With the Norman conquest came innovations in eating utensils (the fork), a new language (French), new people (Normans, Jews), different animals (wild boar, red deer). William and his Norman conquerors ("a French bastard landing with an armed banditti," said Tom Paine) bypassed the customs of the forests that had prevailed from Anglo-Saxon times. Forests were not necessarily wooded. "The forest has its own laws, based, it is said, not on the Common Law of the realm, but on the arbitrary decree of the King."[16] It was the supreme status symbol of the king, a place of sport. The Domesday Book (1086) shows that only about half of the English settlements possessed woodland. In July 1203 King John instructed his chief forester, Hugh de Neville, to sell forest privileges "to make our profit by selling woods and demising assarts."[17] In 1215 there were 143 forests in England. Half of them were wood pasture. Few forests were declared in England after 1216. An authority writes that the principal grievances behind Magna Carta were two, "the malpractices of the sheriff and the extent of the forest."[18]

Having summarized the charter's chapters and having invoked the wooded basis of the material life at the time, we now

15. Nancy Lee Peluso and Peter Vandergeest, "Genealogies of the Political Forest and Customary Rights in Indonesia, Malaysia, and Thailand," *Journal of Asian Studies* 60, no. 1 (August 2001): 761–812.

16. J. R. Maddicott, "Magna Carta and the Local Community," *Past & Present* 102 (February 1984): 37, 72.

17. Holt, *Magna Carta,* 52.

18. Maddicott, "Magna Carta," 27.

return to the fate of King John. Scarcely had the mud of Runnymede dried on his boots than John resumed war on the barons and began to plot with the pope against them. Innocent III vacated the charter as null and void and prohibited the king from observing it. Louis, later to become king of France, invaded England at the barons' invitation in May 1216. King John died in October.

The story of his death became the stuff of legend among the peasant commoners, conveyed by word of mouth and remembered as oral history even by William Morris, the wonderful nineteenth-century craftsman, socialist, and poet, whose version I paraphrase. Fleeing his enemies King John lost all his baggage in an onrushing tide of the sea, and in a foul mood took shelter in Swinestead Abbey, Lincolnshire. "How much is this loaf sold for?" he asked at dinner, and when told one penny he answered, "by God, if I live for one year such a loaf shall be sold for twelve pence!"

One of the monks nearby heard this and considered that his own hour and time to die had come, and that it would be a good deed to slay so cruel a king and so evil a lord. So he went into the garden and plucked plums and replaced the pits with venom. Then he came before the king and knelt saying, "Sire, by St. Austin, this is the fruit of our garden." The king looked evilly on him and said, "Eat first, monk!" So the monk ate but changed countenance not one whit. So the king ate too. Presently right before the king's eyes the monk swelled, turned blue, fell down, and died. Then waxed the king sick at heart, and he also swelled, sickened, and died.

This is history from below, and like history from above (or in between), it must be examined. The herbaria and orchards of the

English monasteries, besides being early examples of collective labor, were also progenitors of communal living upon natural resources held in common. Thus, when the monk offered King John a fruit of the garden, it was a fruit in the double sense of both a product of human labor and a product of the earth, rain and sunshine—which belong to all—as the peasants who told this story and as William Morris who repeated it well understood. Plums originated in Byzantium and came to England at the time of Magna Carta with returning crusaders. King John thus suffered a poetic death caused by a kind of biological blowback.

After the death rattle of John and during the minority of the new king, Henry III, only nine years old, the fate of Magna Carta, indeed its whereabouts, was uncertain. France controlled half of England. The papal legate to England at the time of the death of King John and the coronation of the nine-year-old Henry III was Cardinal Gualo, who had been active in the extirpation of the Albigensians. Henry III granted the Charter of the Forest by the counsel of Gualo (and the English bishops). Did the woods nurture heresy? Was the pope's principal hunter of heretics brought to England to prevent the growth of heresy by promoting this charter?

"The French invasion saved the Great Charter," says McKechnie.[19] It was not until 11 September 1217 that France and England made peace, at an island in the river Thames near Kingston. Barefoot and shirtless, Louis was required to renounce all claim to the English throne, and to restore the Charters of Liberties granted by King John. The treaty put an end to two

19. William Sharp McKechnie, *Magna Carta: A Commentary on the Great Charter of King John* (Glasgow: J. Macklehose and Sons, 1914), 141.

years of civil war. The Victorian constitutional historian Stubbs concluded of the Treaty of Kingston, "in practical importance, scarcely inferior to the charter itself."[20] In contrast to its treaty-like function during the baronial wars, the reissue of the charter in time of peace established it as a basis of government.

Respecting the relationship between the Charter of the Forest and the Magna Carta, Wendover, the leading contemporary chronicler, said King John granted a separate forest charter but Blackstone argues this was unlikely because, among other reasons, the dimensions of the parchment of the great charter were sufficient to add forest clauses. William Blackstone published a scholar's edition of both, *The Great Charter and the Charter of the Forest* (1759). He was the first to print accurate texts of the charters, as they were known to him. "There is no transaction in the antient part of our English history more interesting and important, than the rise and progress, the gradual mutation, and final establishment of the charters of liberties, emphatically stiled THE GREAT CHARTER and CHARTER OF THE FOREST; and yet there is none that has been transmitted down to us with less accuracy and historical precision."[21]

Blackstone noted that the archbishops of Canterbury and Dublin "apprehend the generality of chapter 48 endangered the very being of all forests declaring that it was not the intention of the parties that the general words of the charter should extend to abolish such customs of the forests, without the existence of

20. William Stubbs, *The Constitutional History of England* (Oxford: Clarendon Press, 1894), 2:25.

21. The originals of the Charter of the Forest are in the Bodleian Library, Oxford, and in Durham Cathedral, the regent's seal in green, the papal legate's in yellow.

which the forests themselves could not be preserved." The forest clauses settled nothing. They provided grounds for renewal of war. The issue of disafforestation kept Magna Carta alive.[22]

A charter was a material object with a physical history.[23] At seventeen and three-quarters inches wide and eighteen and one-quarter inches long, the term *magna carta* is surprising. First used in 1218, it distinguished the charter from the companion, but smaller, Charter of the Forest. We should quote the preface to the second of Coke's *Institutes of the Laws of England* (1642). "It is called Magna Charta, not that it is great in quantity, for there be many voluminous charters commonly passed, specially in these later times, longer than this is; nor comparatively in respect that it is greater than Charta de Foresta, but in respect of the great importance, and weightiness of the matter, as hereafter shall appeare: and likewise for the same cause *Charta de Foresta* is called *Magna Charta de Foresta,* and both of them are called *Magnae Chartae Libertatum Angliae"*—the great charters of English liberties.[24] They were published by reading aloud four times a year, at the feast of St. Michael's, Christmas, Easter, and feast of St. John's. They were read in Latin certainly, in Norman French translation probably, and in English possibly.

The date 11 September recurs in this study four times altogether. First in 1217; second, when the Scot William Wallace defeated England in 1297; third, on that day in 1648 when the English Levellers submitted the Large Petition that called for

---

22. Holt, *Magna Carta,* 275.

23. Four originals remain preserved, one in Salisbury Cathedral, another in Lincoln Cathedral, and the others in the British Library.

24. Holt, *Magna Carta,* 18.

popular sovereignty, reparations, juries, religious toleration, and the opening of enclosures; and fourth, when the South Sea Company congratulated itself on that day in 1713 for receiving the license (or *asiento*) to trade African slaves to Spanish colonies in America. The date associates the charters with the forest commons, with greater Britain, with the Levellers, and with the slave trade.

The two charters were reissued together in 1225. McKechnie states, "it marked the final form assumed by Magna Carta."[25] Subsequently, the two were confirmed together. By 1297 Edward I directed that the two charters become the common law of the land. After a law of Edward III in 1369, the two were treated as a single statute. Both charters were printed together at the commencement of the English *Statutes-at-Large*. Blackstone concludes, "the final and complete establishment of the two charters, of liberties and of the forest, which from their first concession under King John in A.D. 1215, had been often endangered, and undergone many mutations, for the space of near a century; but were now fixed upon an eternal basis."

One of those mutations, occurring between 1215 and 1217, modified chapter 7, "and she shall have meanwhile her reasonable estovers of common." What are "estovers of common"? Coke explains, "When estovers are restrained to woods, it signifieth housebote, hedgebote, and ploughbote." Botes do not imply a common wood; they could as well appertain to field or hedgerow. *Firebote* and *hedgebote* are quotas for fuel and fencing; *housebote* and *cartbote* are rights for building and equipment. Coke goes on to say

25. McKechnie, *A Commentary*, 415.

that estovers signify sustenance, aliment, or nourishment. Technically then estovers refer to customary gatherings from the woods; often they refer to subsistence generally. Magna Carta defined limits of *privatization*. In Chapter 33, the clause "Henceforth all fish weirs shall be removed from the Thames and the Medway and throughout all England, except along the seacoast," refers to the right of fishing in another's water in common with the owner and others ("in common of piscary"). The UN's International Covenant on Economic, Social and Cultural Rights declares, "In no case may a people be deprived of its own means of subsistence."[26]

In continent after continent the humble figure of the old woman bent from carrying a burden of sticks that she has gathered from the woodlands has been the quintessential figure of an epoch in reproduction. Her protection is one of the oldest injunctions of written human history from the Mosaic codes onward ("When you reap the harvest in your field and forget a swathe, do not go back to pick it up; it shall be left for the alien, the orphan, and the widow," Deuteronomy 24:19). Wherever the subject is studied, a direct relationship is found between women and the commons. The feminization of poverty in our own day has become widespread precisely as the world's commons have been enclosed.

What happened between 1215 and 1217 to cause this clause to be inserted in chapter 7? The answer is war. The civil war continued. France invaded. War was fought by mounted knights,

---

26. Gerrard Winstanley, *Works,* ed. George H. Sabine (Ithaca: Cornell University Press, 1941), 519; and *International Covenant on Economic, Social and Cultural Rights* (1966, 1976), pt. 1, art. 1, chap. 2. Edward Coke, *The Second Part of the Institutes of the Laws of England* (London: W. Clarke and Sons, 1809), 17.

powerful units of war, terrifying, expensive, and ubiquitous. The king wanted to reward followers with endowments and lands in order "to raise men from the dust." War was fought by crossbowmen; it was fought by sailors; it was fought by many thousands of churls and villeins. Monstrous weapons of mass destruction hurled terror from the sky—the mangonel cast mill-stones, the trebuchet launched bombards, the catapult threw darts, the ballista (like the crossbow) hurled stones and missiles, and the arbalest discharged all manner of arrows, stones, and bolts. They destroyed cities, blinded soldiers, burned houses, razed towns, maimed and mutilated people without discrimination. War produced death by pestilence, drowning, fire, as well as by direct hits from the sky. War produced widows. The "mutation" (Blackstone) of chapter 7 between 1215 and 1217 reflected this reality.

The assize of Woodstock (1184) permitted the poor to have their estovers, but only under stringent rules. McKechnie comments: "If the rich suffered injury in their property, the poor suffered in a more pungent way: stern laws prevented them from supplying three of their primary needs; food, firewood, and building materials."[27] In Somerset complaint was made, "from the poor they take, from every man who carried wood upon his back, sixpence." In Stratford, a warden took a quarter of wheat "for their having paling for their corn and for collecting dead wood for their fuel in the demesne wood of the lord king." Sometimes a local tyrant established a veritable reign of terror. Inasmuch as the Charter of the Forest (1217) protected

27. McKechnie, *A Commentary*, 426.

the commons it was also, and to that extent, a prophylaxis from terror.

The Forest Charter's 1st chapter saved common of pasture for all those "accustomed" to it. The 7th forbade foresters or beadles from taking sheaves of corn or oats, or taking lambs or piglets in lieu of a feudal tax called *scotale*. The 9th chapter provided agistment and pannage to freemen. The 13th stated that every freeman shall have his honey. The 14th chapter said that those who come to buy wood, timber, bark or charcoal and carry it out in carts must pay *chiminage* (a road tax) but those who carry wood, bark, or charcoal on their backs need not pay chiminage.

Coke warns us not to let pass the least crumb or syllable of this law. The substantive customs referred to in Magna Carta are to the wooded realm that supported a material culture whose structures and architectonics were composed of wood, not steel or plastic. Richard Mabey, the incomparable English naturalist, author, and broadcaster, writes of the English woodlands, "More than any other kind of landscape they are communal places, with generations of shared natural and human history inscribed in their structures."[28]

Herbage is common of pasture, like *agistment,* which permitted livestock to roam in the forest. *Pannage* is the right to let the pigs in to get acorns and beech mast. Assarts and swidden are aspects of arable tillage. Firebote, snap wood, turbary, lops and tops refer to fuel. Estovers, cartbote, and housebote refer to tools and building. Chiminage refers to transportation. The widow's es-

---

28. Gareth Lovell Jones and Richard Mabey, *The Wildwood: In Search of Britain's Ancient Forests* (London: Aurum Press, 1993).

tovers of common is thus the phrase that leads us to a completely different world, a world of use values.

J. M. Neeson describes the uses of woods: lops and tops or snap wood for the household, furze and weeds for fodder, bavins or sprays such as bakers and potters wanted for their ovens and kilns. She notes where bean stakes could be found, how hazel was good for sheepfolds, how to assemble a chimney-sweeping brush. The woodlands were a reservoir of fuel; they were a larder of delicacies, a medicine chest of simples and cures.[29] As for food, hazelnuts and chestnuts could be sold at market; autumn mushrooms flavored soups and stews. Wild chervil, fennel, mint, wild thyme, marjoram, borage, wild basil, tansy made herbs for cooking and healing. Wild sorrel, chicory, dandelion leaves, salad burnet, cats-ear, goats-beard, greater prickly lettuce, corn sow-thistle, fat-hen and chickweed, yarrow, charlock, and goose grass made salads. Elderberries, blackberries, bilberries, barberries, raspberries, wild strawberries, rosehips and haws, cranberries and sloes were good for jellies, jams, and wines.

The medievalist Jean Birrell has described the struggle in the thirteenth century over common rights. She places special emphasis on the range of forest commons. Already they were both old and customary. "Most were long standing, though some were recent; some were precisely defined in writing, but most were defined only by custom." They were threatened by the economic pressures consequent on the growth of towns and the

29. J. M. Neeson, *Commoners: Common Right, Enclosure and Social Change in England, 1700–1820* (New York: Cambridge University Press, 1993), 158–59.

increase of trade, as woods were cleared and assarts were made. The number of commons increased, the amount of common lands diminished, and the lords of the manors attempted to curtail common rights. Intercommoning and *stints* began to emerge; common law and direct action preserved commons. The men of Stoneleigh, Warwickshire petitioned the king in 1290 that they had lost their estovers and pasturage by manorial assarts and were unable to survive.[30]

Often Magna Carta refers to *freemen,* and often in subsequent centuries the term has been decried; Mark Twain, for instance, in *A Connecticut Yankee in King Arthur's Court,* refers to it "as a sarcasm of law and phrase." Hence it is an imposter, a shadow, a superstition, "echoing from the caves of fame." However, if we keep in mind the microeconomy of the woods so well described by Neeson, we can appreciate Shelley's apt reply to the question posed at the beginning of this chapter—"What art thou Freedom?"

> For the labourer thou art bread,
> And a comely table spread.
> From his daily labour come
> To a neat and happy home.
>
> Thou art clothes, and fire, and food

So common rights differ from human rights. First, common rights are embedded in a particular ecology with its local hus-

30. Jean Birrell, "Common Rights in the Medieval Forest: Disputes and Conflicts in the Thirteenth Century," *Past & Present,* no. 17 (1987): 48. In 1970 E. P. Thompson used to speed through this village in his Land Rover on his way to work at Warwick.

bandry. For commoners, the expression "law of the land" from chapter 39 does not refer to the will of the sovereign. Commoners think first not of title deeds, but of human deeds: how will this land be tilled? Does it require manuring? What grows there? They begin to explore. You might call it a natural attitude. Second, commoning is embedded in a labor process; it inheres in a particular praxis of field, upland, forest, marsh, coast. Common rights are entered into by labor. Third, commoning is collective. Fourth, being independent of the state, commoning is independent also of the temporality of the law and state. Magna Carta does not list rights, it grants perpetuities. It goes deep into human history.

Magna Carta was a treaty among contending forces in a civil war; as J. C. Holt says, it was a political document. It attempted to put to rest seven conflicts, namely between church and monarchy, between individual and the state, between husband and wife, between Jew and Christian, between king and baron, between merchant and consumer, between commoner and privatizer. It did not settle these conflicts in the sense of declaring victory. Its chapter 39 has grown to embody fundamental principles, habeas corpus, trial by jury, prohibition of torture. But its work is far from done. Other chapters, too, must grow. We shall find five further principles in the Charters of Liberties: the principle of neighborhood; the principle of subsistence; the principle of travel; the principle of anti-enclosure; and the principle of reparations.

CHAPTER THREE

The Commodity and the Commons

I listen to fellows saying here's good stuff for a novel
or it might be worked up into a good play.

I say there's no dramatist living can put old Mrs.
Gabrielle Giovannitti into a play with that
kindling wood piled on top of her head coming
along Peoria Street nine o'clock in the morning.
Carl Sandburg, "Onion Days," Chicago Poems *(1915)*

The sixteenth century was an age of exploration; it was the century of the Tudor dynasty; it began with the Protestant Reformation and ended with the age of Shakespeare; it was the first age of print; it was an epoch of vagabondage when letters were written in blood and fire; it was the climax of medieval feudalism and the beginning of modern capitalism; it was an era in the separation of town and country, and of journeymen unprotected by guilds; it was an age of terrors and the burning of the witches.

It gave birth to the prison and to the Atlantic slave trade. It was the foundational period of criminalization when the larceny and robbery statutes were enacted: the "crime problem" was created. It was the first great phase of the English enclosure movement: the privatization of England had begun.

As far as the history of Magna Carta is concerned, the twentieth-century English historian Herbert Butterfield noted that, in contrast to the thirteenth and fourteenth centuries of its establishment and the seventeenth century of its political rebirth, the sixteenth century presented a "curious interval."[1] Parallel to this paradox of the actual history of the sixteenth century is a second one found in the theatrical history in the sixteenth century. Shakespeare wrote *The Life and Death of King John* without ever mentioning Magna Carta. Its occlusion from the stage parallels its omission in history.

The Tudor state created institutions of centralized power, it made room for a new class of people, and it ruled by new methods adopting Roman law in which there was little room for custom and in which judicial innovations such as courts like the Star Chamber became a byword of malpractice, misjudgment, and despotism.

George Ferrers printed an English translation of Magna Carta and the Charter of the Forest in 1534, at the beginning of his book of "divers olde statutes." This was the year that he entered Lincoln's Inn (enabling him to practice law), and not long before he became a useful servant to Thomas Cromwell, architect of the Tudor revolution in government. In his brief preface to the reader

---

1. Herbert Butterfield, *The Englishman and His History* (Cambridge: Cambridge University Press, 1945), 10, 29.

of the first printed edition in translation of Magna Carta, Ferrers says that "the most part of them retain their force, and bind the king's subjects unto this day" but remarkably he does not say that they are binding on the king. (Similarly, President George Bush also conceives himself as above or outside the law.)

If not the law, the sovereign of the nation-state had its own reasons, its *raisons d'état,* which were secret, war-making, violent, capable of the double bluff and the double cross. George Ferrers nimbly survived regime change from Catholic to Protestant to Puritan to Catholic to Anglican. He was a page in the personal service of Henry VIII where he studied how to please a prince. He was an MP in 1547 and a JP for Barnstable at the same time. He was appointed lord of misrule for the Christmas revels of 1551–52 at a crisis when annual inflation in London was 21 percent, the price of flour doubled, and the poor were starving. He diverted attention from the execution of Somerset with a brilliant show of state-sponsored spectacle. The Christmas revels were a great success in London—the Tudor propensity to show, the gathering and teasing of crowds. Besides music and morris dancing, with Ferrers himself dressed up as a star in this carnival, a creepy prop list has survived that includes the full array of Tudor terror: gaolers, manacles, locks, stocks, pillory, gibbet, and the block and ax.[2]

Henry VIII, in dissolving the monasteries and their attendant commons, opened the way for a new class, the gentry, to take land and turn it to profit by means of *enclosures.* In 1535 Henry VIII granted George Ferrers the manor of Flamstead, Hertfordshire. He was one among a new class who profited from a

2. *Dictionary of National Biography*, s.v. "Ferrers, George."

huge redistribution of English land. The dissolution of the monasteries took place in 1536, a massive act of state-sponsored privatization. More than any other single act in the long history of the establishment of English private property, it made the English land a commodity.

To introduce this theme we rely on three writers of English social history. William Cobbett (1763–1835), the liveliest, most prolific English language journalist writing between Daniel Defoe and Alexander Cockburn, is an especially valuable witness. At work in the midst of the second most fundamental development of English capitalism, the beginning of the factory system in the early nineteenth century, he was in a good position to understand the primary principle of English capitalism, namely, the removal of people from the land or from their means of subsistence. Cobbett understood the Protestant Reformation simultaneously as a landgrab, as a cause of pauperism, and as a violation of Magna Carta. "Englishmen ... ought, above all things, to endeavor to ascertain, how it came to pass, that this land of roast beef was changed, all of a sudden, into a land of dry bread, or of oatmeal porridge." The dissolution of the monasteries "banished, at once, that 'Old English Hospitality,' of which we have since known nothing but the name; and that, in lieu of that hospitality, it gave us pauperism, a thing, the very name of which was never before known in England."[3]

Cobbett deplores the disenchantment of the land that accompanied the discommoning of the field. He links Magna Carta

3. William Cobbett, *A History of the Protestant Reformation in England and Ireland,* ed. Leonor Nattrass, with introduction by James Epstein (London: Pickering and Chatto, 1998), 108.

and the church and hence favorably quotes the passage on excommunication: in 1253, for instance, in the great hall of the king at Westminster Abbey, in the presence of the king and the barons and the archbishop of Canterbury, "arrayed in Pontificals with tapers burning," the sentence of excommunication was uttered with awful ceremony. "We Excommunicate and Anathematise . . . all those who by any arts or crafts do violate, break, diminish, or exchange the Church's Liberties and free customs contained in the Charters of common liberties and of the Forest . . . and all that secretly or openly by deed, word, or counsel, do make statutes, or observe them being made; or introduce customs, or observe them when they are brought in, against the said liberties, or any of them."[4] Excommunication reaffirmed the right of resistance.

The common people depended on various forms of commoning. How did it work? R. H. Tawney (1880–1962), England's most influential socialist and social historian of the first half of the twentieth century, called attention to the great number of cottagers and day laborers who did not hold arable land but in practice used the commons for pigs, geese, poultry, and cows. "It was the essence of the open field system of agriculture—at once its strength and its weakness—that its maintenance reposed upon a common custom and tradition, not upon documentary records capable of precise construction. Its boundaries were often rather a question of the degree of conviction with which ancient inhabitants could be induced to affirm them, than visible to the mere eye of sense." Hospitality had a definite special importance, in good housekeeping,

4. Boyd C. Barrington, *The Magna Charta and Other Great Charters of England* (Philadelphia: W. J. Campbell, 1900), 299–301.

"a miniature cooperative society" as Tawney calls it inclusive of plowmen, threshers, cowherds, milkmaids, servants, and laborers. The *fellowship* of mutual aid, the partnership of service and protection, which characterized the village community Tawney calls "a little commonwealth." Twice he refers to its "practical communism." Common rights persisted even in closed England.[5]

J. M. Neeson, the University of Warwick collaborator with E. P. Thompson, England's most influential socialist and social historian of the second half of the twentieth century, puts an emphasis on the commoners' agency in the preservation of the practices. She writes, "The fuel, food and materials taken from common waste helped to make commoners of those without land, common-right cottages, or pasture rights. Waste gave them a variety of useful products, and the raw materials to make more. It also gave them the means of exchange with other commoners and so made them part of the network of exchange from which mutuality grew. More than this, common waste supported the economies of landed and cottage commoners too. It was often the terrain of women and children. And for everyone the common meant more than income."[6]

Enclosures were not the only force in the creation of the land market but they destroyed the spiritual claim on the soil and prepared for the proletarianization of the common people, subjecting them to multifaceted labor discipline: the elimination of cakes and ale, the elimination of sports, the shunning of dance,

---

5. R. H. Tawney, *The Agrarian Problem in the Sixteenth Century* (London: Longmans, 1912), 235.

6. J. M. Neeson, *Commoners: Common Right, Enclosure, and Social Change in England, 1700–1820* (New York: Cambridge University Press, 1993).

the abolition of festivals, and the strict discipline over the male and female bodies. The land and the body lost their magics. The working class was criminalized, and female powers were denounced as baleful. George Ferrers's translation of Magna Carta omitted the significant phrase of chapter 7, the widow "shall have meanwhile her reasonable estovers of common." Actual widespread want rather than musty parchment or statute books mobilized the multitudes. The poverty that ensued was deeply feminized. The consequences were immediate in rebellion from below, which frequently took religious expression.

The Pilgrimage of Grace for the Commonwealth (1536) required pilgrims to swear not to search for "particular profit to yourself . . . but by counsel of the commonwealth." Its leaders were called Lord Poverty, Captain Pity, and Captain Charity. The first mention of the York Articles of 1536 found the suppression of religious houses "a gret hurt to the common welthe and many sisters be [put] from theyr levyings and left at large." This needs emphasis for, as Adrienne Rich has written, women's experience has been "wordless or negated experience."[7] The expulsion from the common lands had huge and manifold consequences to the silencing and negation of subsequent experience. The "many sisters" who were put from their living and left at large suffered a double loss—of subsistence and of independence. It prepared the way for the terrorizing of the female body through the witch hunts.[8] Burning faggots replaced estovers of

---

7. Adrienne Rich, "When We Dead Awaken: Writing as Re-Vision" (1971), in *On Lies, Secrets, and Silence* (New York: Norton, 1979).

8. Silvia Federici, *Caliban and the Witch: Women, the Body, and Primitive Accumulation* (New York: Autonomedia, 2004).

common; the witch-hunter's prick and the *branks* (a headpiece used for scolding women) silenced and degraded her.

The rhetoric of the commonwealth had become dangerous to the state. Two verses from "The Pilgrims' Ballad" (1536) illustrate how easily the spiritual powers of the Christian religion with its central emphasis on the redeeming value of sacrifice could support those waging armed rebellion for the preservation of their material commons.

> Crist crucifyd!
> For thy wounds wide
> Us commens guyde!
> Which pilgrames be,
> Thrughe godes grace,
> For to purchache
> Olde welthe and peax
> Of the Spiritualtie
>
> Gret godes fame
> Doith Church proclame
> Now to be lame
> And fast in boundes,
> Robbyd, spoled and shorne
> From catell and corne
> And clene furth borne
> Of housez and landes

More than a decade later, two rebellions in 1549, the Prayer Book Rebellion in the West Country and Kett's Rebellion in East Anglia, took place in the summer, remembered as the *camping* time because the rebels in their tens of thousands set up campsites throughout lowland England rather than march on London. More than eighteen camps were planned and coordinated, the largest at Mousehold Heath near Norwich, containing sixteen thousand tradesmen, yeomen, and commoners. They developed an alternative government there, under the Oak of Reformation. They denounced enclosers who regarded only (to quote a Star Chamber document) "private lucre and peculyere commodyte . . . to the decay and utter destruccone of the Comon welthe." The first article of twenty-nine that Robert Kett and his followers prayed—they didn't "demand"—was, nonetheless, bold. "We pray . . . from henceforth no man shall enclose any more." The third: "We pray your grace that no lord of no manor shall common upon the Commons." They prayed that prices and rents revert to the levels under Henry VII. The eleventh: "We pray that all freeholders and copyholders [who held land tenure by manorial custom] may take the profits of all commons, and there to common, and the lords not to common nor take profits of the same." Perhaps the most powerful demand, or prayer, was the sixteenth, "We pray that all bond men may be made free, for God made all free with his precious blood shedding."[9] "Commons is become a king," people said, and with kingly nonchalance, "grant us this and that and we will go home."[10]

Nicholas Sotherton was a contemporary witness to the "commoyson in Norfolk." Like the women in the Niger River delta when the big oil companies took over their common rights in 2004, who protested by baring their bottoms, the boys of Mousehold Heath turned "brychless and bear arssyde" to the

---

9. Anthony Fletcher and Diarmaid MacCulloch, *Tudor Rebellions*, 4th ed. (New York: Longman, 1997), 144–46.

10. Susan Brigden, *New Worlds, Lost Worlds: The Rule of the Tudors, 1485–1603* (New York: Penguin, 2000), 186.

arrows of their opponents. Sotherton also quotes the prophecy that foretold the end of this great revolt for the preservation of the commons.[11]

> The countrie gruffes, Hob, Dick, and Hick
> With clubs and clouted shoone,
> Shall fill up Dussindale with blood
> Of slaughtered bodies soon.

And so it came to pass. While *clouted shoone* (patched or botched shoes or shoes with nail studs) came to stand for a country clown, a derogatory association with the commons remained. The memory of "the camping time," or massive rebellion, remained.

The specter haunting Europe was of having all things in common. The first great proletarian revolt of modern history, the Peasants' Revolt of Germany in 1526, demanded the restoration of customary forest rights. Robert Crowley addressed his petition to the House of Commons in 1548.[12] "I can scarcely trust that any reformation can be had unless God do now work in the hearts of the possessioners of this realm, as he did in the primitive church. . . . But yet I would wish that the possessioners would consider who gave them their possessions, and how they ought to bestow them. And then (I doubt not) it should not need to have

11. B. L. Beer, " 'The Commoyson in Norfolk, 1549': A Narrative of Popular Rebellion in 16th century England," *Journal of Medieval and Renaissance Studies* 6 (1976).

12. Robert Crowley, *An Information and Petition against the Oppressours of the Poor Commons of This Realm* (1548), in *The Select Works of Robert Crowley*, ed. J. M. Cowper, Early English Text Society, extra series, no. 15 (Millwood, NY: Kraus Reprint, 1973), 151–76.

all things made common. For what needeth it the servant of the household to desire to have their masters' goods common, so long as the steward ministereth unto every man the thing that is needful to him?"

Like William Tyndale, who was burned at the stake for translating the Bible in 1536, Crowley was from Gloucestershire and, like Tyndale, he appealed even to "a boy who driveth the plough." He was the most eloquent of the commonwealth writers, the social conscience of England. He was a poet, a printer, and he became a Puritan. His *Philargyrie* (1550)—the title means "love of silver"—attacked human greed. His celebrated edition of Langland's *Piers Ploughman,* written two centuries earlier, stated: "For human intelligence is like water, air, and fire—it cannot be bought or sold. These four things the Father of Heaven made to be shared on earth in common." Earth too was held in common, both in the 1300s of Langland's time and in the 1500s of Crowley's. A Somerset magistrate complained of the gangs of unemployed during the dearth of the year 1596, "so as men are driven to watch their sheep folds, their pastures, their woods, their cornfields, all things growing too, too common."[13]

Crowley denounced with terrible threats the engrossers of farms, the rack renters, the enclosers, the lease-mongers, and usurers. "If the sturdy fall to stealing, robbing and receiving: then you are the causes thereof, for you dig in, enclose, and withhold from them the earth out of which they should dig and plough their living." He asserted human equality: "Which of you can say

13. A. V. Judges, ed., *The Elizabethan Underworld: A Collection of Tudor and Early Stuart Tracts and Ballads* (London: Routledge, 1930), xviii.

for himself any natural cause why he should possess the treasure of this world, but that the same cause may be found of him also whom you make your slave?"

"More than Turkey the tyranny," he concluded with truly catholic understanding. He inveighed against possessioners with prophetic power: "If I should demand of the poor man of the country what thing he thinks to be the cause of Sedition, I know his answer. He would tell me that the great farmers, the graziers, the rich butchers, the men of law, the merchants, the gentlemen, the knights, the lords, and I cannot tell who; men that have no name because they are doers in all things that any gain hangs upon. Men without conscience. Men utterly void of God's fear. Yea, men that live as though there were no God at all! Men that would have all in their own hands; men that would leave nothing for others; men that would be alone on the earth; men that be never satisfied. Cormorants, greedy gulls; yea, men that would eat up men, women, and children, are the causes of Sedition. They take our houses over our heads, they buy our grounds out of our hands, they raise our rents, they levy (yea unreasonable) fines, they enclose our commons!"[14]

Two competing concepts of social morality prevailed in the mid-sixteenth century, commonwealth and commodity. *Commonwealth* was a specific rhetoric in humanist vocabulary and civic life, related to res publica; it implied paternalism and hospitality. In the minds of the Pilgrims of Grace for the Commonwealth, the ambiguity of the term came forth, as landless commoners sought redress for their loss of common

---

14. Crowley, *The Way to Wealth* (1550), in Cowper, *Select Works* (see note 12), 132–33.

lands.[15] Prices had risen, to the distress of the poor. As Hugh Latimer, bishop of Worcester, put it, "poor men which live of their labor cannot with the sweat of their face have a living . . . we shall at length be constrained to pay for a pig a pound." Everyone knew the importance of the pig, and certainly the custom of pannage was widely practiced even if the Charter of the Forest, 9th chapter ("every freeman . . . shall have his pannage"), was not widely known. In the seventeenth century, it has been estimated that two million pigs lived in England. Cobbett observed of the people in the Forest of Dean, Gloucestershire, "every cottage has a pig or two." Beech mast is "the poor man's great friend because it fats him a Pig or two, and with some help a larger hog, for pickled pork, or bacon, which keeps him from the butcher's shop, great part, if not all the year." The pig, together with the allotment and garden, was one of the three defenses against destitution. It remained this way right into the twentieth century up to the Small Pig Keeper's Council of 1940, which in the crisis of that year called up old memories by recycling kitchen waste.[16]

As the son of a plowman himself who grew up on Blackheath Common, Hugh Latimer fully grasped the complexity of mixed farming and explained it to the king and courtiers with a commoner's know-how and a touch of gallows humor. There are two kinds of enclosing, just as there are two kinds of plowing, of the body and of the spirit, preached Latimer in his famous "Sermon on the Plowers," 18 January 1548. The rich churchman lorded

---

15. Steve Hindle, *The State and Social Change in Early Modern England, c. 1550–1640* (New York: St. Martin's, 2000), 22, 55.

16. Robert Malcolmson and Stephanos Mastoris, *The English Pig: A History* (London: Hambledon, 2001), 36, 37, 56, 125.

and loitered while the giants of the property engrossed and enclosed. The practice of commoning can provide mutual aid, neighborliness, fellowship, and family with their obligations of trust and expectations of security. "They must have swine for their food, to make their veneries or bacon of. Their bacon is their venison, for they shall now have *hangum tuum* ["a hanging," in mock legalese] if they get any other venison; so that bacon is their necessary meat to feed on, which they may not lack. They must have other cattles, as horses to draw their plow and for carriage of things to the markets, and kine for their milk and cheese, which they must live upon and pay their rents. These cattle must have pasture, which pasture if they lack the rest must needs fail them. And pasture they cannot have if the land be taken in and enclosed from them."[17]

The commoner helps the farmer restore nitrates by manuring the land with his sheep. The forest owner compensates the commoner for lack of deer by permitting pannage, or the foraging for pigs in season. The *balks* (unplowed strips of ground), the verges, and headlands become places for grazing cows who give the dairy products for squatters and commoners. Whether we call this an economy of makeshifts, or a mixed economy of welfare, or an economy of diversified resources, it was understood by all within it, who at the time referred to it as the commons.[18] A peasant's

---

17. Allan G. Chester, ed., *Selected Sermons of Hugh Latimer* (Charlottesville: University of Virginia Press, 1968), 37, 149–50.

18. Steve Hindle, " 'Not by bread only?' Common Right, Parish Relief, and Endowed Charity in a Forest Economy, c. 1600–1800," in *The Poor in England, 1700–1850: An Economy of Makeshifts,* ed. Steven King and Alannah Tomkins (Manchester: Manchester University Press, 2003), 65.

economy depended on pasturage—milk, butter, cheese, eggs, and meat. It was indispensable to maintenance of the arable holding, to feed his horses that pull the plow and haul his loads. Tawney again: "to work the ploughland one must have the wherewithal to feed the plough beasts."[19]

The crisis precipitated by the huge rebellions of midcentury produced Latimer's powerful sermon, which was addressed to the apex of power about the lowly details of the agronomy of mixed commoning. The rebellions could not be defeated by terror alone, which was amply illustrated by the Sturdy Beggars Act of 1547 making slavery a punishment for vagabondage, but the state itself intervened to regulate the pace of enclosure and the "freedom" of the market. Thus the legal bulwark of Tudor paternalism, familiar to us as "the moral economy," was the Edwardian statute against forestalling, regrating, and engrossing (5 & 6 Edward VI c.14). These practices are inherent in the capitalist morality of the *commodity:* forestalling was the practice of withholding food from the hungry market in order to force the price to rise; engrossing was the practice of monopolizing the whole market for the same purpose; and regrating—named the central sin of the commodity economy—involved buying in order to sell. Lord Kenyon said of this act in another year of dearth (1795) that it was "coeval with the constitution."[20] The moral economy lasted in many respects into the nineteenth century, despite Adam Smith's best efforts to defeat it; it expressed the principle that none should profit until all had been fed.

19. Tawney, *Agrarian Problem,* 240.

20. Quoted in E. P. Thompson, "The Moral Economy of the English Crowd," in *Customs in Common* (London: Merlin, 1991), 200.

In 1548 Robert Crowley had petitioned Parliament against the oppressions of the poor commons of this realm. He railed against the ministers who usurped tithes for their "private commodity." Taking church taxes, they used the money not to relieve the poor, cure the sick, comfort the dying, or teach children but for their self-interest. He argued that the "possessioners"—those with large possessions, those who seek their own private commodity— must sell their possessions as in the primitive Christian church. He reminded the possessioners both of God's vengeance, that "the whole earth (by birthright) belongeth to the children of man," and that history itself gives no continuity of title, as he summarized the fate of Nebuchadnezzar, Pharaoh, the Roman empire, and the Goths. The only thing that can be claimed is that which "you shall get by the sweat of your faces."

Shakespeare wrote *The Life and Death of King John* in 1596, based on an earlier version he probably also composed. He was loyal to the Tudor dynasty and its established church; anything else was treason. The play is dynastic (death plots and attempted murder of Arthur, heir to the throne), military (war in France, loss of provinces, war in England), and religious (John is excommunicated, then kneels to the pope, placing England in fief to the Vatican). The king of England no less than the king of France trades in villainy while the pope's legate, Pandulph, plays a double game. The earth is made red with the blood of the sons of English mothers.

Like all Shakespeare's other history plays, this one is written in light of the Tudor self-narrative. Henry VIII dissolved the monasteries, called Thomas More a meddling priest, and made himself supreme head of the church. So Shakespeare has John shaking the moneybags of hoarding abbots, referring to the pope as "this meddling priest," and himself as "supreme head," prohibiting papal tithing in England and mocking indulgences.

There is plenty of offstage rebellion—"unsettled humours of the land" (2.1.66)—providing a backdrop of anxiety and fear. Later in the play the king speaks of an "inundation of mistemp'red red humour" (5.1.12). At the time *humours* was a medical term, as if rebellion were a disease rather than a healthy process whose resolution can have such lasting benefits as the moral economy or Magna Carta. Besides in 1594–95, when Shakespeare was working on *King John,* the sixth of his ten historical plays, rebellion was too close for the comfort of the Elizabethan court. The Tudors were insecure in their claim to the throne though they, like King John, occupied it by "strong possession."

Hanging and torture figure in the speech and imagery of the play. And a scene of torture is at the center of the play when hot irons are to be applied to the eyes of Arthur. In the torture chamber an executioner prepares to cut out his tongue. At the scene of horror the choice is presented whether to obey the sovereign's command or the springs of conscience that cry out against cruelty. The crisis of conscience proceeds against a background of rebellion that Shakespeare can only hint at, but hint he does.

Ill-defined plebeian murmuring follows the torture scene. Old men and women prophesy dangerously, whispering among themselves "with wrinkled brows, with nods, with rolling eyes" as another "lean unwash'd artificer" joins the discussion, the blacksmith lets his iron cool on the anvil, the tailor puts his slippers on the wrong feet. One prophet sings "in rude harsh-sounding rhymes." King John orders his hanging. Worse than rebellion, or a plot to replace the monarch or the dynasty, was the danger of revolution, turning the world upside down.[21]

At the center of Shakespeare's account of the reign of King John is not the Charters of Liberties; instead we find two related themes (rumor of proletarian disorder and the practice of torture) and a long speech on the commodity. The commodity, or buying and selling, is the matrix of all themes—spiritual salvation, matrimonial love, and war among nations. It has a religious vector, a commercial one, a monarchical one. The word itself summarizes universal political scheming and oath breaking. As the value of a commodity can change, so the value of words may change, even those uttered in solemn oath. It means self-interest, it is introduced by the Bastard, an illegitimate son of Richard I, a choruslike figure, simultaneously close to the center of events and at a distance from them, who both advises the king and comments on the action.

My point is not that Shakespeare ignores Magna Carta because it is an embarrassment to Queen Elizabeth and England's possessioners. He replaces it with a peculiar disquisition on the commodity, a long nearly incomprehensible soliloquy delivered by the Bastard (2.1.561–98). It begins on a theme of insanity, "Mad world! mad kings! mad composition!" The insanity of the commodity arises from its inherent contradiction or double bind: on the one hand it is useful, convenient, or commodious, on the other hand it is bought and sold for profit and gain. Guile replaces plain dealing. No one seems more honest than the cutpurse; no love more sincere than the prostitute's. Altruism and avarice seem

21. Brigden, *New Worlds,* 176.

identical in form. Caveat emptor; the world is full of cheats. The term is shortened from escheat, the fine owed to the lord of the manor in punishment for some offense.

Gilbert Walker explained in his *Manifest Detection* (1552) that "the first and original ground of cheating is a counterfeit countenance in all things." This explains the title of his pamphlet as well as *A Notable Discovery of Cozenage,* Robert Greene's 1591 tract. The Elizabethan rogue literature featured works of detection and discovery of all that is masked or veiled. The "counterfeit countenance" was inherent in the commodity form, which established "material relations between persons and social relations between things." The Bastard's soliloquy proceeds with a long introduction of a personified commodity, "That smooth-fac'd gentleman, tickling commodity."

Gilbert Walker made it very clear that exploitation was at the basis of the commodity. The cheater lives "by rape and ravin, devouring the fruit of other men's labours." How is sexual violence related to the cheating form of the commodity? The Bastard's soliloquy begins as a rant against violence and bad faith while comparing the dealer to a devil, the devil who wins of all opponents— "Of kings, of beggars, old men, young men," and of young women,

> maids,
> Who, having no external thing to lose
> But the word "maid," cheats the poor maid of that,

Thomas Dekker has a chapter on "the manner of undoing gentlemen by taking up commodities." Robert Greene describes the persons who perform their "cozening commodity." The husband who sells his wife into prostitution calls her a "commodity." The prostitute is called "traffic." The commodity retains this sexual meaning at least in slang well into the eighteenth century, when its meaning expanded to become "the private parts of a modest woman and the public part of the prostitute."

The devaluation of woman's work and the degradation of her body relate directly to the enclosures of open fields, the loss of commons, and the depopulation of villages. Prostitution becomes the synecdoche for commodity production. She is a proletarian (she has "no external thing to lose"). She becomes prostituted and cheated simultaneously by the commodity. Unlike Thomas Dekker, who called all prostitutes "commodities," Robert Crowley emphasized the origin of prostitution of young people and placed it squarely on the possessioners and lease-mongers who let out lands at double and triple rents, sending the young "running headlong into wickedness, the boys to garnish the gallows, and girls to perpetual miserable poverty as sisters of the Bank" and finally "lying and dying in the streets full of all plagues and penury."

Brothels and the "stews" shared neighborhood with the Rose and the Globe. Shakespeare observed a proletarian street scene but not one indoors where, in the suburbs especially, the "domestic system" or the "putting-out system" was replacing the art and mystery of the craft guilds. The chronic poverty and the devaluation and extension of women's work became widespread and invisible. In the economic changes of the sixteenth century women suffered the most, they lost the commons; and in the legal changes of the sixteenth century, their "reasonable estovers of common" was forgotten. What Shakespeare expresses is a third meaning of commodity: the anterior alienation and dehumanization of women's body.

With this pun the Bastard moves from gynephobia to physics. Gravity itself is governed by the commodity, a world otherwise resting in equilibrium finds that its purpose and direction is determined by the commodity ruled by bawd and broker. The Bastard is envious; he wants to be seduced by his own private commodity.

> And why rail I on this commodity?
> But for because he hath not woo'd me yet:
> Not that I have the power to clutch my hand,
> When his fair angels would salute my palm,

In referring to "fair angels" he does not mean celestial messengers bringing divine news but an English gold coin worth ten shillings in Edward VI's time. Divinity and sexuality are reduced to money. Private self-interest and political expedience alike violate the feudal bond in which personal loyalty is the basis of honor, faith, and truth.

> But for my hand, as unattempted yet,
> Like a poor beggar raileth on the rich.
> Well, whiles I am a beggar, I will rail
> And say there is no sin but to be rich;
> And being rich, my virtue then shall be
> To say there is no vice but beggary.

The lines express the volatility of fortune: the social structure turns like a wheel of fortune—now a beggar, now rich—and morality may turn as quickly and as capriciously. Class struggle is reduced to the contrasting vices of greed and envy among the possessioners and the poor, or the haves and the have-nots.

Since kings break faith upon commodity,
Gain, be my lord, for I will worship thee!

As the Bastard genuflects in devotion to the commodity, Shakespeare anticipates Karl Marx's labor theory of value, but where Marx finds value in socially necessary labor time, Shakespeare reduces the commodity to the sexually active woman.

The double nature of the commodity conceals its social hieroglyphics in which "a definite social relationship between people assumes in their eyes the fantastic form of a relationship between things." This is what gives to the commodity its opacity. In Shakespeare's *King John* the term signifies betrayal, greed, bad faith, egotism, aggression, and sexuality. The Bastard makes social relations of the commodity transparent. The bawd, the pimp, the broker, and the usurer act in the name of the commodity. Rape is the reality the commodity conceals.

A flaxwife organized another form of collective resistance in a London suburb about the time when Shakespeare first came to London. "Fuel or firing being a thing necessary in a commonwealth," begins the account, a cozening coal dealer termed a "leger" had emerged who sold coals by "the sack" but whose sacks contained a quarter less than standard. By this means, as well as including stones at the bottom of the sack, the leger practiced the commodity economy. Discovering the cheat, the flaxwife gathered sixteen neighboring women who had similarly been pinched. The next time the leger came to shoot the coals into her coal bin, the women quickly surrounded him. Though armed with cudgels beneath their aprons they refrained from giving him a beating. Instead they formed a jury, indicted him for cozenage, heard evidence, and examined the sacks before pronouncing him guilty. They then sentenced him to a beating and to be turned out of doors without money, coals, or sacks. Collective neighborhood preserved affordable hydrocarbon energy prices.[22]

The other principles of Magna Carta did not fare so well in Tudor times: anti-enclosure had a protracted practice and was a leading, though losing, theme of the age; subsistence commoning met its arch foe in starvation and the commodity; restraints upon state power were fewer than ever; exile or the right of return was generally one way; and not even the established church, much less the Puritan churches, called for reparations for the loss of monastic lands. After a "curious interval" of neglect in the sixteenth century, in the seventeenth century Magna Carta was transformed and became central in the revolutionary struggle of empire. Shakespeare's contemporary Edward Coke made the commodity and the Magna Carta compatible.

22. Robert Greene, *A Notable Discovery of Cozenage* (1591), in Judges, *Elizabethan Underworld* (see note 13), 146–48.

CHAPTER FOUR

Charters Lost and Found

What kind of times are they, when
A talk about trees is almost a crime
Because it implies silence about so many horrors?
  Bertolt Brecht, "To Those Born Later" (1938)

And I won't tell you where it is, so why do I tell you
anything? Because you still listen, because in times like these
to have you listen at all, it's necessary
to talk about trees.
  Adrienne Rich, "What Kind of Times Are These?" (1991)

Bertolt Brecht wrote against enslavement and genocide. They were the horrors against which the antifascist generation fought, postponing friendliness, revolution, and talk of trees. Brecht implored forbearance from "those born later." Adrienne Rich came later, she answered him. To her the trees concealed the memory of a deeper revolution of meeting houses and signified a woman-friendly ecology where mushrooms could be gathered, for example. The relation of enslavement and the war-making state to the

expropriation of the commons and the assault upon women originated in the seventeenth century. Then the ax triumphed in two
senses, namely, by decapitation and defoliation, regicide and
défrichement (as the French call forest removal).

This chapter develops the two themes about the charters, how
one was found and became a constitutional bulwark and how the
other was lost and left only local and customary practices. The
chapter divides the seventeenth century into three periods: the period of Stuart autocracy (1603–40), the period of the English Revolution (1640–60), and the period of the Restoration (1660–1700).

The beheading of Charles I in 1649 sent shivers through royal
palaces of Europe. The king was tried "as a tyrant, traitor and
murderer, and public enemy to the commonwealth," and for
violating "the fundamental constitutions of this kingdom"
including "the law of the land"—a phrase from Magna Carta.
He smiled at the verdict.[1] John Bradshaw, the chief judge of the
High Court of Justice that tried Charles, quoted "the Great Old
Charter of England" in his speech sentencing the king to death.
King John must have been in the thoughts of Charles Stuart. His
favorite ecclesiastic, Archbishop Laud, who preceded the king at
the chopping block by a few years, said, "So the Great Charter
had an obscure birth from usurpation, and was fostered and
showed to the world by rebellion."[2]

1. *The Kingdome's Weekly Intelligencer,* 30 January 1648.
2. David Lagomarsino and Charles Wood, eds., *The Trial of Charles I: A Documentary History* (Hanover, NH: University Press of New England, 1989), 105,
114; and Christopher Hill, *Puritanism and Revolution: Studies in Interpretation of
the English Revolution of the 17th Century* (New York: Schocken Books, 1958), 69.

What was the relation between the fall of the monarchy and forest clearing? The answer lies among the common people. Margaret Harkett, sixty years old, of Stanmore, Middlesex, was hanged in 1585 as a witch. "She had picked a basket of peas in the neighbor's field without permission. Asked to return them she flung them down in anger; since then no peas would grow in the [neighbor's] field. Later William Goodwin's servant denied her yeast, whereupon his brewing stand dried up. She was struck by a bailiff who had caught her taking wood from the master's ground; the bailiff went mad."[3] Keith Thomas casts this as a conflict between neighborliness and a growing sense of private property. Chartered rights to estovers had been part of neighborhood for centuries, but the charter as such was not well known, according to John Manwood (d. 1610), gamekeeper, forest magistrate, and author of the classic book on forest law. He stated, the forest laws "had grown clean out of knowledge in most places."[4]

Many thousands of women were burned or hanged as witches in Britain during the seventeenth century. From the multiple hangings of 1612 in Pendle Forest (Lancashire) to the Salem witch trials of 1692 (nineteen hanged) through the three hundred hangings and burnings by Matthew Hopkins, the Witch-Finder General of 1645, the century of the scientific revolution—the age of reason—saw systematic terror against women, especially the

3. Keith Thomas, *Religion and the Decline of Magic* (New York: Scribner, 1971), 556.
4. John Manwood, *A Treatise and Discourse of the Lawes of the Forrest* (1598; New York: Garland, 1978). This is the enlarged edition of a book on forest laws he wrote six years earlier.

old, the healers, herbalists, counselors, the poor. "They go from door to door for a potful of milk or potage without which they could hardly live," wrote a 1594 observer of such women. Whether a young boy looking for wild plums and falling instead among a witches' conclave, or a weaver charged with stealing turfs (peat), or a beggar charged with sheep stealing, or cow's milk going off, a motif in the evidence against witches was association with common rights of pasturage, pannage, or estovers. Charles I personally examined four witches in 1635.[5]

Over the great arch of English history some parts of Magna Carta, namely chapter 39, evolved in creative response to events while other parts, such as chapter 7 providing the widow with her reasonable estovers of common, and the entire Charter of the Forest, collected dust among the muniments. The smaller charter begins to disappear during the seventeenth-century crisis with the conjuncture of renewal of slavery, colonial conquest, enclosure of common lands, and manifold assaults upon women. Its disappearance and the settlement of Atlantic colonies (Ireland, Caribbean, mainland America) are inseparable.

The crisis of the seventeenth century was a crisis of forestry. With Stuart financial demands, ship building, iron foundry, and a mini-ice age, a transition to coal had begun in the history of hydrocarbons. So the Stuart kings put the squeeze on the forests, reviving forest law when it suited them, extending

---

5. Edgar Peel and Pat Southern, *The Trials of the Lancashire Witches: A Study of Seventeenth-Century Witchcraft* (New York: Taplinger, 1969), 97, 151; Mary Brigg, "The Forest of Pendle in the 17th Century," *Transactions of the Historical Society of Lancashire and Cheshire* 113 (c. 1961).

boundaries of royal forests, prosecuting freeholders, holding forest *eyre* (as the forest courts were called), allocating timber and fuel, and stinting the commons.[6] James I asserted his claims over the copyhold tenants of Pendle Forest in 1608, restricting access to timber, an essential irritant in the Lancashire witch-burning frenzy. Abuse of the forest laws was a major grievance leading to the English Revolution.

Custom belongs at the center of our understanding of English history.[7] The customary rights (pannage, piscary, estovers, chiminage) take on new meanings through these struggles. Billets, elding, bavins, faggots, kids, bush, gorse, furze, peat, whins, cazzons, bracken, sedge, and reeds—once the names for a manifold of natural uses—became reduced to nomenclature for fuel.[8] Part of the crisis of the seventeenth century was reflected in precisely this separation of *statutes* (or "black-letter law") from *common law* (or judges' opinions) and hence also from the custom of the actual commons.

The forest eyre was revived in 1632, first at Windsor and Bagshot, then at the Forest of Dean, then Waltham, the New Forest, and Alice Holt. Charles I's attorney general and lord chief justice, Sir John Finch, was a student of Francis Bacon, and an adept flatterer and outspoken royalist ("Sir, you are the breath of

6. George Hammersley, "The Revival of the Forest Laws Under Charles I," *History* 45, no. 154 (June 1960).

7. Andy Wood, "The Place of Custom in Plebeian Political Culture: England, 1550–1800," *Social History* 22, no. 1 (January 1997).

8. Donald Woodward, "Straw, Bracken and the Wicklow Whale: The Exploitation of Natural Resources in England since 1500," *Past and Present* 159 (May 1998).

our nostrils, and the light of our eyes"). At the Essex assizes he extended the boundaries of the king's forests against local custom. It became one of the articles of impeachment against him. In 1633 in the Star Chamber he sentenced the Puritan and parliamentarian William Prynne (1602–69) to have his ears cut off for seditious libel. At a second trial in 1637 he caused Prynne's ears to be sliced even closer to his skull while his cheeks were branded S and L for seditious libel. Of Finch it was said, "He gave our goods to the King, our lands to the deer, our liberties to the sheriffs." No other court was as hated as the Star Chamber. It was the court that punished a thousand after the Braydon Forest riots in 1631; and it was used against the poor commoners of Gillingham Forest.

Forest perambulations existed since at least the time of Magna Carta. They were ceremonial walks about a territory for asserting and recoding its boundaries, that is, "beating the bounds." A perambulation was a kind of peripatetic map, or walkabout, in which briar-scratched skin, stubbed toes, aching legs aided the memory. Perambulations enlarged royal jurisdiction. Rockingham Forest boundaries extended from six to sixty miles. Large fines against wealthy trespassers were levied in the Star Chamber.[9] The perambulation of the New Forest authorized by Charles II in 1671 resulted in a Latin document that, translated, comprises a single sentence over six pages long, of approximately one thousand nine hundred and eighty words, many hundreds of prepositional phrases (the grammatical unit most having to do with position and direction)—to, from, by, beyond, across, in—

---

9. Kevin Sharpe, *The Personal Rule of Charles I* (New Haven: Yale University Press, 1992), 119.

and human or natural landmarks—ditch, post, hedge, common, vale, pond, gate, river, oak, beech, grave, croft, marsh, lane, road, ford—with current name, alias, and former names, thus making a text layered with semantic history and compact with minute orientation but expressing no action despite huge number of places connected by the tramp of many footsteps. Such was the map of the New Forest whose lawns of chamomile mixed with gorse thickets protected oak and beech seedlings. These aged into the characteristic giant gnarled beeches and oaks perfectly fit, it was said, to the deck beams and curved timbers of English shipping.[10]

If the perambulation was a kind of mapping, it was also a contested act because some walkers brought along axes to chop down enclosures along the way.[11] The walk could become an assertion of popular right, even equality, as it did in 1744 when William Good urged that the annual perambulation become an anti-enclosure protest: "all tenants in the commonable woods in the forest have . . . an equal right of common with those that have houses and lands of their own, and as good a right by custom, and the laws of the land, as the owners of the woods have to timber and underwoods."[12]

10. Richard Mabey, *Flora Britannica* (London: Chatto and Windus, 1996), 371, 78; and Percival Lewis, *Historical Inquiries Concerning Forests and Forest Laws, with Topographical Remarks Upon the Ancient and Modern State of The New Forest* (London: T. Payne, 1811), 178.

11. Bob Bushaway, *By Rite* (London: Junction Books, 1982), 83.

12. Steve Hindle, " 'Not by bread only?' Common Right, Parish Relief and Endowed Charity in a Forest Economy, c. 1600–1800," in *The Poor in England, 1700–1850: An Economy of Makeshifts,* ed. Steven King and Alannah Tomkins (Manchester: Manchester University Press, 2003), 52–53.

Cottagers, artisans, laborers, and poor farmers rioted to preserve their commons against the attempts by Charles I to enclose them, for during the bad harvests and stagnation in the cloth trade, they depended on income supplements from the forests—pannage, grazing, firewood, construction timber, game. Authorities complained that common right, and common of pasture in particular, supported beggars and gave license to thieves, rogues, and "naughty and idle persons." There was much taking of game and timber during scarcities and harsh winters.[13]

Women played a central role in the preservation of common right. The bold Captain Dorothy led the women of Nidderdale against the enclosure of Thorpe Moor. Gleaning was the ancient practice of gathering leftover stalks of grain after the main harvest was completed. It was almost entirely in the control of women, who when they went into the harvested field were led by their own, the gleaners' queen. Gillingham Forest riots in 1626–28 were led by women, saying, "Here we were born and here will we die." An observer of the Leicester Forest riots in 1627, obviously of scholastic bent, noted that it was led by "a certain number of ignorant women." The Forest of Dean riot of 1632 was led by the mythical figure Lady Skimmington. Cannon was brought from Bristol but the gunners prevaricated and refused to fire the guns. In 1633 a second wave of persecution of women swept over Pendle Forest.[14]

13. Buchanan Sharp, *In Contempt of All Authority: Rural Artisans and Riot in the West of England, 1586–1660* (Berkeley: University of California Press, 1980), 5.

14. Peter King, "Customary Rights and Women's Earnings: The Importance of Gleaning to the Rural Labouring Poor," *Economic History Review,* 2nd s., 44, no. 3 (1991): 462.

During the 1607 uprising in Rockingham Forest more than fifty people defending common right were massacred. The commotion of forest commoners was a major step in the history of class struggle in England. New kinds of writing arose describing the class struggle, such as the seditious writing wrapped around a ball of wax ("living the poor doth want and living they shall have") and thrown into a church choir, or such as Shakespeare's treatment of the hard-hearted ruler faced with a starving populace in his Roman play *Coriolanus* (1608).

In the high weald of east Sussex in 1680 the commoners who had had right of common of pannage, grazing, estovers, and stone for building and marl for fertilizer, petitioned against enclosure of Ashdown Forest. In 1689 they pulled down the fences and tossed away the court injunction: "and after he had thrown down the Hedge into the ditch he threw the said paper upon it and covered it with earth." Praxis buried lex. Its enclosure was a process of protest, negotiation, and compromise over a period of fifty years with the result that the forest was never totally enclosed and a large amount of land remains open today.[15]

Edward Coke was the leading constitutionalist of Parliament, a man of lawyers, property, and commerce.[16] An individualist, he wrote that "the house of an Englishman is to him as his castle."

---

15. Linda Merricks, "'Without Violence and by Controlling the Poorer Sort': The Enclosure of Ashdown Forest, 1640–1693," *Sussex Archaeological Collections* (1994): 132

16. Christopher Hill, *Intellectual Origins of the English Revolution* (Oxford: Clarendon Press, 1965).

In debate Coke said, "Magna Charta is such a fellow, that he will have no sovereign."[17] He wrote "there is no law to warrant tortures in this land." Dismissed as chief justice of the King's Bench in 1616, imprisoned in the Tower in 1621, he helped draw up the Petition of Right of 1628. Debating the petition, Rudyeard said, "I shall be very glad to see that good old decrepit law of Magna Carta. . . . I shall be glad to see it walk again, with new vigor and luster."[18] Coke put it on its feet.

The crackdown on the forests was preceded by the tug-of-war between king and Parliament. The Magna Carta was transformed from a medieval document rarely cited, though frequently confirmed, into a modern constitutional law, from a feudal particularization of privileges into a charter suitable to commerce, property, and individualism. Edward Coke helped to transform it, first by amalgamating habeas corpus with chapter 39, second by inserting it into the colonial charters of Atlantic colonies, third by affirming that Magna Carta's *nullus liber homo* (free man) equaled all the people, including women, and fourth by linking Magna Carta to Parliament.[19]

In 1631 Charles I heard that Coke was working on a book on Magna Carta and prohibited it. As Coke lay dying, his law chambers were ransacked and his manuscripts were confiscated. Parliament ordered their recovery at the beginning of the English

17. *Cobbett's Complete Collection of State Trials* (London: R. Bagshaw, 1820), 3:194.

18. J. R. Tanner, *English Constitutional Conflicts of the Seventeenth Century, 1603–1689* (Cambridge: Cambridge University Press, 1928).

19. Michael E. Tigar and Madeleine R. Levy, *Law and the Rise of Capitalism* (New York: Monthly Review Press, 1977), 258.

Revolution, and they were published posthumously in 1642. These were the *Institutes of the Laws of England,* whose four parts influenced subsequent jurisprudence. From its ornate title page, a masterpiece of intertwined architectural intricacy, to the extravagant design of the textual page with commentary upon Magna Carta line by line in both Latin and English, with footnotes, marginal notes, and explanatory notes, the work was a rococo tour de force. English reformers wished to show that they were restorers of ancient custom, not innovators.

Coke included the Charter of the Forest in his discussion of Magna Carta and referred to it as "a declaratory law restoring the subject to his former right." As lawyers do, he began by defining his terms: the forest is composed of eight things: soil, covert, laws, courts, judges, officers, game, and certain bounds. Three of these might be termed natural, whereas the rest pertain to human society. "Generally a man may common in a forest," he says. Stressing the use of *common* as a verb, Coke wants us to understand it as a customary activity, not as a thing or resource. In contrast to the law—understood since the early sixteenth century by Thomas More and others to be a vast conspiracy among the rich to oppress the poor—custom traditionally belonged to manor courts, "little Commonwealths" as Coke called them, and could actually protect the poor.[20]

"A man may have common for his sheep within the King's forest." "Every man in his own woods within the forest may take housebote and heybote" or "otherwise according to custom." Coke explained the *drifts* of the forest, or roundups of cattle.

---

20. Edward Coke, *Complete Copyholder* (London: W. Lee, 1650), 203.

"First, to see whether those that ought to common do common with such kind of cattle as by prescription or grant they ought. Secondly, if they common with such cattle as they ought, whether they do surcharge or no. Thirdly, if the cattle of any stranger be there, which ought not to common at all." On the one hand Coke recognized that the Forest Charter, like the Magna Carta, restored "the subject to his former right"; on the other hand he said that forest law was bounded by the common law and that it could not stand against laws enacted by Parliament. As he elevated Magna Carta to fundamental law, he subordinated the Charter of the Forest to statute and judges' law.

Once the English Revolution began, one of its early acts rolled back royal encroachments on the forest to preserve it, not so much for the poor as for rich commoners. So the 1641 Act for the Certainty of Forests (17 Charles I c.16), among other things, "provided tenants, owners, and occupiers . . . shall or may use and enjoy such common and other profits and easements within the forests as anciently or accustomarily they have used and enjoyed" and restored the boundaries set by the perambulations of 1623. Commissioners might be appointed by the Lord Chancellor to set these boundaries as "commonly known."[21] The Grand Remonstrance of December 1641, the huge petition from the House of Commons, contained 204 points of remonstrance, number 21 referring to "the enlargements of forests, contrary to *Carta de Foresta.*"

Magna Carta became a revolutionary tract, its possibilities expanding with the progress of the revolution. The 1641 act for the

---

21. S. R. Gardiner, ed., *The Constitutional Documents of the Puritan Revolution, 1625–1660* (Oxford: Clarendon Press, 1906), 192–96.

abolition of the Star Chamber (17 Charles I c.10) began by quoting Magna Carta's chapter 39. Pamphlets in Thomason's collection grew from 24 in 1640, to 721 the following year, to 2,134 in 1642. In that year John Milton wrote *The Reason for Church Government* against church hierarchy and the "merchants of Babylon," who "by their corrupt and servile doctrines" will establish slavery and "repeal and erase every line and clause of both our great charters."[22]

John Lilburne (1615–57), champion of the people, pamphleteer, agitator, and prisoner, organized the first democratic political party, the Levellers, which by means of sacrifice, direct action, and symbolic performances linked the Magna Carta to the concept of the nation.[23] Tub preachers and talk in the inns and gatherings conveyed the words to eager hearers, and pamphlets conveyed them to those "sitting at studious lamps." Lilburne was the first to go to prison on behalf of the view that self-incrimination was a violation of Magna Carta, as William Walwyn pointed out. In the Tower he listened for the tramp of feet and the ring of horses' hooves as Thomas Fairfax (1612–71), commander of Cromwell's New Model Army, entered London. When Fairfax entered the Tower, he called for Magna Carta saying, "this is that which we have fought for, and by God's help we must maintain."[24]

22. John Milton, *Complete Poems and Major Prose,* ed. Merritt Hughes (New York: Odyssey, 1957), 685.

23. Pauline Gregg, *Free-born John: A Biography of John Lilburne* (London: George Harrap, 1961), 95.

24. William Walwyn, *England's Lamentable Slaverie* (1645), in *Tracts on Liberty in the Puritan Revolution, 1638–1647,* ed. William Haller (New York: Columbia University Press, 1933), 3:311–18.

The goal of the Levellers was "the right, freedome, safety, and well-being of every particular man, woman, and child in England." Magna Carta became "the Englishman's legal birthright and inheritance." Lilburne said, "the liberty of the whole English nation" is in chapter 39. He addressed the soldiers, "we are at best but your hewers of wood and drawers of water. The ancient and famous magistracy of this nation, the Petition of Right, the Great Charter of England . . . which our ancestors at an extraordinary dear rate, as with abundance of their blood and treasure, purchased for the inheritance of us and of the generations after us."[25]

Coke, we saw, gave Magna Carta its legs. One Leveller, Richard Overton, actually put his legs to use in protecting it. He and his wife were dragged to prison. "They would have forced me along up the hill on my feet, yea, they intreated me, but at that time I was not minded to be their DRVDG, or to make use of my feet to carry the rest of my body to the jail, therefore I let them hang as if they had not been one of my own, or like a couple of farthing Candles dangling at my knees." The copy of Coke's *Second Institute* upon Magna Carta that Overton clutched in his hands was taken: "by an assault they got the great Charter of *Englands Liberties and Freedoms* from me . . . and forthwith without any warrant poor Magna Charta was clapt up close prisoner in Newgate, and my poor fellow prisoner derived of the comfortable visitation of friends."[26]

25. John Lilburne, *Just Defense* (1653), 14; and his *Young Men's and the Apprentice's Outcry* (1649), in *The English Levellers,* ed. Andrew Sharp (London: Cambridge University Press, 1998).

26. Richard Overton, *The Commoners Complaint: or, Dreadful Warning from Newgate to the Commons of England* (1646), reprinted in *Tracts on Liberty in the Puritan Revolution, 1638–1647,* ed. William Haller (New York:

On 11 September 1648, the Levellers submitted to Parliament the Large Petition (with 40,000 signatures), which raised questions of the commons and reparations. Among its twenty-seven demands were ones for popular sovereignty; opposition to forcing "any sort of men to serve in wars"; religious toleration even toward atheists, Muslims, and Jews; punishment for monopolizing and engrossing; reparations to persons oppressed by "Monopolizers or Projectors"; trial by jury of peers; no conviction but by two witnesses; no self-incrimination; release of debtors from prison; and the opening of "all late enclosures of Fens and other Commons." Losing common rights led to the criminalization of the commoner. Thus safeguards against tyranny were becoming linked to preservation of commoning.

In May 1649 thousands of women beseeched the House of Commons with a Petition of Women, reminding the MPs that they were worthy petitioners created in the image of God and had an equal interest in the freedoms of the commonwealth, as stated in the Petition of Right and other good laws.[27] They could not stay at home but rallied to protest the imprisonment of the Levellers, to condemn the death of Robert Lockyer (who had mutinied against armed service in Ireland), to denounce martial law, and to

---

Columbia University Press, 1934), 3:385–86, 393. Coke's contemporary Robert Cotton collected the surviving original charters. There is poetic justice to one story that he saved one from a tailor whose shears were about to transform the parchment into a pattern for a suit of clothes; the sheepskin, the epidermis of a creature once nourished in a commons, was to be turned into a means to make the tailor's "cabbage," a customary right to the excess cuttings.

27. A. S. P. Woodhouse, *Puritanism and Liberty* (Chicago: University of Chicago Press, 1951), 367 69.

call for reparations. Granted, the petition comes "unto you by the weak hand of women, it being a usual thing with God, by weak means to work mighty effects." Here we can continue with one of the most eloquent passages of the era, "God favors all weak things and hath a special regard to tender ones when under darkness or oppression. And in order hereto he lays the axe to the root of the tree and strengthens our weak principle; he lays the foundation of freedom within us and so proceeds to blow up the fire till the room be too hot for unrighteousness and wrong." It was written by John Warr, a radical with special interest in law.[28]

With Gerrard Winstanley (1609–76), the liberation theologian, clothier, cowherd, and communist who founded the colonies of *Diggers* on wasteland at midcentury, indeed, the fire grew hot, and it had to do with *who* might lay the ax to the trees. With forty-three other people he signed *A Declaration from the Poor Oppressed People of England* (1649) that resolved "to plant the Commons withal . . . seeing the Earth was made for us, as well as for you." Addressed to the lords of the land who "do cause the Trees and Woods that grow upon the Commons, which you pretend a Royalty unto, to be cut down and sold; for your own private use, whereby the Common Land, which your own mouths doe say belongs to the poor, is impoverished, and the poor oppressed people robbed of their Rights, . . . while you, and the rich Free-holders, make the most profit of the Commons, by your overstocking of them with Sheep and Cattle; and the poor . . . are checked by you, if they cut Wood, Heath, Turf, or

28. John Warr, *The Privileges of the People; or, Principles of Common Right and Freedom* (February 1649), in *A Spark in the Ashes: The Pamphlets of John Warr,* ed. Stephen Sedley and Lawrence Kaplan (London: Verso, 1992), 80.

Furseys, in places about the Common, where you disallow." Just before Easter 1649 the parson of the parish and the lord of the manor led hired men "to pull down a poor mans house, that was built upon the Commons, and kikt and struck the poor mans wife, so that she miscarried of her Child." Winstanley negotiated an understanding with the lord that both houses and trees remain. However on Good Friday the lord returned with fifty men to burn them out, which they did, throwing their belongings "up and down the Common, not pittying the cries of many little Children, and their frighted Mothers."[29]

While Winstanley thought Magna Carta was over-emphasized—"the best Laws that *England* hath (viz. *Magna Carta*) . . . are yoaks and manicles, tying one sort of people to be slaves of another"[30]—Thomas Tany, writing as "a commoner of England," argued that "Magna Charta is the being of our being." He was influenced by the alternativists of the day, those who thought and lived as though another world were possible. Homeless, Tany pitched his tent where he might in and about London. He refused to take his hat off at the bar of the House of Commons and was imprisoned for blasphemy.[31] He died at sea

29. *An Humble Request to the Ministers of Both Universities and to all Lawyers in every Inns-a-Court* (April 1650), in *The Works of Gerrard Winstanley,* ed. George H. Sabine with an introduction (Ithaca: Cornell University Press, 1941), 433.

30. Gerrard Winstanley, *An Appeal to the House of Commons, Desiring their Answer; Whether the Common People shall have the quiet enjoyment of the Commons and Waste Lands* (1649), in Sabine, Works, 274.

31. Thomas Tandy, *The Nations Right in Magna Carta Discussed with the Thing called Parliament* (1650), ed. Andrew Hopton with an introduction (repr.; London: Aporia Press, 1988).

in an attempt to recover Jerusalem for the "true Jews," namely, anyone ready to "feed the hungry, clothe the naked, oppress none, and set free them bounden."

After the execution of the king and after the proclamation of the republic, John Warr published *The Corruption and Deficiency of the Laws of England soberly discovered; or, Liberty Working Up to Its Just Height.* As there is no such thing as too much freedom, it follows that laws were made to bridle princes or parliaments. To him, "fundamental law" is a false idol. He rests his case upon history, which shows that the will of the conquerors in their successive invasions can be repelled only "by fury of war of incessantness of address" by the people. The Normans brought in landlord, tenant, and tenure, which were "slavish ties and badges upon men, grounded originally in conquest and power." His position is close to that of the Diggers. However, he departs from Winstanley in his estimation of Magna Carta. Indeed, while he mentions it, what he emphasizes, almost alone within the teeming discussions of the English Revolution, is the Charter of the Forest. He praises the Forest Charter for abridging the king's power to enlarge himself in the forests. Although John Warr wrote in June 1649, just months after the defeat of the Levellers and the massacre of the Diggers, he holds that the people, like a worm when trod upon, will turn again.

Adrienne Rich found the memory of revolution and the ghosts of the persecuted among stands of trees. She might have been expressing the condition of England after the Restoration, not the condition of America at the end of the twentieth century. She walked at the edge of dread in the sense that at the boundary of the commons lay genocide, enslavement.

this is not somewhere else but here,
Our country moving closer to its own truth and dread
Its own ways of making people disappear.

The condition of dread during the English Restoration included the Clarendon Code, disenfranchising dissenters and forbidding them to meet, the restrictions upon forests and commoning, the Atlantic slave trade, the colonial carceral archipelago—Bunyan jailed, Milton harassed, the witches of Salem consumed. The repression began earlier when the wealthier freeholders had turned decisively against the customary rights of the poor.[32] Cromwell's Council of State was informed in 1654 that "the principal end" of enclosure of forests is "advantage to husbandry and tillage, to which all commons are destructive." Two acts of 1653 and 1654 authorized the disafforestation of all remaining royal forests.[33]

The Restoration also brought a counterinterpretation to Coke's expanded, generous, revolutionary Magna Carta. Coke's first comment on the *nullus liber homo* clause of chapter 39 was emphatic, "this extends to villeins," opening the way to democratic constructions that the Levellers developed. Robert Brady, physician to Charles II and James II, composed *A Complete History of England* in 1685 as "an Impregnable Rock against the pretended Sovereignty and Power of the People in this Nation."[34] To him the

32. Wood, "Place of Custom."

33. C. H. Firth and R. S. Rait, eds., *Acts and Ordinances of the Interregnum* (London: HMSO, 1911), 2:782–812, 993–99.

34. J. G. A. Pocock, *The Ancient Constitution and the Feudal Law* (Cambridge: Cambridge University Press, 1957), is a development of the author's 1952 thesis, "The Controversy over the Origin of the Commons," a study of Brady and the House of Commons, not common right or common lands.

nullus liber homos clause of chapter 39 referred to freeholders of property. He showed that the condition of "ordinary people" was the same before and after the Norman Conquest. At Runnymede Norman barons made the "noise" culminating in "liberty," by which they meant a relaxation of feudal dues, and it had nothing to do with fundamental rights and liberties or with an Englishman's birthright. The archbishop and bishops led them in this "dance," but Coke, the Levelers, the Diggers, and others created new steps for it during the English Revolution.

Brady approached the composition of the working class by means of philology—the ancient Latin authors use terms such as *villein* and *rustic*—and then he distinguishes among various terms according as the person paid rent or labor for access to land. The struggle for access to customary rights is thus a struggle to preserve the working day. Later sources refer to cottagers and customary tenants, servants and bondsmen, and *operarii,* "poor miserable labourers that wrought at all times and seasons, and did all manner of Works at the command of their Lords." They were under socage tenures, that is, they paid money rent or did labor services but did not have to go to war at the lord's bidding. The charter made no difference to the majority of English people who "were as much Hewers of Wood and Drawers of Water, as truly *vassals* and *Slaves* after, as before this Great Charter."[35]

To the authoritarian and materialist philosopher Thomas Hobbes (1588–1679), law is the command of the sovereign, noth-

---

35. *Daily Gazetteer* in 1735 arguing against *The Craftsman,* and quoted in Anne Pallister, *Magna Carta: The Heritage of Liberty* (Oxford: Clarendon Press, 1971), 53.

ing more, nothing less, while to the philosopher of global empiricism and private property John Locke (1632–1704), law is the agreement of the propertied. Neither says much, if anything, about the Charters of Liberties. "Sir Edward Coke doth not care to hear of the Feudal Law as it was in use at this time, and hath a fine fetch to play off the Great Charter and interpret it by his Modern-law." The thought is that the distance in time between feudalism and modernity is too great for continuity. In wave mechanics, however, the "fetch" of a wave derives its power from the distance it has traveled, and the distance in space could be oceanic.

Magna Carta took on an Atlantic dimension. Coke helped to draft the royal charter of the Virginia Company in 1606. The royal charters establishing other English colonies in America—Massachusetts in 1629, Maryland in 1632, Maine in 1639, Connecticut in 1662, Rhode Island in 1663—also alluded to Magna Carta. Whereas those colonists used the Magna Carta against the authority of the crown (New York's charter of liberty quoted Magna Carta's chapter 39), they ignored its forest provisions when it came to their own intrusions into the woodlands of the indigenous peoples. Magna Carta became an instrument of both colonial independence and acquisitive empire.[36]

While the Diggers were being burned off the commons, Roger Williams, an Englishman gone to Massachusetts, recorded a conversation with the Indians. "Why come the Englishmen hither? And measuring others by themselves; they say, It is because you want *firing:* for they, having burnt up the *wood* in one place . . . they are faine to follow the *wood;* and so to remove to a fresh new place

36. Louise P. Kellogg, *The American Colonial Charter* (Washington DC: GPO, 1904).

for the *wood's* sake." English forests were cut down at such a rate that toward the end of the century John Evelyn despaired of the national security, inasmuch as the navy provided the island's "wooden walls." The expansion of the British empire was by means of wood products and it was to the end of acquiring wood products.

The indigenous people recognized that the composition of North American forests was the result of many natural changes and interaction with human history. The biannual burning altered the composition of forest stands to fire-tolerant species, such as loblolly, longleaf, and slash pine. The land was not virgin land, it was widowed land! The settlers' survival depended on knowledge of the "many ancient & knowing Indians." Indians cultivated tobacco, sweet potatoes, tomatoes, squash, watermelons, kidney beans, sunflowers, and maize. "Beyond the fields and in the forest, fallen or dead wood was collected for fuel, mainly by the women, so that it was generally known as 'squaw wood.' "[37] Estovers, again.

The Restoration diarist and gentleman environmentalist John Evelyn (1620–1706) inherited a fortune that his grandfather had accumulated under James I and Charles I through his royal monopoly on saltpeter, essential ingredient (with sulfur and charcoal) to gunpowder. The "saltpeter man" forcibly ransacked stables, barns, dovecots, pigeon houses in search of potassium nitrate. The grandson's project was to make an inventory of English trees in terms of their use values, and to convey this knowledge from commoners to commercial, scientific, and military markets. Not once does Evelyn mention the Forest Charter. Enclosed woods thrive better than unfenced forest. He wrote disdainfully of "satisfying of

37. William Cronon, *Changes in the Land: Indians, Colonists, and the Ecology of New England* (New York: Hill and Wang, 1983), 48.

a few clamorous, and rude Commoners."[38] He could not escape a millennium of custom, but he could bury it within Latin and Greek obscurantism. He concluded by quoting a Latin proverb of Erasmus, who was paraphrasing the Greek poet Theocritus, *Praesente Quercu ligna quivis colligit,* "In the presence of an oak everyone collects firewood."[39] Referring to An Act for the Punishment of Unlawful Cutting or Stealing or Spoiling of Wood (15 Charles II c.2), he coolly noted that ancient law punished the "beheading" of a tree by the forfeiture of a hand.[40] Nevertheless, the view persisted that wood could be taken "by hook or by crook." The criminalization of customary rights became a principal theme of the social history of England for the next century and a half.[41]

If the commoners' charter was lost, the Magna Carta was strengthened in three ways: preservation of the jury, habeas corpus, and prohibition of torture.

In 1680 John Hawles wrote *The Englishman's Right; or, A Dialogue between a Barrister at Law and a Juryman,* which defined an essential part of the array of rights understood in the concept to be "free-born." The jury originated "time out of mind." It was "cotemporary with the nation itself." These liberties were recited and confirmed by the Magna Carta, chapters 14 and 39: "The end

38. John U. Nef, *Industry and Government in France and England, 1540–1640* (Ithaca: Cornell University Press, 1957), 92, 319.

39. Erasmus, *Adages* 3.1.86.

40. John Evelyn, *Sylva: or, A Discourse on Forest Trees and the Propagation of Timber in His Majesty's Dominions* (London: Royal Society, 1664), 206.

41. Robert W. Bushaway, "From Custom to Crime: Wood-Gathering in 18th and Early 19th Century England: A Focus for Conflict in Hampshire, Wiltshire and the South," in *Outside the Law: Studies in Crime and Order, 1650–1850,* ed. John Rule (Exeter: University of Exeter Press, 1982), 74.

of Juries is to preserve men from oppression," said Coke. In December 1667 the House of Commons found the Lord Chief Justice arbitrary and illegal in his use of power by fining juries, that he hath "undervalued, vilified, and corrupted Magna Charta, the great Preserver of our lives, freedom, and property." Lord Chief Justice Keeling had aroused the wrath of the Commons by fining a grand jury of Somerset and forcing it to return a verdict of murder rather than manslaughter; when one of the jury referred to Magna Carta in protest, he replied, 'Magna Farta, what ado with this have we?' "[42] No longer stretching its legs, the great charter was becoming hobbled.

In August 1670 William Penn preached in Gracechurch Street in London to a crowd of three or four hundred. He was indicted for disturbing the peace "to the great *terror* and disturbance of his liege people and subjects." He pleaded not guilty. The jury found him guilty of "speaking," which was not a crime. Detained through Saturday and Sunday, on Monday the jury persisted in rendering a verdict of Not Guilty. The court fined the jurors forty marks each. Edward Bushel brought a writ of habeas corpus against "that torturous illegal imprisonment" and, reversing its stance, the court found for him.

King Charles and his *cabal* repressed the plots and risings during the Restoration by banishing suspects to Barbados, Virginia, and Tangier.[43] When the Habeas Corpus Act was passed in 1679 it was called "an Act for the better securing the liberty of the subject, and for prevention of imprisonment beyond the seas." It

---

42. Pallister, *Magna Carta,* 29–30.

43. Robert L. Greaves, *Enemies Under His Feet: Radicals and Nonconformists in Britain, 1664–1677* (Palo Alto: Stanford University Press, 1900), 83.

provided that no English subject "may be sent prisoner into Scotland, Ireland, Jersey, Guernsey, Tangier, or into parts, garrisons, islands or places beyond the seas." The British constitution was formed during a transcontinental recomposition of the labor force: transportation of felons, penal policy, slave trade, plantation agriculture, penal laws in Ireland, migration to America, and indentured servitude. Brecht wrote,

> For we went, changing countries oftener than our shoes
> Through the wars of the classes, despairing
> When there was injustice only, and no rebellion.

In 1680 *The Great Charter of the Forest, Declaring the Liberties of It* was published, and a contemporary manuscript hand subscribes, "A declaration of ye Liberties of ye English Nation with respect to Forrests." In *The Spirit of the Laws* some eighty years later Montesquieu, citing Tacitus, praised the English government by saying "this beautiful system was invented first in the woods."

The Charters of Liberties had found their legs and were preserved by scholarship, politics, and direct action, by "dancing," as Robert Brady complained (in his *Complete History*). But the Cinderella dance, where even the drudge may be beautiful, shuts down at midnight. Although aspects of Magna Carta survived in the Habeas Corpus Act (1679), Bushel's case (1671), and the Bill of Rights (1689) one of its legs was lamed. Its companion, the Charter of the Forest, like Cinderella's missing shoe was, for all practical purposes, lost. Adrienne Rich again,

> I won't tell you where the place is, the dark mesh of the woods
> Meeting the unmarked strip of light—
> Ghost-ridden crossroads, leafmold paradise:
> I know already who wants to buy it, sell it, make it disappear.

CHAPTER FIVE

The Charters in Blackface and Whiteface

I wander thro' each charter'd street,
Near where the charter'd Thames does flow,
And mark in every face I meet
Marks of weakness, marks of woe.

William Blake, "London" (1792)

The enclosure movement and the slave trade ushered industrial capitalism into the modern world. By 1832 England was largely closed, its countryside privatized (some even mechanized), in contrast to a century earlier when its fields were largely open—"champion" country, to use the happy technical term—and yeomen, children, women could subsist by commoning. By 1834 slavery had been abolished in the British empire whereas a century earlier, on 11 September 1713, the *asiento* licensed British slavers to trade African slaves throughout the Americas. Together the expelled commoners and the captured Africans provided the labor power available for exploitation in the factories of the field (tobacco and sugar) and the factories of the towns (woolens and cottons). Whether indentured servant, West African youngster, former milkmaid, or woodsman without his woods, the lords of humankind looked upon them indifferently as laboring bodies to produce surplus value, and so emerged the Atlantic working day, which entirely depended upon a prior dis-commoning.

The legal cliché is that the American constitution is written, while the English is unwritten. Strictly speaking this is untrue inasmuch as both have stemmed from the Magna Carta of 1215. The important difference between English and American constitutional development is not that one is unwritten and the other is written. The difference is Africa. The maintenance and expansion of unwaged labor on the plantation where slaves produced surplus value was indispensable to American constitutional and revolutionary history, whereas the salient English development was the statutory enclosure of lands and privatization of all attempts at commoning. The Atlantic multitudes were divided by race in the emerging *constitution*.[1] The Charters of Liberties were contested in this process. The enclosure movement, opposed by English commoners, conveniently ignored the Forest Charter. The movement to abolish slavery used Magna Carta and helped to put it back into the English working-class movement.

Two episodes of the eighteenth-century Enlightenment reveal how the struggle to preserve commoning in England intersected

---

1. David Roediger, *The Wages of Whiteness: Race and the Making of the American Working Class* (New York: Verso, 1991).

with trans-Atlantic slavery. First, some English commoners blackened their faces as "sham Negroes" in 1722, to protect customary rights. This resulted in the passage of the infamous Waltham Black Act (9 George I c.22), part of a movement that tended to racialize crime and to criminalize race. The act made disguising (or *blacking*) a crime, and it did so at an important moment in the development of white supremacy. Second, half a century later in 1774, a former African slave in England whitened his face in order to obtain a writ of habeas corpus against the enslavement of a fellow worker. The former episode criminalized the disguise of going Black. The latter episode arose at the beginning of the abolitionist movement when the scholar and activist Granville Sharp (1752–1813) proved that Magna Carta prohibited slavery.

The analysis of charters was central to the Enlightenment. The year 1681 was "truly a great one in the history of the human mind," wrote the twentieth-century French historian Marc Bloch, because in that year the Benedictine monk Jean Mabillon published *De re diplomatica,* which stated the principles of verification of documents. Mabillon studied medieval charters in particular. *Diplomatics* became the foundation of historical criticism, which also included chronology, epigraphy, paleontology, handwriting, and philology.

William Blackstone (1723–1780) made law an academic discipline. He was a professor at All Souls College, Oxford; he reformed the university press; he wrote a four-volume commentary on the laws of England (1765–69), "the most influential law book ever published in the English language."[2] In 1759 he published

2. *Dictionary of National Biography,* s.v. "Blackstone, William."

The Great Charter and the Charter of the Forest, which for the first time applied to the charters the critical, comparative method made known by Mabillon.[3]

He showed, first, that there were both prequels and sequels—preceding articles and subsequent reissues—and, second, he showed that by analyzing these chapter by chapter, comparing them to the articles, or *capitula*, preceding, and to the versions of Henry III of November 1216 and 1217 following John's of 1215, a text was established by the third reissue in 1225 which the numerous subsequent confirmations of Magna Carta accepted.[4] Only after 11 September 1217 when the articles of peace concluding the civil war were agreed on did Henry III grant a new charter and also a charter of the forest. The charter of the forest expands, amplifies, or amends chapters of the great charter, and this is why as documents they were published together. According to Blackstone, "this original charter of the forest, and all authentic records of it, are at present lost." He prints from an original in Durham

3. Marc Bloch, *The Historian's Craft,* trans. Peter Putnam (Manchester: Manchester University Press, 1954), 81. Blackstone was involved in scholarly dispute with Dr. Lyttleton, dean of Exeter and later bishop of Carlisle, who possessed an ancient roll containing both charters. Blackstone did not accept it as original, and controversy raged in the Antiquarian Society.

4. We can make these comparisons ourselves thanks to J. C. Holt, *The Magna Carta,* 2nd ed. (Cambridge: Cambridge University Press, 1992), which reprints the relevant documents. "Diploma" etymologically came from a Greek word meaning the doubling of parchment by folding it in half. While inspecting the earlier document's chapter 32, Holt found "a few letters are worn out by the folding or the original." They pertained to what became chapters 12 and 13 of Magna Carta, saying no scutage or aids (taxes) "except by the common counsel of our realm" and preserving the "ancient liberties and free customs" of London.

cathedral whose green seal is "still perfect, but the body of the charter has been unfortunately gnawn by rats." Other flaws were attributed to "the haste of the ancient amanuenses." He collated this mutilated original with an inspeximus of 25 Edward I (1297). A month after the charters were renewed in 1225, a perambulation was made of the bounds of the forests of England. The king confirmed them again under threat from the barons, "the yoke of slavery was now heavier than ever, especially with regard to the forest." Chapter 7 of the great charter was modified to include *rationabile estoverium suum interim de communi,* allowing widows reasonable estovers of common.

While Blackstone preserved the scholarship of estovers and forest customs, the practice was preserved by *blacking.* Blacking, wrote its first historian, commenced "about the times of general confusion, when the late pernicious schemes of the South Sea Company bore all things down before them, and laid waste what the industry and good husbandry of families had gather'd together."[5] The 1720 South Sea Bubble, when the speculative mania of get-rich-quick seized the quality in society, opened the rankest period of corruption in English history.

The commercial-economic conjuncture was characterized by the expansion of trade following the Peace of Utrecht (1714), which put an end to one of those early dynastic wars that were really global wars between European empires for colonies; this one was called the War of Spanish Succession. Which royal behind sat on the throne was the least of it. New instruments of state power, like the bank, the coinage, the insurance companies, and

5. *The History of the Blacks of Waltham in Hampshire and those under like Denomination in Berkshire* (1723).

the national debt permitted the most intense concentration of capital ever amassed. Furthermore, finance capitalism permitted violent swings of attention to wherever expropriations from common lands were most profitable. "Britain was sunk in lucre's sordid charms," wrote Alexander Pope.

The political-military conjuncture was dominated by the threat to the Protestant succession posed by the exiled Stuart pretender in France, a Catholic. It was a short sail from France across the Channel to the southern coasts of England. From the Norman Conquest to the aerial combat during the Battle of Britain these were vulnerable stretches in the island's bulwarks. Hence the English imaginary, as Raymond Williams pointed out, locates the national essence not far from these white cliffs. The sturdy yeoman described by the journalist William Cobbett (1763–1835), the peaceful ornithology described by the ecologist Gilbert White (1720–93), or the mannered gentry of the novelist Jane Austen (1775–1817) were conceived near Farnham, precisely where blacking began.[6] Round about Farnham timber was wanted for the construction of men-of-war and East Indiamen that stopped in Portsmouth for repairs or were built there from scratch, for the purpose of the globalization of commodity trade.

Here's how a flashpoint in the episodes of the Waltham Blacks began: "Mr. Wingfield who has a fine Parcel of growing Timber on his Estate near Farnham fell'd Part of it: The poor People were admitted (as is customary) to pick up the small Wood; but some abusing the Liberty given, carry'd off what was not allow'd, which that Gentleman resented; and, as an Example to others,

6. Raymond Williams, *The Country and the City* (New York: Oxford University Press, 1973), chap. 11.

made several pay for it." The passive voice helps confuse the issue: who adjudicated disputes on the commons? Was the "Liberty" one that was customary, or was it at the pleasure of Wingfield? Who decided the allowances? The presumption here is that the customs belonged to Wingfield. But this was disputed from two directions. The first line of opposition is suggested by Charles Withers, surveyor general of woods, who observed in 1729 "that the country people everywhere think they have *a sort of right* [emphasis added] to the wood & timber in the forests, and whether the notion may have been delivered down to them by tradition, from the times these forests were declared to be such by the Crown, when there were great struggles and contests about them, he is not able to determine." He does not say that he read the Charters of Liberties.[7]

William Waterson was the vicar of Winkfield. He said, "the great inducement of late years to purchasing and building in the Forest has been the relaxation or rather annihilation of the Forest Laws." He inquired into the use and abuse of common rights of his parishioners. When he first came to the parish, "the people did not know by what title they held their estates, or in what respects they were *free from,* or subject to, the *forest laws.*" He actively defended the right to turf cutting. He was the local historian searching for legitimating documentation such as the Elizabethan patent, Chancery decrees (1605), or the survey of 1613.

The second type of opposition that the proprietor of Farnham Park faced was the direct action of the Blacks. The account continues, "Upon which, the Blacks summon'd the Myrmidons

7. E. P. Thompson, *Whigs and Hunters: The Origin of the Waltham Black Act* (New York: Pantheon, 1975), 239. I rely on this complete account, although it is narrow in scope.

[constables, in 18th-century cant], stripp'd the Bark off several of the standing Trees, and notch'd the Bodies of others, thereby to prevent their Growth; and left a Note on one of the maim'd Trees, to inform the Gentleman, that this was their first Visit; and that if he did not return the Money receiv'd for Damage, he must expect a second from . . . the Blacks."

The Blacks had Jacobite sympathies and *might* be loyal to the pretender across the sea. Their leader declared his intention to swear near a public house in Waltham Chase his loyalty to the Hanoverian settlement, "which he accordingly did; but 15 of his Sooty Tribe appear'd, some in Coats made of Deer-Skins, others with Fur Caps, &c. all well armed and mounted: There were likewise at least 300 People assembled to see the *Black Chief* and his *Sham* Negroes." So the Waltham Blacks *may* not be loyal to the Whigs.

Three hundred people was a considerable crowd. Advance word would have gone out—"the Blacks are coming." Why does he say "*Sham* Negroes"? The blacking was not only disguise, it was disguise *as Negroes,* that is, Africans. And why *sham?* It was a recent slang and cant term of imposture and hoaxing, suggesting trickery. More was involved than concealment. Something was up.

In Hampshire commoners took snap wood pretty freely, not distinguishing between forests and private woods. They crossed them daily, watching nuts and berries ripen, taking a few rabbits. "The co-existence of turbary in forests and commons, with the hedges, spinneys and woods of landowners, make the getting of wood in particular seem to be a general right." The defense of commoning was integral to class consciousness. The Waltham Blacks protested: they "had no other design but to do justice, and to see that the Rich did not insult or oppress the poor." They were assured that the chase (a term for a tract of open country used for breeding animals to hunt) was "originally design'd to feed Cattle, and not to fatten deer for the clergy, &c."[8]

The central common right was access to pasture for livestock, "common of herbage," as the Forest Charter says. Keeping a cow was possible on two acres, and on a smaller plot in a forest or fen. Half the villagers of England were entitled to common grazing. As late as the eighteenth century, "all or most householders in forest, fen, and some heathland parishes enjoyed the right to pasture cows or sheep." The whole family commoned. It provided subsistence, a safety net against unemployment or low wages, and social security for the old. Landless laboring families opposed enclosure: "they gathered fuel, they gleaned after harvest, and their children went nutting and berrying, scared crows from the crops, watched the pigs at mast harvest, tended the sheep and gathered wool from the pastures." "From underwood came quick-growing hazel to make hurdles for folding sheep, to mend hedges and make fences. The thin tributary branches made good beanstakes, and a long hazel rod tied around with holly sprigs made a good chimney-sweeping brush."[9] Bulrushes were woven into baskets, mats, hats, chair seats. Rushes were also used for thatch, as netting for wall plaster, good for bedding, and a wrapping for soft cheeses. Sand was used for scouring and strewn on cottage floors once a week to absorb dirt, dust, grease. Commoners derived menthol from mint, digitalis from foxglove, aspirin from willow bark; buckthorn was

8. J. M. Neeson, *Commoners: Common Right, Enclosure, and Social Change in England, 1700–1820* (New York: Cambridge University Press, 1993), 163.

9. Neeson, *Commoners,* 317, 283–84.

a purgative, henbane a narcotic sedative; comfrey good for bruises, celandine said to remove warts, dandelion a diuretic and laxative, feverfew helped those suffering from migraine.

The *flora Britannica* of today is a product of these struggles. Take for instance the medlar. It tastes like baked apple and is used for jellies, preserves, and pie filling. Medlars should never be planted in new hedgerows because "it is bad policy to increase temptations to theft; the idle among the poor are already too prone to depredations, and would still be less inclined to work, if every hedge furnished the means of support."[10] Many medlar trees are relics of orchards or parks. Others are results of the practice that was once widespread of peasants planting orchard trees in the wild. The allure of commoning arises from the mutualism of shared resources. Everything is used, nothing is wasted. Reciprocity, sense of self, willingness to argue, long memory, collective celebration, and mutual aid are traits of the commoner.

These were not the preferred traits of the proletarian who, apart from possessing nothing, was to be nothing but a compliant slave. The commissioners inquiring into the state of Windsor Forest in 1809 observed that "The absence of compact villages, and the dispersal of foresters, made social discipline impossible." The inhabitants "enlarged their claims upon browse wood, fallen timber, lops and tops, and rootage."[11] Commoning could seem inevitable, part of the order of nature, even to someone like William Blackstone, the magisterial expounder of private

---

10. Thomas Rudge, *General View of the Agriculture of the County of Gloucester* (1807), quoted in Neeson, *Commoners,* 29; and Richard Mabey, *Flora Britannica* (London: Chatto and Windus, 1996), 209.

11. Thompson, *Whigs and Hunters.*

property. He argued that as an animal pulled the plow, and as animals manured the fields, so their herbage was necessary to agriculture, part of "the necessity of the thing."

Timothy Nourse, the theorist of the English garden as a walled enclosure, denounced commoners at the beginning of the century. They were "rough and savage in their Dispositions." They held "leveling Principles." They were "insolent and tumultuous" and "refractory to Government." Commoners belonged to a "sordid race."[12] They were compared to the Indian, to the savage, to the buccaneer, to the Arab. In September 1723 Richard Norton, the warden of the Forest of Bere, wished to "put an end to these arabs and banditti." Blackstone records that the pope had excommunicated the barons "as being worse than the Saracens," the crusaders' Muslim and Arab enemies.

Blacking thus must be understood in an Atlantic racial context as well as the local microhistory of copse and coppice. The disguise was a blackface performance, but not the licensed song and dance of nineteenth-century minstrelsy. These were not yet stage gestures. The Herefordshire turnpike rioters of 1736 called themselves "Levellers" and blacked themselves. Moll Flanders took on male dress, like the pirates Ann Bonny and Mary Read. Macheath transformed himself as Marrano, to join the West African slaves.[13]

---

12. Timothy Nourse, *Campania Foelix, or a Discourse of the Benefits and Improvements of Husbandry* (1700), English Landscape Garden series (New York: Garland, 1982), 15–16.

13. The primary function of blacking was disguise, and this was not the first prohibition of disguise. During the first year of the Tudor monarchy, an act was made law (Henry VII c.7 [1485]), providing "if any person or persons hereafter be convicted of any such hunting with painted faces, visors, or otherwise disguised . . . at night," they are guilty of felony.

The meanings of the Waltham Blacks are confidently proclaimed at an inn, their intentions are clearly announced and inscribed in the woods, a note tacked onto a tree trunk. Advanced semiology is not required. It is otherwise with their *persons.* Dressed in animal skins with fur attached, their visages blackened, they emerged from the woods as creatures of the forest, differentiated from the powdered wigs, the rouged cheeks, the silk stockings of the Whigs. They lived with the wild animals of the forest. There is something of the vagabond and the rogue in their performance that is brazen and forceful, as well as of the commoner negotiating for turf, heath, kindling, or grazing. These commoners are hunters and gatherers who have counterparts in the Americas and Africa.

The Waltham Blacks were arrested in May. Forty altogether were held for trial in 1723. When the Special Commission of Oyer and Terminer opened in June 1723, some had died in prison, four were transported to Maryland. Walpole, the prime minister, locked the gates and set the mantraps of Richmond Park. He was only the grandest of these rich and their show-off parks. But a mantrap? In the early twentieth century the memory of these engines of mutilation was still strong: in *The Woodlanders* (1887) Thomas Hardy provides a description. They could lame the unwary traveler for life.

The South Sea Company was formed to exploit the Caribbean and South Atlantic riches permitted by the *asiento,* or license to deal in slaves. England became "the supreme slaving nation in the Atlantic world."[14] The agent at Cape Coast Castle in the first decade of the century said, "nothing can make colonies thrive but

14. James A. Rawley, *Transatlantic Slave Trade: A History* (New York: Norton, 1981), 163.

the cheapness of labor, and this is as certain [that] negroes are the only laborious people to be depended on." In the South Sea Company ships six out of every seven slaves were to be adults, and the rest were to be boys and girls between ten and fifteen. Thumbscrews and jaw openers were used in force-feeding. Human beings had become commodities, bought and sold, shipped and delivered in the eighteenth century across the ocean from continent to continent. "Each factory had its own brand, usually a replica of its initials. . . . The branding iron was made of gold or silver. The traders preferred gold irons because they were said to make a sharper, more distinctive scar."[15]

In Virginia a permanent brand was realized, namely, the white skin, for the time of the bubble coincided almost to the year with "the invention of the white race," to give the title of Ted Allen's extraordinary thesis. When and how did the "wages of whiteness" originate? It was not during Bacon's Rebellion of 1676, when in Virginia both European and African bond servants combined to overthrow servitude and escape (to the western commons). A buffer stratum between planters and bonded proletarians was to be created by offering material advantages to white proletarians, to the lasting detriment of black proletarians. Decisive in the attainment of this goal were laws in Virginia making Africans and Anglo-Africans and their heirs slaves forever. The bonded people objected in 1723 to the bishop of London and the king "and the rest of the Rullers." "Releese us out of this Cruell Bondegg" they cried. In the same year Richard West, the attorney general, objected to the same law, "I cannot see why

---

15. Colin Palmer, *Human Cargoes: The British Slave Trade to Spanish America, 1700–1739* (Urbana: University of Illinois Press, 1981), 59, 69.

one freeman should be used worse than another, merely upon account of his complexion." But the governor understood the necessity of "a perpetual Brand" and in this way, Ted Allen tells us, a "monstrous social mutation" occurred.[16]

Rediker estimates that 2,400 vessels were captured and plundered in the ten years between 1716 and 1726, the golden age of piracy. They blockaded ports, disrupted the sea lanes. At any one time one to two thousand pirates were active. The pirate ship "might be considered a multiracial maroon community." Hundreds were African. Sixty of Blackbeard's crew of a hundred were black. Rediker quotes the Negro of Deptford who in 1721 led "a Mutiny that we had too many Officers, and that work was too hard, and what not." They also prevented the slave trade from growing. This was the complaint of Humphrey Morice, MP, governor of the Bank of England, owner of a small fleet of slavers, who led the petitioning to Parliament and who suffered severe losses in 1719, the year that serious blacking commenced. A naval squadron was sent to West Africa. Four hundred and eighteen pirates were hanged in the period.[17]

Daniel Defoe was preoccupied with the issues of Atlantic labor power, white and black. *Robinson Crusoe, Mariner* was published in 1719. The book dramatizes the labor theory of value, glories in the intricacies of the division of labor, and puts the European foot (Crusoe) on the African neck (Friday). Alexander Selkirk, the actual person who was prototype of

16. Ted Allen, *The Origin of Racial Oppression in Anglo-America,* vol. 2 of *The Invention of the White Race* (New York: Verso, 1997).

17. Marcus Rediker, *Villains of All Nations: Atlantic Pirates in the Golden Age* (Boston: Beacon Press, 2004), 140–41.

Robinson Crusoe, died in February 1721 as a sailor in a naval squadron that was sent to West Africa to extirpate the piracy interrupting the slave trade. *The Adventures and Misadventures of Moll Flanders,* published in 1722, treats the issues of criminalization of the commons and large-scale cooperative labor. Upward social mobility was not accomplished by affirmative action but negative criminality, as Moll Flanders hooked up with highwaymen as the first step in the ladder of success whose final rung—a Virginia tobacco plantation—she at last attained, so she too could put the boot to the African enslaved. If we see Crusoe and Flanders as exponents of the white race (where race is precisely defined as the stratum between bonded labor and planters), it is in contrast to *both* Africans and commoners.

The New-England Courant began in inspiration by *The London Journal,* itself created to expose the fraudulence of the South Sea Bubble. The Boston paper contained news of ships "cleared out for Barbadoes, Jamaica, Virginia, Surinam." Regular postal service across the Atlantic began in 1721. Its summer issue of 23 July 1722 (no. 52) sought to rectify the stupidity of the countrymen by quoting the famous chapter 39 of Magna Carta and commented, "No Freeman shall be taken, &c. These words deserve to be written in letters of gold, and I have often wondred that they are not inscribed in Capitals in all our Courts of Judicature, Town-halls, and most publick edifices; they being essential to our English Freedom and Liberties." Already the worm was in the apple. "No man ought to be put from his Livelyhood without answer" rings hollow to the unemployed, or to the Indians who were proclaimed rebels in the same newspaper for attacking fifteen fishing vessels and whose women and children were taken in captivity to Dunstable. "No man can be exiled or banished out of his native country" was hypocrisy to the men and women and children enslaved in America from the west coast of Africa. Its sole advertisement reads, "A likely Negro Woman to be sold by Mr. *Thomas Selby* at the Crown Coffee-House, the lower end of Kingstreet."

Did the themes of blacking and slaving actually overlap? They did so by geography, economics, and law. Geographically, Waltham Chase is near Portsmouth and thus close to the sea routes of the empire. Indeed, if you wanted to get from Portsmouth to London in the eighteenth century, one of the main routes took you through the forests of Hampshire and Berkshire, the locations of blacking. Percival Lewis, the local nineteenth-century antiquary, noted the proximity of the New Forest to Normandy, and it was William the Conqueror's first forest. Of the seven Waltham Blacks hanged at Tyburn in December 1723, three were from Portsmouth. Economically, the shipyards of Portsmouth were enormous consumers of timber. The purveyor of the navy maintained his residence in the New Forest. The cutting trees for timber by commoners in this forest became especially acute in 1719 when "Navy Trees" were taken for lodge repairs. It was a stone's throw from the wild wood to the seven seas. In terms of law, the relation between slaving and blacking is personified by the solicitor general, Philip York, who in 1723 prosecuted seven of the forest commoners under the Waltham Black Act. Five years later as attorney general he ruled that baptism does not bestow freedom on the slave, and his ruling permitted slave masters to compel slaves in England to return to the plantations.[18]

18. Percival Lewis, *Historical Inquiries, Concerning Forests and Forest Laws* (London: T. Payne, 1811), 46.

Pirates and poachers held mock trials, and in the rituals of the trials they preserved the forms of Magna Carta. In 1722 on an island off Cuba a pirate crew under Captain Thomas Antis diverted themselves with "a Mock Court of Judicature to try one another for Pyracy." The trial took place before judge and jury. "He that was a Criminal one Day was made Judge another." The pirate Charles Bellamy inveighed against the rich men, "they rob the Poor under the Cover of Law, forsooth, and we plunder the Rich under the Protection of our own Courage." The same year the Windsor Forest Blacks held a mock court in the spring of 1723 to try Rev. Thomas Powers, a wife beater and informer for Walpole against the Blacks. Men in blackface and pirates, commoners and Africans, practiced a histrionic class consciousness of legalistic countertheater.

In 1760, a year after Blackstone published his scholarly diplomatics on the Charters of Liberties, Tacky's revolt among the slaves of Jamaica initiated a cycle of resistance among slaves throughout the Caribbean, with significant reverberations among the workers of London and the commoners of England, and culminated in the American Revolution. The expansion of the slave empire would be joined with the simultaneous expansion of the manufacturing working class in England.[19]

On the river Thames in 1762 the Nigerian slave Olaudah Equiano told his master, who was getting ready to sell him to a West Indiaman, that he was free. The oarsmen on the riverboat taking him to his new ship "pulled against their will" and told him he could not be sold. Encouraged, Equiano continued to

---

19. Peter Linebaugh and Marcus Rediker, *The Many-Headed Hydra* (Boston: Beacon Press, 2000), chap. 6.

argue on the deck of the *Charming Sally.* " 'You are now my slave,' said the captain. I told him my master could not sell me to him, nor to any one else. 'Why,' said he, 'did not your master buy you?' I confessed he did. But I have served him, said I, many years, and he has taken all my wages and prize-money, for I only got one sixpence during the war; besides this I have been baptized; and by the laws of the land no man has a right to sell me: and I added, that I had heard a lawyer, and others at different times, tell my master so. They both then said that those people who told me so were not my friends: but I replied—It was very extraordinary that other people did not know the law as well as they. Upon this Captain Doran said I talked too much English; and if I did not behave myself well, and be quiet, he had a method on board to make me."[20]

In Oxford meanwhile William Blackstone began *The Commentaries on the Laws of England,* which appeared between 1765 and 1769, a period when another link between Magna Carta and the abolition of slavery began to be forged.

Thomas Lewis, born on the Gold Coast (Ghana), was sold to a Danish slave trader; he worked by turns for a nobleman, a hairdresser, and a judge; he lived in New York, Carolina, Jamaica, New England, and Florida before coming to London. In 1770 slave catchers in Chelsea attempted to force him back to slavery, first endeavoring "to gag him, by thrusting a stick into his mouth." But his cries "reached the ears of some servants" who were able to get in touch with Granville Sharp the abolitionist, Greek scholar, and musician. Thence events proceeded swiftly.

20. Olaudah Equiano, *The Interesting Narrative and Other Writings,* ed. Vincent Carretta, with an introduction (London: Penguin Books, 1995), 93–94.

As Sharp began his legal appeals, the slavers carried Lewis by riverboat to the slave ship that began to sail down river to the sea. "The promptitude of head, heart, and hand, in this transaction, can scarcely be surpassed." The turning point occurred on the fourth of July. His journal jots down the attempt to attain, if not a nation's, then a slave's independence:

> July 4. Went to the Lord Mayor, and to Justice Welsh, also to Judge Willes and Baron Smith, for a writ of Habeas Corpus, in behalf of Thomas Lewis.

The wind died, the writ was served, Lewis rescued, his putative owner brought to trial, where the jury found for Lewis, and the cry went up from assembled onlookers, *"No property, no property."*

Private property was very near to divinity in the mind of the English ruling class of the time. True, Blackstone admitted in his *Commentaries* that there are elements such as light, air, and water, which "must still unavoidably remain in common." But otherwise, he defined private property as "that sole and despotic common which one man claims and exercises over the external things of the world, in total exclusion of the right of any other individual in the universe."

For Granville Sharp it was a triumph, not least because Lewis's counsel held up in his hand Sharp's tract *On the Illegality of Tolerating Slavery in England,* having one finger in the book, to keep open a particular part. Sharp wrote, "there are many honest weather-beaten Englishmen, who have as little reason to boast of their complexion as the Indians." The least toleration of slavery in some leads to the "general bondage of the common people." He quotes 28 Edward III c.3, to prove that in law a Negro slave cannot be not a man, "and no man of what estate or condition that he be shall be put out of land or tenement, nor taken, nor imprisoned, nor disinherited, nor put to death, without being brought in answer by due process of the law."[21]

Sharp provides twenty-four pages of footnotes analyzing colonial slave statutes, comparing them to those for indentured servants. He contrasts Saxon times with the feudal tyranny after the Norman conquest. Such barbarous customs as villeinage "had no other foundation than the violent and unchristian usurpation of the uncivilized barons in the age of darkness; and that religion and morality, reason and the law of nature were obliged to give place to the imaginary (tho' mistaken) interest, and uncontrollable power of these over-grown landholders." Later Granville Sharp devised in 226 pages a system of local democracy based upon the *frankpledge,* the Anglo-Saxon form of community local government. It was not purely of antiquarian or utopian interest however. The seventeenth-century jurist and scholar John Selden showed that the *court leet* (comprising the residents of a neighborhood) evolved from the frankpledge, and the court leet did such local business, he said, as the regulation of how many cows or sheep shall be put in the common. The frankpledge, thus, was the administrative term for local commoning.[22]

Granville Sharp became a giant for Magna Carta. "The wisdom of ages has made [Magna Carta] venerable, and stamped it with an authority equal to the Constitution itself, of which it is, in reality, a most essential and fundamental part; so that any attempt

21. Granville Sharp, *A Representation of the Injustice and Dangerous Tendency of Tolerating Slavery* (London, 1769).

22. Adam Hochschild, *Bury the Chains: Prophets and Rebels in the Fight to Free an Empire's Slaves* (Boston: Houghton Mifflin, 2005), 146.

to repeal it would be treason to the State! This glorious Charter must, therefore, ever continue unrepealed: and even the articles which seem at present useless, must ever remain in force."[23]

The judge in Thomas Lewis's trial was William Murray, Lord Mansfield, who was determined not to make a general ruling against slavery. As he told Lewis's counsel, "for I would have all Masters think them free, and all Negroes think they were not, because then they would both behave better." Granville Sharp was furious. The judgment displayed

> Open contempt of the principle of the Constitution . . . preferring private to public advantage, pecuniary or sordid property, as that of a master in a horse or dog, to inestimable Liberty, and abusing a noble statute intended from the freedom of injured subjects from imprisonment, to render it on the contrary, an instrument of oppression for delivering up poor innocent men into absolute unlimited slavery, dragging them up like horses or dogs to a private individual as mere property.[24]

In January 1772 James Somerset's case was brought to the King's Bench on a writ of habeas corpus and six months later the celebrated judgment was given. Somerset was born in Africa, sold as a slave in Virginia, became the property of a Boston customs official who brought him to London, where he ran away. However, he was caught but a habeas corpus writ prevented him from being sent away again as a slave and brought the case to trial. The decision itself was ambiguous, even "crabbed." Nevertheless, it was

23. Granville Sharp, *A Declaration of the People's Natural Right to a Share in the Legislature* (London: B. White, 1774), 202–3.

24. Peter Fryer, *Staying Power: The History of Black People in Britain* (London: Pluto, 1984), 120.

widely believed that "the judgement thus pronounced by Lord Mansfield has established the following axiom, as proposed by Mr. Serjeant Davy: As soon as any slave sets his foot on English ground he becomes free."[25]

The notion that "English ground" bestowed freedom appears again in Blackstone's infamous vacillating passage on slavery. Somerset's counsel invoked the passage from the *Commentaries,* "And this spirit of liberty is so deeply implanted in our constitution, and rooted even in our very soil, that a Slave or a Negro, the moment he lands in England, falls under the protection of the laws, and with regard to all natural rights becomes *eo instanti* a freeman." So says the 1766 edition, but the second edition a year later adds a qualification that was suggested to Blackstone by Mansfield, "though the Master's right to his service may possibly still continue."

It is a peculiar notion that the ground confers freedom, all the more so since this figure of speech was being introduced precisely at the moment when the ground—fenced, divided, hedged, enclosed—was less free than ever. Blackstone and Mansfield were old friends. Mansfield was a deep admirer of the *Commentaries* (he helped draft the first edition) and contrasted their author to Coke, "an uncouth, crabbed author."[26]

The commons comes up in the case in two ways. Somerset had a nephew who, hearing the news of his freedom, ran away from his own situation as a servant. The master wrote complaining, "I don't

25. Prince Hoare, *Memoirs of Granville Sharp, Esq.* (London: Henry Colburn, 1820), 92.

26. James Oldham, *The Mansfield Manuscripts and the Growth of English Law in the Eighteenth Century* (Chapel Hill: University of North Carolina Press, 1992), 2:1225.

find that he has gone off with anything of mine. Only carried off all his own cloths which I don't know whether he had any right so to do." It was a custom known as *vails* for servants to have the clothes. Indeed, English workers during this industrial transition time who no longer had access to agrarian or wooded commons discovered or created numerous trade usages and customary perquisites such as vails.[27] That was the first way commoning arose in the case.

The second was this. Mansfield's nephew, Sir John Lindsay, fathered a child named Dido, a black, whose mother Lindsay had been taken prisoner from a Spanish vessel. Lord Mansfield took care of the girl. Dido was literate and occasionally played the role of amanuensis to the judge, writing in a regular, legible hand. The daughter of an African American slave was also a commoner who, superintending the dairy and poultry yard at Mansfield's big house, Kenwood, overlooked stock that enjoyed common of herbage on Hampstead Heath.[28]

In the spring of 1774 Olaudah Equiano signed up on the *Anglicania* bound for Smyrna, Turkey, and he recommended "a very clever black man, John Annis, as a cook." And thus began a tragedy. On Easter Monday six men with two wherry boats forcibly took Annis for a slave ship. Equiano reacted swiftly and wholeheartedly. Another mad rush, the ships chasing over the water, the writs over the land. "My being known to them obliged

27. The technical literature here is large. See Peter Linebaugh, *The London Hanged*, 2nd ed. (London: Verso, 2003).

28. Oldham, *Mansfield Manuscripts*. He quotes a contemporary: "Mansfield "knows he has been reproached for showing fondness for her—I dare not say criminal" (1239).

me to use the following deception: I whitened my face, that they might not know me, and this had the desired effect." He was able to serve the writ of habeas corpus. Yet despite whitening his visage, despite passing the literal and racial line of the threshold to Annis's master, alas! Equiano lost his case. His attorney proved unfaithful. The slave ship sailed for St. Kitt's, where Annis was cut, flogged, staked to the ground, loaded with irons, and killed.[29]

History, however, is not all tragedy. Not only did the experience lead to Equiano's own prominence in defining the abolitionist movement in England, but habeas corpus became part of the struggle in America in the Shadrach Minkins case (1851) and the Anthony Burns case (1854). Both men were Virginia slaves who ran away by shipping to Boston, where they were recaptured. Habeas corpus petitions on their behalf challenged unsuccessfully the Fugitive Slave Law (1850). However, direct action of habeas corpus—"you shall have the body"—by entering the courthouse (using a battering ram in the case of Burns) and releasing the prisoner was attempted in both cases, successfully in the case of Minkins. When William Lloyd Garrison sounded the note of jubilee in 1829, calling the Fourth of July "the worst and most disastrous day in the whole 365," he had not known of Lewis's and Sharp's victory on that day in 1770.

Thanks to the struggle in England, Magna Carta became part of the abolition of slavery in America. The Forest Charter was forgotten or consigned to the gothic past. Although there was certainly a lively struggle in America for rights of common,

29. Equiano, *Interesting Narrative*, 179–81.

there was no suggestion after the revolution that they could become a constitutional basis of society.[30]

Of the three jurists I have mentioned in this chapter, one was a parish vicar, one a professor, and one an abolitionist. William Waterson pursued an antiquarian's path searching for the documentary basis of common rights. William Blackstone stood for Magna Carta and private property; Granville Sharp showed how Magna Carta could be used against slavery. Blackstone called common rights "incorporeal hereditaments" because he restricted the commoning to what could be inherited; Sharp showed that in English history villeinage was transformed into the status of copyholder who might enjoy immemorial commoning. Sharp opposed slavery; Waterson was an advocate of commoning; Blackstone equivocated on both.

Granville Sharp wrote an alternative history thanks to what he learned from the ex-slave abolitionists: he turned to Magna Carta and he turned to the time before it, finding in the frankpledge of the Angles and Saxons a pure form of democracy that he recommended to the French revolutionaries, to the free blacks settling in Sierra Leone, and to those intent on leveling the Hindu caste system. It was a form of self-government for all, "be he free, be he serf" (Bracton), which kept watch and ward, which maintained "free engagement of neighbor for neighbor," which evolved into the court leet, making such bylaws "as that a man shall put so many cows or sheep in the common."

---

30. Alan Taylor, *Liberty Men and Great Proprietors: The Revolutionary Settlement on the Maine Frontier, 1760–1820* (Chapel Hill: University of North Carolina Press, 1990); and Allan Kulikoff, *From British Peasants to Colonial American Farmers* (Chapel Hill: University of North Carolina Press, 2000).

CHAPTER SIX

1776 and *Runnamede*

Now, when the frost was past enduring,
And made her poor old bones to ache,
Could any thing be more alluring
Than an old hedge to Goody Blake?
And now and then, it must be said,
When her old bones were cold and chill,
She left her fire, or left her bed
To seek the hedge of Harry Gill.

William Wordsworth, "Goody Blake
and Harry Gill" (1798)

Thomas Jefferson's original draft of the Declaration of Independence from June 1776 is preserved as a "Charter of Freedom" in the Rotunda of the National Archives in Washington DC along with the U.S. Constitution, and the Bill of Rights. Harry S. Truman dedicated the rotunda in December 1952, warning against the documents becoming idols. In September 2003 George W. Bush rededicated the rotunda, praising the signers of the Declaration of Independence for becoming "the enemy of an empire."

Skirting on idolatry himself, he went on to imply heaven-sent significance. "The true revolution was not to defy one earthly power, but to declare principles that stand above every earthly power—the equality of each person before God, and the responsibility of government to secure the rights of all."

After the Texas billionaire Ross Perot bought a version of the Magna Carta from Edward I's reign (ca. 1297) for $1.5 million in 1984, he placed it on permanent loan in this rotunda among the other charters of freedom. And there it sits, separated by thousands of miles from its centuries-long companion, the Charter of the Forest: Magna Carta, a charter of English empire, alongside the American ones.

In *Common Sense* (spring 1776) Tom Paine wrote as if freedom were a damsel in distress, and the political project of independence a version of knight errantry: "Every spot of the old world is overrun with oppression. Freedom hath long been hunted round the globe. Asia, and Africa, have long expelled her. Europe regards her like a stranger, and England hath given her warning to depart. O! receive the fugitive, and prepare in time an asylum for mankind." Such thoughts can no longer be easily applied to the ports of entry into the United States and not to Heathrow either, but at the time Paine wrote, the experience of many immigrants was as fugitives and asylum seekers, who had been expelled from their subsistence by the enclosure movement. It hadn't yet fenced in every spot of the old world but the tendency was well begun by 1776 in Ireland, Scotland, and England. To imagine in the winter of 1775–76 that freedom was womanly was warming to soldiers whose fingers were cold to the bone. (Paine asked that the money raised by the sale of the first edition be used to buy them mittens.)

Common Sense linked the argument for independence with the argument for a republic. A king is "the principal ruffian of some restless gang." He remembers the Norman Conquest in 1066. "When William the Conqueror subdued England, he gave them law at the point of the sword," which of course was changed by Magna Carta. William of Normandy (who founded the line of English monarchy) was "a French bastard landing with an armed banditti." Calling him a bastard—"the plain truth is, that the antiquity of English monarchy will not bear looking into"—reflects on his mother as if her conduct scandalized the colonists. Female virtue is necessary to *Common Sense,* which seeks to rescue wronged womanhood.

Paine calls on Americans to frame "a continental charter, or Charter of the United Colonies (answering to what is called the Magna Carta of England)." This charter will secure "freedom and property to all men, and above all things, the free exercise of religion, according to the dictates of conscience; with such other matter as is necessary for a charter to contain." *Common Sense* mobilized the colonies to war and suggested drawing up a charter of some kind, "to be understood as a bond of solemn obligation, which the whole enters into, to support the right of every separate part, whether of religion, personal freedom, or property." He appeals to the commodity owners, farmers, craftsmen, and tradesmen, men who understood Paine's praise of such a charter—"A firm bargain and a right reckoning make long friends"—exactly because they had commodities to bargain and reckon.

He describes a ceremony. "Let a day be solemnly set apart for proclaiming the charter; let it be brought forth placed on the divine law, the word of God; let a crown be placed thereon, by which the world may know, that so far as we approve of monarchy, that in America THE LAW IS KING. For as in absolute governments the King is law, so in free countries the law ought to be King; and there ought to be no other. But lest any ill use should afterwards arise, let the crown at the conclusion of the ceremony be demolished, and scattered among the people whose right it is." He refers to the Bible but not by name, as the support of the crown or the law and the crown.

He concludes with the suggestion that a manifesto be published "setting forth the miseries we have endured" and advocating independence in order that "we take rank with other nations." The pamphlet ends with "nothing can settle our affairs so expeditiously as an open and determined declaration for independence," and he gives four reasons that all amount to the same, independence is necessary to getting help from allies. The new meaning of diplomatics would now extend from the charter to the nation.[1]

Blackstone was a jurist of the Atlantic ruling class during the huge upheaval that began in the 1760s. His *Commentaries on the Laws of England* helped to provide written law with the appearance of sovereign supremacy. With the independence of the colonies, now the United States of America, diplomatics ceased to be a technical term of documentation and began to mean diplomacy, since the relations among states had become documentary in such a novel way. Diplomacy concerns relations among states. The last paragraph of the Declaration of Independence, with its appeal to the supreme judge, with its authority

---

1. Thomas Paine, *Common Sense* (1776), in *Thomas Paine: Collected Writings,* ed. Eric Foner (New York: Library of America, 1995), 17, 33–34, 43.

from the good people, soberly describes the operation of the "Free and Independent States." It mentions levying war, concluding peace, contracting alliances, establishing commerce. The relation that Paine anticipates is the relation of commerce. But the commerce in question is unlike that in the Charter of the Forest—which points not to nations but to the commons—and in this document commoning is understood only in relation to producing and to consuming. Indians, slaves, and women had pursued happiness in various informal commons. In contrast to all that is open in the commons, commerce hides production (its mechanization, its divisions, its prolongation) and it hides as well the poverty or luxury of the consumer. Thomas Paine and the Declaration of Independence imagine the independent state as a consumer society.

The Declaration of Independence lists about twenty-seven "facts" or "usurpations" illustrating the despotic absolutism of George III. Some of these derive directly from Magna Carta, such as trial by jury (chapter 39) or the taking away of charters (chapter 49), and others come indirectly. We can name several. The declaration refers to Admiralty Courts as a special jurisdiction; Magna Carta refers to Forest Courts as special jurisdiction as well. The king "constrained our fellow Citizens taken Captive on the high seas" without habeas corpus. The reference to "the free system of English laws" pertains to *due process of law*. The declaration finds that the king has cut off overseas trade; Magna Carta specifically protects merchants when they travel. The declaration complains that the king and Parliament tax without consent; and the Magna Carta says that no scutage or aid may be levied without common counsel. Finally, the declaration objects to king and Parliament "for transporting us beyond Seas to be tried for pretended offences."[2] The Coercive Acts that permitted such "renditions" was Parliament's response to the Boston Tea Party.

There are important differences between Magna Carta and the Declaration of Independence. The purpose of the declaration is to *justify* the powers of state that relate to war, peace, alliances, and commerce. The purpose of Magna Carta is to *curtail* the powers of the sovereign. Magna Carta put an end to a war; the Declaration of Independence intended to win allies and stiffen the resolve of soldiers to fight. They presuppose different conceptions of property. Magna Carta is a document of reparations, returning the forest, whereas the declaration is a document of acquisition. It is a continental landgrab that allows for the defense of "our frontiers" against what Paine termed "the merciless Indian Savages, whose known rule of warfare, is an undistinguished destruction of all ages, sexes and conditions."

Tom Paine has wrested common sense from the commoners. The project of independence that his pamphlet *Common Sense* propounded is a project of privatization. African slaves are excluded, the indigenous people are excluded, and women, apart from rhetoric, are excluded. Although he calls for "a large and equal representation," their occlusion is related to the privatization of the commons, even when it is not the consequence of expropriation.

2. Carl Becker, *The Declaration of Independence* (New York: Knopf, 1942), 86; the philosophy of the declaration, Becker writes, was "good old English doctrine." Pauline Maier finds no colonists of that generation actually transported beyond the seas for trial. *American Scripture: Making of the Declaration of Independence* (New York: Knopf, 1997), 118.

The expropriation of the commons diminished the economic role of women. Gleaning, Ivy Pinchbeck reckoned, could provide half a dozen bushels of grain; this aspect of breadwinning was the work of women and children. Estovers, or the acquisition of fuel, was largely women's work. Herbage, or the grazing rights that permitted the keeping of a cow, was also her work, and thus she provided the cheese, butter, and milk for a healthy diet, and her livestock provided manuring to replenish nutrients in garden and field. Access to commons conferred two kinds of independence. For one thing "laborers with livestock, with gardens, and with rights of turbary and estover were not always at the farmer's beck and call." For another thing, commoning provided her independence within the family. Commoning was gregarious. The loss of the commons had epistemological effects—how you see the world, what you know of the world—that surface in the poetry, for instance, of John Clare.[3]

If the faculty of common sense is practical, it is formed by social interactions in the praxis of the world. The nature of that world was changing, and the primary social interactions—reproduction and production, in a word, labor—were changing as well in the fencing, hedging, planting, manufacturing, clearing,

---

3. Ivy Pinchbeck, *Women Workers and the Industrial Revolution* (1930; repr. New York: A. M. Kelley, 1969), is the classic account. J. M. Neeson, *Commoners: Common Right, Enclosure and Social Change in England, 1700–1820* (New York: Cambridge University Press, 1993), is the most thorough and humane. Jane Humphries, "Enclosures, Common Rights, and Women: The Proletarianization of Families in the Late Eighteenth and Early Nineteenth Centuries," *Journal of Economic History* 50, no. 1 (March 1990). John Barrel, *The Idea of Landscape and the Sense of Place, 1730–1840: An Approach to the Poetry of John Clare* (London: Cambridge University Press, 1972).

road making, canal digging that we loosely call the industrial revolution. Joseph Priestley (1775) defined common sense as "the capacity for judging of common things." John Beattie (1770) said common sense was truth perceived not by argument but by irresistible impulse derived from nature, not education. A few years earlier Thomas Reid, Adam Smith's successor at Glasgow University, published *An Inquiry into the Human Mind: On the Principles of Common Sense* (1764). He derived the phrase from Cicero, not from the traumatic experiences of those burned out of the Scottish highlands or removed from communal runrig fields, even though this was the dominant experience of his generation of Scots.

The phrase was thus in the air when Paine wrote. His pamphlet, warming and timely as it was, nevertheless suffered from three contradictions. First, he insisted, "Oppression is often the *consequence,* but seldom or never the *means* of riches." Such a sentence could not be written after the widespread use of the factory; that it is written after the plantation reminds us that he excludes slaves from independence. Second, part of the condemnation of England is that it "stirred up the Indians and Negroes to destroy us, the cruelty hath a double guilt, it is dealing brutally by us, and treacherously by them." Third, he had an argument which we might call the "peak wood" phenomenon, the notion of a limit to the principal hydrocarbon energy source that may put the project of independence in crisis. The forests are disappearing, he argued, hence the ability to build ships, the weapons of war, will diminish in the future.

On the one hand the United States relied on the Magna Carta (a form of solemn publication of separation and independence), on the other hand, as an aggressive power it was hungry to privatize the lands (the virgin forest) to pay its soldiers, to reward its allies. "The least fracture now will be like a name engraved with the point of a pin on the tender rind of a young oak; the wound will enlarge with the tree, and posterity read it in full grown characters."

In the most eloquent, modern plea for independence from England, Paine refers to the most fundamental, gothic part of the English constitution. Why? The first element in the colonists' notion of liberty was Magna Carta, followed by the Peasants' Revolt of 1381, and the overthrow of Charles I in 1647.[4] In 1761 James Otis gave a speech—"a flame of fire" John Adams called it—against the British writs of assistance (allowing the government access to citizens' homes and personal records) in which he brought together natural rights and Magna Carta. "American independence was then and there born," concluded Adams. In a sermon preached in 1766, Rev. Edward Barnard of Haverhill, Massachusetts likened the resistance to the Stamp Act to the struggle for Magna Carta.[5] Indeed, the Massachusetts Assembly declared the Stamp Act null and void, as being "against the Magna Carta and the natural rights of Englishmen." Paul Revere designed paper money for Massachusetts in 1775 showing a colonist holding "Magna Charta," which in the next year has become (misspelled) "Independance."

In Britain meanwhile, Magna Carta was receiving another theatrical telling. John Logan was born in 1748 south of Edinburgh.

---

4. Edward Countryman, " 'To Secure the Blessings of Liberty': Language, the Revolution, and American Capitalism," in *Beyond the American Revolution: Explorations in the History of American Radicalism,* ed. Alfred F. Young (DeKalb: Northern Illinois University Press, 1993).

5. Harry S. Stout, *The New England Soul: Preaching and Religious Culture in Colonial New England* (New York: Oxford University Press, 1986), 267.

Figure 2.   Paper money designed by Paul Revere, 1775 and 1776.
Courtesy American Antiquarian Society.

He attended University of Edinburgh. In 1783, the year of the Treaty of Paris when the United States joined the independent nations, the attempt was made to perform his tragedy, *Runnamede,* at Covent Garden but it was prevented by an order from the Lord Chamberlain, "occasioned by the unfavorable allusion that some passages were supposed to bear to the Court politics of the time, which for ten years had been hostile to the spirit of independence that wrested from Great Britain her American colonies—the same spirit," his editor explained—"which had wrested the Charter of liberty from king John."

Woman's role in this interpretation relates to the elimination of actual production: she has a romantic value, not one of labor nor of reproduction. She is also without needs, hence no mention of estovers. The fact that she might be widowed is not stated. She is a means of racial integration, Normans and Saxons united to form the Britons, or in the last speech of the play delivered by Stephen Langton, archbishop of Canterbury, she reaches an apotheosis as Britannia, goddess of the British empire. As America's motley crew is absent from *Common Sense,* so Britain's commoners do not appear among the dramatis personae of *Runnamede.*

His recent valor as a crusader in the holy land distinguishes the warrior protagonist. Thus England is defended and united in opposition to the figure of the Moor. Albemarle is a Norman lord who had fought in the Crusades, defeated Saladin, raised the cross over the crescent; Arden is the Saxon lord. But Albemarle's daughter, Elvina, could reconcile the Norman and Saxons if she would marry Arden: "I hail the day / That makes one nation of the British race." The overthrow of that Norman yoke Tom Paine described is to come about through an embrace: one nation from two races.

The lover of her youth, Elvine, however, has just been in the holy war. The French invade England and Elvine is with them. The papal legate has tricked Elvina to declare for the dauphin, not the prince, and she appears to be a traitor. She is brought to the gallows, "enter at the side scene Elvina dressed in white," emblem of innocence. Elvine rescues her. He too has been falsely accused. Deprived of his baronial rank, he becomes a champion of "a cause / That down the course of time will fire the world."

Rather than accept slavery under the Roman empire, the Goths exclaim,

> Give us again the wildness of our woods,
> And the fierce freedom of our great forefathers!
> Stephen Langton, the quasi narrator says,
> From such commotions revolutions rise,
> And still will rise, congenial to the isle.

Elvine takes leadership of the English army, "England arming in the cause of freedom." Dialogue between John and Elvine:

> The rights of Britons, and the rights of men
> Which never king did give, and never king
> Can take away. What, if a tyrant prince
> May rule at will, and lord it o'er the land,
> Where's the grand charter of the human kind?
> Where the high birthright of the brave? And where
> The majesty of man?

In general the freedom is of mind, person, and property. The particulars include Parliament ("the common voice / And general suffrage of th' assembled realm"), habeas corpus ("Disclose the secrets of the prison walls, / And bid the groanings of the dungeon strike / The public ear"), and trial by jury ("The heaven-conferred palladium of the isle, / To Britain's sons, the judgement of their peers"). The bombast reaches a conclusion in the female personification of the nation.

> The Queen of isles behold,
> Sitting sublime upon her rocky throne,
> The region of the storms! She stretches forth
> In her right hand the sceptre of the sea,
> And in her left the balance of the earth.
> The guardian of the globe, she gives the law:
> She calls the winds, the winds obey her call,
> And bear the thunder of her power, to burst
> O'er the devoted lands, and carry fate
> To kings, to nations, and the subject world.
> Above the Grecian or the Roman name,
> Unlike the great destroyers of the globe,
> She fights and conquers in fair Freedom's cause.

Her song of victory the nation's song:
Her triumphs are the triumphs of mankind. (189)

The rule of the waves, the command of the sky, the bombs bursting in air, the apotheosis on high: Magna Carta has become an instrument of full-spectrum domination.

John Logan was the tutor of John Sinclair, who became in 1793 the first president of the quasi official Board of Agriculture, an organization that conducted agricultural surveys of the counties of England and spearheaded the passage of Parliamentary enclosure bills. In 1795, when the Parliamentary Select Committee on Waste Lands reported, Sinclair wrote, "The idea of having lands in common, it has been justly remarked, is to be derived from that barbarous state of society, when men were strangers to any higher occupation than those of hunters or shepherds, or had only just tasted the advantages to be reaped from the cultivation of the earth."[6] The commons belonged to a distant irretrievable past, cave man.

John Logan's play *Runnamede* could not obtain license from the Lord Chamberlain for performance in London on the grounds that it favored arguments in the Magna Carta employed by the American revolutionaries. The problem was solved by John Millar, who wrote an interpretation of Magna Carta resting on economics and class conflict. Magna Carta could be venerated as a foundation of stability of little threat to the social order of property, as long as it is placed as a class conflict within an economic,

6. J. L. Hammond and Barbara Hammond, *The Village Labourer, 1760–1832* (1911; repr. New York: A. M. Kelley, 1967), 30.

or technological, context that had its own invariable stages of development. Detachment was attained by sequence.

Millar had access to the high theory of capitalism, which at that time referred not only to the "invisible hand" and the "division of labor" of Adam Smith but to an argument of inevitability. Adam Smith's leading student was John Millar, a supporter of the American cause, who wrote *An Historical View of the English Government* (1787), which provided the first materialist interpretation of Magna Carta. He applied the theory of four stages to history, to wit, savagery, barbarism, feudalism, and commercial society. These were based on hunting, domestication of animals, agriculture, and manufacturing. Property, kinship, language, manners, and political institutions depended on the progress of the mode of production. Thus, the times conditioned human nature itself.[7]

Millar's account of Magna Carta does not differentiate it from the many other charters of the time except by "a greater variety of particulars." These pertain both to the chief nobles or barons and "persons of a lower rank," as illustrated by chapter 20 of Magna Carta, that even a villein may not be deprived of his carts and implements of husbandry. His analysis of the particulars also reveals "the interest of another class of people." He means the mercantile portion of the population; chapter 41 provided protections for their immunities, their weights and measures, and security to foreign merchants.

7. Christopher J. Berry, *Social Theory of the Scottish Enlightenment* (Edinburgh: Edinburgh University Press, 1997), 116. C. George Caffentzis, "The Scottish Origin of 'Civilization,'" in *Enduring Western Civilization: The Construction of the Concept of Western Civilization and Its "Others,"* ed. Silvia Federici (Wesport: Praeger, 1995).

The Magna Carta had a few chapters concerning the forest laws that were expanded in 1217 with the Charter of the Forest, "as the great charter came to be thus divided." Millar says, "The charter of the forest, how insignificant soever the subject of it may be thought in the present age, was then accounted a matter of the highest importance." He explains how the "Gothic nations" replaced the Roman empire and they remained in a "rude and military state, which disposed them to bodily exercise, while it produced such a contempt of industry, and profound ignorance of the arts, as were the sources of much leisure and idleness." The gentry and their subordinates were hunters. Independent proprietors endeavored to ensure the exclusive privilege of killing game on their own grounds. British insularity protected it from war, hence more leisure sports; it also led to the extirpation of "the fiercer and more hurtful species of wild animals," so hunting became a refined pursuit.

William and his Norman troops "laid waste very extensive territories, in different parts of England, in order to convert them into forests; having for that purpose demolished many houses, and even villages, and expelled the inhabitants. New and savage penalties were inflicted upon such as encroached upon the king's game, or committed any trespass in his forests; and the laws upon this subject were executed in a manner the most rigorous and oppressive." "The erection of great forests, even though these had been confined within the demesnes of the king, was likely of itself to occasion much popular clamour; as in our own times, the change of a large estate from tillage to pasturage, by which many tenants are deprived of their livelihood, is frequently the source of much odium and resentment." William the Conqueror's forest policy, Millars states, was based on "the violations of private property." No pannage, herbage, chiminage, no estovers. These are "insignificant" particulars.

Three factors enlarge the meaning of the charter, to the advantage of the whole community: progress of arts or technological innovation; increases in industriousness or productivity; and change of the peasantry's circumstances. "Though the freedom of the common people was not intended in those charters, it was eventually secured to them; for when the peasantry, and other persons of low rank, were afterward enabled, by their industry, and by the progress of arts, to emerge from their inferior and servile condition, and to acquire opulence, they were gradually admitted to the exercise of the same privileges which had been claimed by men of independent fortunes; and found themselves entitled, of course, to the benefit of that free government which was already established." Upward social mobility is possible, careers are open to talent (in the slogan of the day), opportunities are equal (in the slogan of our day), but equality based on the commons is assiduously excluded.

The Scottish philosopher David Hume wrote an influential history of England. He accepted the seventeenth-century interpretation of Magna Carta: it "granted or secured very important liberties and privileges to every order of men in the kingdom; to the clergy, to the barons, and to the people." Just as the king submitted to a necessity, so did the barons, who were "necessitated to insert in it other clauses of a more extensive and more beneficent nature: They could not expect the concurrence of the people, without comprehending, together with their own, the interests of inferior ranks of men." As if to prove the point, he noted accurately that "even a villein or rustic shall not by any fine be bereaved of his carts, ploughs, and implements of husbandry. This was the only article calculated for the interests of this body of men, probably at that time the most numerous in the kingdom."[8]

The view helps to explain John Millar's perspective on the Magna Carta. While it protects property, there is no reference to actual agrarian or pastoral or woodland economies. Despite the title of John Logan's play, there is hardly any reference to the actual meadow that was anciently used for assemblies, the council mead. The Saxon word for council is rune. In 1814 the 160 acres of good soil (24s. an acre and tithe-free) of Runnymede were owned by ten people who had sole use of it from March to 12 August, when it became common to the parishioners of Egham who turned out "an indefinite number of cattle." At the end of August it (together with some adjacent enclosed land) was used for two-mile horse races. "These amusements, with the erection of tents, trampling of horses, &c., destroy the herbage for the time, though it soon springs up again much improved and in great abundance."[9]

American independence conducted in the name of Magna Carta occurred in the midst of Atlantic expropriation of common lands, from the Scottish highlands to Irish rundale to Parliamentary enclosure acts, and it is consistent with these forms of privatization. It is no wonder that Ross Perot forgot to buy the

8. David Hume, *The History of England* (1778; repr. Indianapolis, IN: Liberty Clarion, 1983), 1:450.

9. Owen Manning and W. Bray, *The History and Antiquities of the County of Surrey* (London: Printed by J. White, for J. Nichols, 1814), 3:249.

Forest Charter when he purchased the English charter of liberty to display with the Declaration of Independence. Whereas President George W. Bush idolizes the result (it is "above every earthly power"), this was not possible at the end of the eighteenth century, when the justification for the disappearance of the commons was argued in secular terms with the creation a theory of inevitability in the interpretation of Millar's four-stage theory of history. The working class in England, however—from the radicals of the 1790s to the Chartists of the 1830s—was by no means ready to ignore the particulars of the commons allowed by Magna Carta.

Proponents of the landed commons yet survived. Thomas Spence was born in 1750 in Newcastle, in the north of England. He was influenced by James Murray's *Sermons to Asses* (1768), which highly praised Magna Carta. In 1775 he gave a famous lecture at the Philosophical Society arguing for the equal restoration of land to all the people. He was thrown out of town, moved to London, and became an innovating propagandist and popular theorizer of agrarian communism, but he also called for an intellectual commons in his opposition to patents. Among reformers and radicals he distinguished himself from Tom Paine, who did not go far enough in respect to equality of resources. "The country of any people is properly their common, in which each of them has an equal property, with free liberty to sustain himself and family with the animals, fruits, and other products thereof." Spence's argument was never based on law, custom, or contract. There is no reference to the Forest Charter or Magna Carta. However, he was imprisoned three times when habeas corpus was suspended. In 1803 he related an affair in the countryside near Hexham, up the river Tyne, gathering hazelnuts. A forester threatened to arrest him for trespassing on the Duke of Portland's land but Spence replied that he could not arrest the squirrel, for the nuts "are the spontaneous Gifts of nature ordained alike for the Sustenance of Man and Beast, that choose to gather them, and therefore they are common," and as for the Duke of Portland he must look sharp if he wants any nuts.[10]

Hazel nuts were highly esteemed by Celtic people. In legend they are emblems of concentrated wisdom, which they pass to the salmon and people who feed on them. In the seventeenth century they fetched at market the same price as a bushel of wheat. But evidence from the owner of Hatfield Forest, Essex, complained in 1826 that "as soon as the Nuts begin to get ripe . . . the idle and disorderly Men and Woman of bad Character . . . come . . . in large parties to gather the Nuts or under pretence of gathering Nuts to loiter about in Crowds . . . and in the Evening . . . take Beer and Spirits and Drink in the Forest which affords them an opportunity for all sorts of Debauchery." On Nutcrack Night the nuts could be taken into church and cracked noisily during sermon.[11]

The county association for the reform of Parliament was formed in 1779, at "a second Runnymede." Its members believed that the Americans were fighting for "an American Magna Carta."[12] On 20 January 1794 at a general meeting of the London

10. "The Rights of Man" (1793), in *Pig's Meat: Selected Writings of Thomas Spence,* ed. G. I. Gallop (Nottingham: Spokesman, 1982), 59. This is a version of his 1775 lecture.

11. Richard Mabey, *Flora Britannica* (London: Chatto and Windus, 1996), 88–91.

12. Anne Pallister, *Magna Carta: The Heritage of Liberty* (Oxford: Clarendon Press, 1971), 65.

Corresponding Society, the first working-class organization in England, an "Address to the People of Great Britain and Ireland" was read and agreed to. It argued, "the provisions of the Magna Carta and the 1689 Bill of Rights have been eroded by the practice of letting judges assess fines, by basing trials on a charge made by the Attorney General or an informer, by annulling verdicts of juries, by demanding exorbitant bail." John Richter, a leader of the LCS, arrested in 1794, defended himself as follows, "we have referred to Magna Charta, to the Bill of Rights, and to the Revolution, and we certainly do find that our ancestors did establish wise and wholesome laws: But we as certainly find, that, of the venerable Constitution of our ancestors, hardly a vestige remains."[13] In the decade of the 1790s various "friends of the people" might offer toasts tying Magna Carta to the English Revolution ("May the exertions of the people during the reigns of John, Charles, and James, never be forgotten by their descendants") or alluding to the Waltham Black Act ("A speedy abolition of the Slave Trade and Game Laws") or to "the rights of juries and may they ever exercise their authority in favor of liberty."[14] The working-class radicals' project was tied to the reform of Parliament.

The winter months of 1816–17 were extremely hard, for handloom weavers especially. The "blanketeers" were to march from Manchester to London, sleeping in the rough (thus the blankets) to present the regent with petitions for relief of distress. "John Bagguley, an eighteen-year-old Manchester apprentice and a leader of the march, insisted that although their meetings

13. Mary Thale, ed., *Selections from the Papers of the London Corresponding Society, 1792–1799* (Cambridge, Cambridge University Press, 1983), 106.

14. *Toasts and Sentiments: Adapted to the Times* (London, n.d.).

might soon be shut down, 'the law says that [if] the King did not give an Answer to the Petition within the space of 40 Days, He was liable to be seiz'd & all his Familey and confined in a prison till he give an Answer.' " Bagguley supported the point by references to Magna Carta.

Writing in the first number of *The Black Dwarf* in 1817, Thomas Wooler struck the right note. "As the power is always on the side of the people, when they choose to act, it followed as a matter of course that whenever a single point was put to the test of the sword, the people were always ultimately victorious. . . . The country has boasted of being free because Magna Carta was enacted, when the least share of penetration would have taught us that Magna Carta was only enacted because our ancestors were determined to be free." Republicans such as William Sherwin and Dr. James Watson, a former Spencean, were prepared to argue in 1818 that "the great Charter of our Liberties, commonly called MAGNA CHARTA," was "a RECOGNITION OF POSITIVE RIGHTS antecedently existing and inherent in the People; of Rights, which no King or Government can lawfully give or take away."[15] William Hone's "Political House That Jack Built" uses the form of children's poetic game to defend Magna Carta at the classic moment of English working-class formation, the Peterloo Massacre of 1819.

Addressing a huge rally on Heartshead Moor in 1838, the Reverend Joseph Raynor Stephens declared " 'We stand upon our rights—we seek no change—we say give us the good old laws of England unchanged'; and when he received the shout of Magna

15. James A. Epstein, *Radical Expression: Political Language, Ritual, and Symbol in England, 1790–1850* (New York: Oxford University Press, 1994), 15, 21.

Charta to his question 'What are these laws?' he replied: 'Aye, Magna Charta! The good old laws of English freedom—free meetings—freedom of speech—freedom of worship—freedom of homesteads—free and happy firesides, and no workhouses.'"

John Phillippo called the Act of May 1833 abolishing slavery in the British empire "the Magna Carta of negro rights." Thomas Clarkson wrote of the abolition bill of 1807 abolishing the British slave trade, a "Magna Carta for Africa in Britain."[16] These were not merely figures of speech: Granville Sharp had proved the connection. In America the labor periodicals of the 1830s, *The Workingman's Advocate* and *The Man,* proclaimed "our Constitution, the Magna Charta of our *boasted* liberties."[17] As for the English working class, Karl Marx wrote of the Ten Hours Act (1848), "In place of the pompous catalogue of the 'inalienable rights of man' comes the modest Magna Carta of a legally limited working day."[18] Again, more is involved than a figure of speech. Marx began his study of economic conditions with the expropriation of forest customs in the Rhineland. Furthermore, his mature expression of the importance of the prolongation of the working day to the capitalist system linked the extension of the day to the removal of European common rights.

16. Thomas Clarkson, History of the Rise, Progress, and Accomplishment of the Abolition of the African Slave Trade by the British Parliament (London: Longman, Hurst, Rees, and Orme, 1808), 2:580.

17. Merle Curti, "Reformers Reconsider the Constitution," *American Journal of Sociology* 43, no. 6 (May 1938): 881.

18. Karl Marx, *Capital,* trans. Samuel Moore and Edward Aveling, ed. Dona Torr (London: George Allen and Unwin, 1946), 1:288.

"Goody Blake and Harry Gill" is the most pathetic expression ever written of the importance of widow's estovers. It expresses both the feminization of poverty and the feminine strengths of the commons. Part of the power lies in the personal narrative that introduces a moralizing discourse whose only redress is the curse. Human sympathy would fall into an ooze of sentimentality were it not so clear that sentiment, moral values, and common sense were losing their material base.

Walter Scott refers to the Charter of the Forest in *Ivanhoe* (1820), a story based on ethnicities and nationalism. The story of Robin Hood opens with description of the English woods, "hundreds of broad-headed, short-stemmed, wide-branched oaks." Gurth is the Anglo-Saxon swineherd whose pigs banquet on beech mast and acorns. He explains, "little is left us but the air we breathe, and that appears to have been reserved with much hesitation, solely for the purpose of enabling us to endure the tasks that they lay upon our shoulders." He curses the Norman conqueror, "I will teach them that the wood was disforested in terms of the great Forest Charter."

In 1822 Thomas Love Peacock wrote *Maid Marian,* another Robin Hood tale. Peacock was a clerk in the East India Company, said to have been responsible for bringing steam navigation to India. Robin Hood is king of the forest with its "swinish multitude of wild boars." His secretary, Little John, reads the four articles of legitimacy, the three articles of equity, the two articles of hospitality. There is a reference to the widow's estovers: "every forester shall . . . aid and protect maids, widows, and orphans, and all weak and distressed persons whomsoever." There is a reference to chiminage. "Postmen, carriers, and market-folk, peasants and mechanics, farmers and millers, shall pass through our forest dominions without let or molestation."

William Morris wrote in *A Dream of John Ball* (1888) of how the peasants spoke of Robin Hood, and how they sang,

> So over the mead and over the hithe,
> And away to the wild-wood wend we forth;
> There dwell we yeomen bold and blithe
> Where the Sheriff's word is nought of worth.
> We shall bend the bow on the lily lea
> Betwixt the thorn and the oaken tree.
>
> With stone and lime is the burg wall built,
> And pit and prison are stark and strong,
> And many a true man there is spilt,
> And many a right man doomed by wrong.
> So forth shall we and bend the bow
> And the king's writ never the road shall know.

Morris turned the dream to purposeful collective human action. While waiting for John Ball to preach, he "pondered . . . how men fight and lose the battle, and the thing that they fought for comes about in spite of their defeat, and when it comes turns out not be what they meant, and other men have to fight for what they meant under another name."[19] Commons—commune—communism—commons again.

By 1803 the imperial project had become intimately tied to the expropriation of the commons. Sinclair again, "Let us not be satisfied with the liberation of Egypt, or the subjugation of Malta,

---

19. William Morris, *A Dream of John Ball* (New York: Oriole Chapbooks, n.d.), 12–13.

but let us subdue Finchley Common; let us conquer Hounslow Heath, let us compel Epping Forest to submit to the yoke of improvement."[20] An essential part of suppression at home was expansion abroad. The fate of the English commoner was determined in the jungles of India.

20. Quoted by Anne Janowitz, "Land," in *An Oxford Companion to the Romantic Age: British Culture, 1776–1832,* ed. Iain McCalman (New York: Oxford University Press, 1999), 160.

CHAPTER SEVEN

The Law of the Jungle

If ye kill before midnight, be silent, and wake not the woods with your bay,
Lest ye frighten the deer from the crops, and the brothers go empty away.
The Kill of the Pack is the meat of the Pack. Ye must eat where it lies;
And no one may carry away of that meat to his lair, or he dies.

Rudyard Kipling, "The Law of the Jungle" (1895)

"A frightful hobgoblin stalks throughout Europe. We are haunted by a ghost, the ghost of Communism"—is the opening of the *Communist Manifesto* in its first English translation.

The translator was Helen MacFarlane, a Lancashire Chartist, whose choice of words derived from the forest commons— "Hob" was the name of a country laborer, "goblin" a mischievous sprite. Thus communism manifested itself in the *Manifesto* in the discourse of the agrarian commons, the substrate of language revealing the imprint of the clouted shoon in the sixteenth century who fought to have all things common. The trajectory from the commons to communism can be cast as the passage from past to future. For Marx personally it corresponded to his intellectual progress. The criminalization of the woodland commons of the Moselle Valley peasantry provided him with his first experience with economic questions and led him directly to the critique of political economy.[1]

The "science" of political economy provided a specious universal built upon the axioms that commodity exchange and private property were natural laws and humankind's summum bonum. Actually, some of its major proponents, James Steuart, Thomas Malthus, James Mill, and J. S. Mill, were employees of the East India Company.[2] The hobgoblin may have had ghostly existence in Europe but in India the forest commons, or jungle, and the creatures therein, were thriving. "Causes which were lost in England might, in Asia or Africa, yet be won," wrote E. P. Thompson in the midst of the colonial revolt.[3]

In 1867 the Lord Chief Justice of England, Alexander Cockburn, argued in the notorious Governor Eyre controversy that the summary hanging of hundreds of people during the Morant Bay uprising in Jamaica the previous year was criminal. Referring to the Petition of Right as well as to the great charter, he enunciated the principle of the rule of law, "every British citizen, white, brown, or black in skin, shall be subject to definite, and not indefinite powers," and added "What is

1. Karl Marx, *A Contribution to the Critique of Political Economy,* trans. N. I. Stone (Chicago: Charles H. Kerr, 1904).

2. John Roosa, "Orientalism, Political Economy, and the Canonization of Indian Civilization," in *Enduring Western Civilization: The Construction of the Concept of Western Civilization and Its "Others,"* ed. Silvia Federici (Westport: Praeger, 1995), 138.

3. E. P. Thompson, preface to *The Making of the English Working Class* (New York: Vintage Books, 1963).

done in a colony today may be done in Ireland tomorrow, and in England hereafter."[4] This is the boomerang, or blowback, of imperialism.

Sumit Guha sums up the modern ecological history of India by saying that at the end of the twentieth century about half the surface area of India was under cultivation while actual woodlands made up 13 or 14 percent of the total area—wooded islands in a sea of tillage. The ratio two centuries earlier—archipelagoes of cultivated field in a sea of modified forest—had been reversed.[5] What happened? Rabindranath Tagore, the Nobel prize–winning poet of Bengal, published a volume of poetry, which he translated into English as *Stray Birds* (1916). He wrote, "The woodcutter's axe begged for its handle from the tree. The tree gave it." It is a gentle metaphor for imperialism.

Here's how it worked. In 1802 the Crown arrogated to itself sovereignty over the Indian forests. Teak trees provided planking for the decks on naval and commercial ships that exported the produce of India: it was teak that defeated Napoleon. They were ripped wholesale from the hills to provide railway ties, "sleepers," for the iron rails that carried Indian wealth from the interior to the port cities, and whose steam engines voraciously consumed more and more wood. The steamships and iron railways of the British raj, useless without the Indian timbers and

---

4. Alexander James Edmund Cockburn, *Charge of the Lord Chief Justice of England to the Grand Jury at the Old Bailey* (April 1867); Bernard Semmel, *Jamaican Blood and Victorian Conscience: The Governor Eyre Controversy* (Boston: Houghton Mifflin, 1963).

5. Sumit Guha, *Environment and Ethnicity in India, 1200–1991* (Cambridge: Cambridge University Press, 1999), 40.

fuel for their construction, carried away the wealth of India. India seemed to provide the substances of its own undoing.

Indian famine joined the English enclosures, the American frontier, the Scottish clearances, African slavery, and the Irish famine as historical synecdoches of primitive accumulation when terror accompanied the brutal separation from the means of subsistence, Victorian holocausts all. After the Indian Mutiny of 1857 "English fury" took over. In English parlance the word "nigger" began to prevail.[6] The sanguinary rod of rule rang the iron triangle formed by terror, racism, and expropriation. The frequency, extent, severity, and nature of Indian famines changed for the worse. They became less localized owing to the extension of the railways; many millions perished by starvation, cholera, smallpox, and fever; and a new cause exacerbated the scarcities directly proceeding from lack of rain, to wit, lack of purchasing power. Agricultural wage laborers suffered the most. Government offered public works at starvation wages—breaking stones, digging ditches, and preparing railway beds. Those with strength and opportunity fled to the jungle.

One million five hundred thousand people died in Madras presidency during the Great Famine of 1876–78. Women and children who stole from gardens or gleaned in fields were "branded, tortured, had their noses cut off, and were sometimes killed." In Poona leading an aborted conspiracy in 1879, B. B. Phadke became "the Maratha Robin Hood," the father of militant Indian nationalism.[7] Jotirau Phule (1881) said, "The cun-

6. V. G. Kiernan, *The Lords of Human Kind* (Boston: Little, Brown, 1969).

7. Mike Davis, *Late Victorian Holocausts: El Niño Famines and the Making of the Third World* (London: Verso, 2001).

ning European employees of our motherly government have used their foreign brains to erect a great superstructure called the forest department. With all the hills and undulating lands as also the fallow lands and grazing grounds brought under the control of the forest department, the livestock of the poor farmers does not even have place to breathe anywhere on the surface of the earth."[8] The nationalist Dadabhai Naoroji wrote at the end of the nineteenth century: "The Europeans are and make themselves strangers in every way. All they effectually do is to eat the substance of India, material and moral, while living there, and when they go, they carry away all they have acquired, and their pensions and future usefulness besides." He continued, "How strange it is that the British rulers do not see that after all they themselves are the main cause of the destruction that ensues from droughts; that it is the drain of India's wealth by them that lays at their own door the dreadful results of misery, starvation, and deaths of millions."[9]

Government in its Indian Famine Commission's report offered the view that "the mortality, whether it be great or little, was due to the ignorance of the people, to their obstinacy and their dislike for work." The famine commissioners blamed the Indian forest commoner whose alleged "improvident denudation" destroyed the topsoil, removed the forest cover, and lowered the water table. Government must step in "to turn to the best account the vast resources provided by nature." "Measures

8. Madhav Gadgil and Ramachandra Guha, *This Fissured Land: An Ecological History of India* (Berkeley: University of California Press, 1993), 150.
9. Dadabhai Naoroji, *Essays, Speeches, Addresses and Writings* (Bombay: Caxton, 1887), 466, 473.

must be taken" to prevent people who are *accustomed* to taking forest produce from doing so. Such practices were "recklessly destructive of the public property." The commissioners concluded, "so far as any immediate advantage is to be sought from the extension of forest in respect to protection against drought, it will, in our opinion, be mainly in the direction of the judicious enclosure and protection of tracts."[10] The raj criminalizes custom, and it does so in the context of famine, which it blames on the ignorance, obstinacy, and laziness of Indian commoners.

Commons in the forest provided the basis of subsistence agriculture in times of plenty and of dearth. *Kumri* was a system of shifting cultivation practiced in western India. *Jhum* was a similar system of forest cultivation under which a tract of forest is cleared by fire, occupied and cultivated for a time, and then abandoned for another tract. Among the Baigas this form of agriculture is called *bewar.* It is swidden agriculture—burning clearings in the forest, and seeding in the scattered ashes. They say, "the axe is our milk-giving cow."[11] The forest was the people's safety net. The preservation of this net was partly the responsibility of the *panchayat,* the local jury or assembly. During famine, seeds of the *sál* tree were in considerable demand as an article of food. After the thorns had been cut off the prickly pear tree and it had been chopped up, it could be given to cattle in time of scarcity. As for the karkapilly tree, "the leaves and twigs furnish a never-failing

10. *Report of the Indian Famine Commission,* vol. 3, *Famine Histories* (London: HMSO, 1885), 181; and vol. 2, *Measures of Protection and Prevention,* 177–78.

11. Verrier Elwin, *The Muria and Their Ghotul* (Calcutta: Oxford University Press, 1947), 24.

forage for the poverty-stricken feeder of milch goats; birds, beasts, and boys scramble for the plump arillus which encases its seeds." Wild acacia tree provides "bark eaten in times of scarcity." The Indian horse chestnut "is given as food to cattle and goats, and in times of scarcity the embryo is soaked in water and then ground and eaten mixed with flour by the hill people." And as for sandalwood, "the leaves were eaten to a considerable extent in famine seasons in the Ceded Districts."[12]

The Dang of Gujarat tell an old story of a sahib who was spotted with a telescope. "He said, 'these are forests of gold. I must get them for myself.' Moving through the jungle he asked for the names of trees, which he wrote down immediately in his book. With the names in his book, he did not need the rajas any longer, for he knew everything about the forest himself."[13] Naming and expropriation go together. Like Adam before him, John Bull sat down to name the species of creation. In 1902 James Sykes Gamble published *A Manual of Indian Timbers: An Account of the Growth, Distribution, and Uses of the Trees and Shrubs of India and Ceylon.* Gamble belonged to the Indian Forest Department. Four thousand seven hundred and forty-nine species were identified and described, the "deracinated particulars" of the European sci-

---

12. James Sykes Gamble, *A Manual of Indian Timbers: An Account of the Growth, Distribution, and Uses of the Trees and Shrubs of India and Ceylon,* 2nd ed. (London: S. Low, Marston, 1902); and Dietrich Brandis, *Indian Trees: An Account of Trees, Shrubs, Woody Climbers, Bamboos and Palms Indigenous or Commonly Cultivated in the British Indian Empire* (London: Constable, 1911), 117.

13. Ajay Skaria, *Hybrid Histories: Forests, Frontiers and Wildness in Western India* (Oxford: Oxford University Press, 1999), 178.

entific fact.[14] He provided a three-part index, one for the European name, one for the Latin name, and one for the Indian vernacular. One of its purposes, he explains, was to help the English forester "be free from the obvious danger of having to rely on the diagnosis of a subordinate or workman."[15] Why was this obvious?

Arundhati Roy leads us to the answer. She records a conversation with a man of the forest. "In Vadaj, a resettlement site I visited near Baroda, the man who was talking to me rocked his sick baby in his arms, clumps of flies gathered on its sleeping eyelids. Children collected around us, taking care not to burn their bare skin on the scorching tin walls of the shed they call a home. The man's mind was far away from the troubles of his sick baby. He was making me a list of the fruit he used to pick in the forest. He counted forty-eight kinds. He told me that he didn't think he or his children would ever be able to afford to eat any fruit again. Not unless he stole it."[16]

And indeed after naming came law. The Indian Forest Department was formed in 1864 with Dietrich Brandis, a German forester, as the first inspector general of forests. The first Forest Act (1865) contained provisions for the "definition, regulation, commutation, and extinction of customary rights." The Indian Forest Act of 1878 was an act of massive, intercontinental confiscation. It destroyed the village forest commons by undermining subsistence

14. Mary Poovey, *A History of the Modern Fact* (Chicago: University of Chicago Press, 1998), xiv.

15. Gamble, *Manual of Indian Timbers,* xix.

16. Arundhati Roy, *The Cost of Living* (New York: Modern Library, 1999), 53–54.

cultivation as well as hunting and gathering. Ramachandra Guha writes, "one stroke of the executive pen attempted to obliterate centuries of customary use by rural populations all over India."[17] Brandis expressed one of the consequences: "the rich shoal land in the ravines down which the streams descend attracted coffee planters who destroyed the magnificent timber, and this let in the wind which has extended the mischief done by the axe." Brandis advocated "the formation of village forests for the exclusive use of the people." In the debates preceding the 1878 Forest Act, Henry Baden-Powell advocated total state control over the forests of India with the extinction of existing customary rights, norms, and practices and the denial of access to the land and resources of the forest. Baden-Powell, an Indian high court judge, regarded these as unwritten privileges rather than as ancient rights. He did so on the basis of the theory of "Oriental despotism."[18]

An opposing view prevailed in Madras, whose board of revenue reported in August 1871, "There is scarcely a forest in the

17. Ramachandra Guha, "An Early Environmental Debate: The Making of the 1878 Forest Act," *Indian Economic and Social History Review* 27, no. 1 (1990): 78.

18. That theory perhaps derives from monarchical claims of land ownership, which were deliberately perceived as legal titles. Customary "rights" to use and work the forest were therefore seen as "privileges" granted by the monarch to the subjects in his kingdom. Sir Thomas Munro in 1800 said, "the only land in Kanara that can in any way come under the description of *Sirkar* land is unclaimed waste." A suit by the king of Mysore in 1870 about forests on river Kalanadi said they "were claimed *first* by virtue of certain sanads [official documents, deeds] alleged to have been granted by Tippoo sultan, *second* by virtue of the claimants having exercised the right of cutting trees, gathering forest produce, and cultivating kumri."

whole of the Presidency of Madras which is not within the limits of some village, and there is not one in which, so far as the Board can ascertain, the State asserted any rights of property—unless royalties in teak, sandalwood, cardamom, and the like can be considered as such—until very recently. All of them, without exception, are subject to tribal or communal rights which have existed from time immemorial and which are as difficult to define and value as they are necessary to the rural population. Nor can it be said that these rights are susceptible of compensation, for in innumerable cases, the right to fuel, manure and pasturage, will be as much a necessity of life to unborn generations as it is to the present. Here the forests are, and always have been, a common property."

The Madras Forest Act was delayed to 1882 because of the debate over "customary uses." The governor of Madras stated that the 1878 Forest Bill "is framed for the purpose of the acquisition by government and ultimate extinction of all such private or village rights." Among the British governors the debate over forest policy was conducted with the parallel to the Norman Conquest of England in mind. The parallel was mentioned in an 1878 minute, "the system we are following and now seeking to legalize is worthy only of the times of the Norman Conquest." According to the eighth article of the minute by Governor Buckingham and Chandos, "This is probably much the same process which the Norman Kings adopted in England for their forest extension." Remarkably, this debate, now archived in Delhi, was printed.[19] The discussion was haunted by the ghost of the Norman yoke and Magna Carta.

19. D. Brandis, *Memorandum on the Demarcation of the Public Forests in the Madras Presidency,* National Archives of India, Delhi, 1878, passim.

In 1885 a petition to the governor of Bombay from the cultivators of the mountain ranges of the Tannah District provided a list of subsistence uses that could be compared with those mentioned in the English Charters of Liberties. The hearths burn fuel hewn from the forest, the simple huts from time to time need new rafters gathered from the woods, the cattle require grazing grounds, wood is needed to make farm implements such as the plow. In seasons without grain petitioners require the fruits and vegetables of the jungle, its "wild productions," the ability to sell flowers and mangoes from the open land provides some cash. Its ninth article noted, "the powers proposed to be given to the police are arbitrary and dangerous, arrest without warrant of any person suspected of having been concerned at some unknown time of being concerned in a forest offence (taking some wild bee's honey from a tree or the skin of a dead animal)."[20] The petition linked the two principles of subsistence and freedom from arbitrary arrest: chapter 39 of Magna Carta and the 13th chapter of the Forest Charter, which says "Every freeman . . . may also have honey that is found in his woods."

In 1875 Henry Baden-Powell launched the *Indian Forester,* with a German forestry expert, W. Schlich. It combined scientific enterprise (observation and experimentation) with assiduous record keeping ("every forest officer who is worthy of the name keeps a note-book"), and abject loyalty to authority ("we are suppliants at the threshold of every temple of government"). Its first article was

20. The petition is reprinted in Indra Munshi Saldanha, "Colonial Forest Regulations and Collective Resistance: Nineteenth Century Thana District," in *Nature and the Orient: The Environmental History of South and Southeast Asia,* ed. Richard H. Grove, Vinita Damodaran, and Satpal Sangwan (New York: Oxford University Press, 1998), 730–32.

hostile toward *kumri* agriculture. Henry Baden-Powell sent impressions from Dehra Dun, warning against "the frightful injury caused by fire," issuing forest diktats ("I would simply prohibit, as far as possible, ALL CUTTING"), and in these emphatic terms of general prohibitions ("From therein fire MUST ABSOLUTELY be kept out and GRAZING.") we hear the slap of the sahib's swagger stick.[21] As one hill man of Dehra Dun put it, "the forests have belonged to us from time immemorial: our ancestors planted them and have protected them: now that they have become of value, government steps in and robs us of them."[22]

Baden-Powell and his compatriots wrote with the blind superiority of the imperialist. The prologue to the journal emphasized the "utilization of forests"—the harvesting of produce, the extraction of rubber, the production of fruits, the charcoal burning, "the transport of forest produce by land and water, dragging, carrying, carting, snow-sledges, timber slides, floating and boating, and of all things road making" and it mentions the different methods of disposal of forest produce by sale, by permit, by government agency, and by auction. *Kumri, jhum* and other Indian agricultural practices are left out entirely. "Next we mention protection of the forests and their produce against men and beasts." The cat is out of the bag. The prologue concludes with the characteristic imperial elision of knowledge and force, "the field is a wide one; let us try and occupy it successfully."

Powell published his *Forest Law* in 1893. At near five hundred pages it had every appearance of the definitive: twenty-seven

21. *The Indian Forester* (July 1875): 4–5.

22. Madhav Gadgil and Ramachandra Guha, "State Forestry and Social Conflict in British India," *Past and Present,* no. 123 (May 1989): 165.

lectures, schematic conspectus of each part, liberal footnotes to German experts. Although it considered the rights of litter, of lopping, of grass cutting, of wood for building, for fuel, for industrial and agricultural implements, and for minor forest produce, its definition of a "right" was anything but reassuring to the Indian *ryot* or forest dweller. Rights, it explained, have to be established and defined in order to be legal. Custom is recognized insofar as it is uniform, uninterrupted, and longstanding. Although he mentions Manwood on *Lawes of the Forrest* (1598) there is never a mention of the Forest Charter. There is no evidence that he ever consulted the *panchayat*. Forest laws are required, he says, "A forest is really as much the subject of property as an orchard or a garden; but owing to its natural origin, in most cases, the ignorant population has an inveterate tendency to regard it as 'no man's goods,' or as free to all: and the feeling is, that it is theft to steal a gold ring from a shop, or even apples from an orchard or roses from a garden, but it is not harm to cut a tree or turn in some cows to graze in a forest."[23]

The forest was also haunted by the specter of communism. Baden-Powell was part of a worldwide debate following the Paris Commune of 1871. His study of *The Land Systems of British India* argued that there was no tribal stage in the formation of villages and hence no such thing as tribal property. His book was reviewed by Thorstein Veblen, forming part of the international discussion. Since such property did not legally exist, there was no "need for its explanation in an a priori assumption of 'collective ownership,' or holding 'in common.'" This scholarship gave

23. B. H. Baden-Powell, *Forest Law* (1893), 184–85.

backing to privatization by doubting the existence, past or present, of social commoning. The village commons was entirely nugatory. Dietrich Brandis discussed the communal forests of French and German villages at the conclusion of his *Memorandum on the Demarcation of the Public Forests in the Madras Presidency* (1878): "they are not based on theories and Utopian schemes."[24]

After naming, after law, comes science.

Darwin buckled down to writing *The Origin of Species* during the summer of the India Mutiny in 1857, including the evidence of his correspondents stationed in India. Colonel Poole reported from the northwestern frontier of India that the Kattyar breed of horses is generally striped. Mr. Blyth and Captain Hutton of India kept whole flocks of hybrid geese descended from the common goose and the Chinese goose. In 1849 his friend Hooker was kidnapped in Sikkim returning from Tibet through a mountain pass. He had been collecting rhododendron seeds for Kew Gardens. In response, a regiment was moved toward Darjeeling, while Sikkim was annexed for the Crown—thereby making "botanizing," as this biopiracy was called, more secure. Meanwhile the rhododendron seeds, collected at different altitudes in the Himalayas, were found to possess "different constitutional powers of resisting the cold" in England and provided Darwin with an example of plant acclimatization at different temperatures, in his chapter on the laws of variation. In *The Origin of Species* Darwin refers to childhood observation of Scotch fir ecology on both enclosed and unenclosed heath that was later confirmed by similar observation near Farnham, Surrey, where heaths were both enclosed and un-

---

24. Brandis, *Public Forests in the Madras Presidency*.

enclosed.[25] In 1876 an article in the *Indian Forester* quoted Darwin to the effect that for tree plantations to flourish, browsing cattle and human woodcutters alike should be excluded.[26]

And after science comes myth.

Rudyard Kipling wrote "The Law of the Jungle" in 1895 as a poetic, oracular coda to his *Second Jungle Book*. It has found its way into the pep talks of American football coaches, into the handbook and lore of the United States Marine Corps, as well as into the rituals and games of the Wolf Cubs. It is a masculine, predatory creed whose rhythms of solidarity might be mistaken for the sound of marching boots,

> As the creeper that girdles the tree-trunk the Law runneth
> forward and back—
> The strength of the Pack is the Wolf, and the strength of the
> Wolf is the Pack

Despite its numbing rhythm a closer study reveals a socialist code of conduct. It is against accumulation, primitive or otherwise, and it provides a moral economy for the pack, the cub, the mother, and the father. It is based on the jungle commons. The eighteen stanzas of "The Law of the Jungle" enjoin one to wash, to sleep, to keep the peace, to live unobtrusively, and to sit down in order to

25. Charles Darwin, *The Origin of Species* (New York: Modern Library, 1993), 182, 205, 369. Adrian Desmond and James Moore, *Darwin* (New York: W. W. Norton, 1991), 343.

26. Kavita Philip, *Civilizing Natures: Race, Resources, and Modernity in Colonial South India* (Rugers: New Brunswick, 2004), 29, 57. *The Indian Forester* (October 1876).

prevent war. One takes no pleasure in killing, one leaves food for the weak, one shares the kill, hoarding is forbidden, the children may draw on the food of the pack, the mother is given privilege to food. Yet fear pervades the jungle. It provides a guide to virtuous conduct during the crisis of privatization when violence is inherent in all aspects of environmental losses.

The Mowgli series originated in a tale Kipling had written about the Indian Forestry Department. Mowgli is a boy brought up by wolves. "How Fear Came" is a version of the fall where Satan is replaced by "Man," or the people of the plains and the empire. They brought catastrophe to the creatures. Hathi the Elephant explained, "Ye know what harm that has since been done to all our peoples—through the noose, and the pitfall, and the hidden trap, and the flying stick, and the stinging fly that comes out of white smoke, and the Red Flower that drives us into the open."[27] Malthusian gloom set in and like kept to like.

Rudyard Kipling was born in Bombay in 1865, descended from three generations of Methodist preachers. The Mowgli stories owe something to his evangelical background (Bunyan's *Pilgrim's Progress*). He was devoted to his *ayah,* and as a child he dreamt in Hindustani. His father worked at a Bombay arts college named after a Parsi benefactor who also endowed a neighboring Jainist animal hospital reputed in England to illustrate the Indian "love of animals." In 1891 his father, John Lockwood Kipling, wrote *Beast and Man in India.* European observers, however, "mostly look at nature along the barrel of a gun." "In India," he believed,

27. Harry Ricketts, *The Unforgiving Minute: A Life of Rudyard Kipling* (London: Chatto and Windus, 1999), 206.

"we are nearer the time when creatures spoke and thought";[28] accordingly he has a short chapter on animal calls.

That was also the year that he shipped his son, Rudyard, to England, and an abusive upbringing by puritanical guardians. This childhood uprooting was marked in his memory by the miserable cruelty suffered by the dogs at the neighboring hospital. At the United Service College, whose headmaster was sympathetic to the socialist outlook of William Morris, young Kipling was in touch with the agricultural laborers and small cottagers from whom he heard about poaching, smuggling, wrecking, community forms of appropriation that are halfway between moral economies and social banditry.[29] This tale occurs during famine, and the suggestion is that scarcity is the time when the law especially is needed. Kipling's description is remarkable for its ecological signs—a tree (mahua) does not bloom, wild yams dry up—and it is remarkable for the water truce, during which predatory animals stop hunting and the water hole is a peaceful gathering place for all, an *encuentro*.

George Shaw-Lefevre of Wimbledon Common founded the Commons Preservation Society in 1865. Within fifteen miles of the center of London there were seventy-four such commons. The society had two purposes, "that the people should have some interest in the land of the country"; and "that the amenities of

28. John Lockwood Kipling, *Beast and Man in India: A Popular Sketch of Indian Animals in Their Relations with the People* (London: Macmillan, 1891), 10, 15, 19.

29. Angus Wilson, *The Strange Ride of Rudyard Kipling: His Life and Works* (New York: Viking, 1977), 42.

everyday life should be placed within reach of rich and poor alike."[30] The society soldiered nobly in defense of the great parks of London as "amenities" for the health of the urban proletariat, not as a platform of social and economic equality.

Robert Stephenson Smyth Baden-Powell, the founder of the Boy Scouts, similarly wanted to improve the health of the slum children in the English industrial cities. He denigrated the book by his half brother, Henry Baden-Powell, as "his manual on forest law, whatever that may be." *Scouting for Boys* was published in 1908 and the Wolf Cubs were started in 1916; their activities and rituals were based on the anthropomorphic stories of Mowgli in the *Jungle Books*.[31] Robert Baden-Powell also served in India. A code of conduct for twentieth-century Anglo-American boys—mediated by Rudyard Kipling and Baden-Powell—thus emerged from the Indian subcontinent jungles just at the time when those forests and the human cultures they sustained were falling under the ax. The Indian forest was enclosed and its commoners expropriated at the same time that English workers found relaxation in the parks developed from the ancient English commons. The exotic imaginary of the Indian forest as evoked in Kipling's *Jungle Books* provided the template of healthy activity for proletarian children in the English Cub Scout movement even as the vast safety net in the forests of India was expropriated in the midst of famine.

30. Lord Eversley [George Shaw-Lefevre], *Commons, Forests, and Footpaths,* rev. ed. (New York: Cassell, 1910), vii.

31. Tim Jeal, *Baden-Powell* (New Haven: Yale University Press, 1989), 54, 500.

Kipling stayed with friends in Allahabad who introduced him to the Seoni jungle. Kipling may be contrasted with Verrier Elwin, who went out to India from Oxford to join a mystical Christian ashram, then became a follower of Mohandas Gandhi and the non-cooperation movement, finally abandoned the independence movement, and lived with the Gond people in the Seoni, becoming an Indian citizen after independence. He records several talking animal stories collected by these "tribals." Whereas the gender of activities in the Mowgli stories tends to be male, the gender of commoning in the English forests tended to be female—gathering, nutting, gardening, gleaning, pig keeping, cow caring. A big difference between Kipling's Mowgli story and reality was described by Verrier Elwin: there is no "subjugation of woman in a Gond village." In 1939 reformers warned Gandhi of "immoralities" there—women dancing, alcohol allowed—and when his reform movement reached the Seoni, it impoverished them all as much as the expropriations of the Forest Department had.[32]

Jungle is a Hindi word in origin meaning waste or forest. Among the forest people of western India the *jangli* is associated with a discourse of wildness as well as with a particular ecosystem. Ajay Skaria refers to "the cathexis of the forest" or to its affect and energy as provided or discerned by the indigenous Dang. The Dang periodized history as two epochs, the time of

---

32. Verrier Elwin, *Leaves from the Jungle: Life in a Gond Village,* 2nd ed. ([1936]; New York: Oxford University Press, 1958), 12, 23; and Verrier Elwin, *The Tribal World of Verrier Elwin* (New York: Oxford University Press, 1964), 115–18. G. S. Ghurye, *The Aborigines—'So-Called'—and Their Future* (Bombay, 1943), opposed Elwin's policies and advocated the modern integration of the "tribals" under Hindu terms.

tax collectors, land demarcation, and forest guards, and the time before, when freedom prevailed, along with hunting, fishing, gathering, shifting cultivation, and collecting mahua flowers and seeds. This time was called *moglai*.[33] Thus Kipling in his Mowgli stories summons up not a golden age nor a garden of Eden but a specifically Indian characterization of a recently lost commons. While it is true that Kipling was the bard of British empire, his "underground" or "Mowgli" self should not be seen ethnically or even nationalistically, but in sympathetic relation to the people who came before. The boy named Mowgli brought up in a wolf pack personified the epoch of historical freedom known as *moglai* that was passing before their eyes.[34]

Mowgli was a hobgoblin but not a communist. Kipling's accomplishment, with Baden-Powell's help, was to displace the ancient discourse of commoning and the modern political discourse of communism into childhood. Early in the twentieth century in the heyday of the privatized nuclear family, the human relations of the commons were repressed (as if in a kind of Freudian commons) or consigned to the bedroom and nursery in the children's utopias of *Peter Pan, Treasure Island, The Land of Oz,* and *The Wind and the Willows.* The *Jungle Books* end with Mowgli rejoining human society and taking a position in the Indian Forestry Department, the "great superstructure" of discommoning.

Gandhi arrived in England in 1888 in order to study law in one of the Inns of Court and to become a barrister. To pass his exams (1891) he had to read Broom on *Common Law* and Williams on

33. Skaria, *Hybrid Histories,* 15, 63.

34. Zohreh T. Sullivan, *Narratives of Empire: The Fictions of Rudyard Kipling* (New York: Cambridge University Press, 1993), 11.

Real Property. In Broom he would read that the forest laws were insupportable until "the people of England" passed "the immunities of *carta de foresta* as warmly contended for, and extorted from the king with as much difficulty, as those of *magna carta* itself." Knowledge of the Norman Conquest at the time stressed the violent creation of the royal forests. The king pulled down houses and churches, lectured Joshua Williams at Gray's Inn in 1877. He also stressed as the first thing mentioned in the Forest Charter "all forests which King Henry our grandfather afforested should be viewed by good and lawful men" in order to disafforest them.[35] Although Gandhi wrote that Williams on *Real Property* "read like a novel," he'd find in it no references to herbage or pannage and only two to estovers, unless Gandhi read Joshua Williams's lectures delivered ten years earlier at Gray's Inn on *Rights of Common,* in which case he'd become acquainted with the Forest Charter and its numerous references to customary usufructs (28 citations to herbage, 21 to estovers, 8 to pannage).[36] He was more interested in vegetarianism, theosophy, ballroom dancing, and the punctilio of an English gentleman's fashion than he was in English law. Gandhi may have just read "the rights of common . . . are, for the most part, rights which arose in a primitive state of society, and which are unfitted for society as it now exists."[37] Communism is childish: Mowgli must grow up.

35. Herbert Broom and Edward A. Hadley, *Commentaries on the Laws of England* (London: W. Maxwell, 1869), 2:102.

36. Joshua Williams, *The Rights of Common and Other Prescriptive Rights: Twenty-Four Lectures* (London: H. Sweet, 1880), 230.

37. Mohandas Gandhi, *An Autobiography: The Story of My Experiments with Truth* (Boston: Beacon Press, 1957), 80.

In the theory of John Locke useful human activity confers prescriptive right; property right arises directly from labor. Joshua Williams in his Gray's Inn lectures expressed it like this. "The right to take fuel to burn in a house, if claimed by prescription must be claimed in respect of an ancient house; for prescription is a title acquired by a use, for time whereof the memory of man runneth not to the contrary."[38] The issue of memory is important because it can be disturbed by trauma, such as famine, when those quickest to succumb are the elderly, vulnerable holders of the community's customary knowledge. This from a forest settlement report of 1916. "The notion obstinately persists in the minds of all, from highest to the lowest, that Government is taking away their forests from them and is robbing them of their own property. . . . The oldest inhabitant therefore and he naturally is regarded as the greatest authority, is the most assured of the antiquity of the people's right to uncontrolled use of the forest. . . . My best efforts however have, I fear, failed to get the people generally to grasp the change in conditions or to believe in the historical fact of government ownership." Elwin observed the result of failure to resist: "He became both timid and obsequious, and it was almost impossible to develop in his mind a sense of citizenship, for he no longer felt at home in his own country."

In May 1913 a village clerk petitioned for exemption from forced labor. "They are not allowed to fell down a tree to get fuel from it for their daily use and they cannot cut leaves of trees beyond certain portion of them for fodder to their animals." Social order began to be monitored by the statistics of wood theft,

38. Williams, *Rights of Common,* 186.

which no more foretold the coming storm of *satyagraha* than the Moselle River statistics foretold the 1848 revolutions. Defiance of forest regulations formed part of the campaign led by the Indian National Congress in 1920–22 and 1930–32.[39] Women and children committed the bulk of "forest offences."[40] In 1911 Sonji wanted wood to rebuild his house but forest regulations required that he ask permission from the English authorities. Instead he told his chief, who said take the teak since he was "master of the forest." Sonji duly took the wood, he was challenged, the commoners assembled, and incendiarism spread.[41]

While the nonviolence, the passive resistance, and the spiritual purity of the concept of satyagraha has had powerful effects in Indian independence movement as well as the America civil rights struggle, yet it left the commons behind. Satyagraha did not include estovers. A British missionary wrote in 1921, "the ignorant have been stirred up by the [Congress] agitators to believe that Gandhi is King now, and that the British rule is at an end— the results being that the villagers have been trespassing in the reserved forests and taking leaves and branches for firewood ad lib."[42] Ad libitum meaning at one's pleasure, but villagers did not take just as much as they pleased. We saw that Sonji consulted his chief before cutting down the teak to rebuild his house.

---

39. Sumit Sarkar, "Primitive Rebellion and Modern Nationalism: A Note on Forest Satyagraha in the Non-Cooperation and Civil Disobedience Movements," in *A Critique of Colonial India* (Calcutta: Papyrus, 1985), 79–85.

40. Ramachandra Guha, *The Unquiet Woods: Ecological Change and Peasant Resistance in the Himalaya* (Berkeley: University of California Press, 1989), 121.

41. Skaria, *Hybrid Histories,* 269.

42. Skaria, *Hybrid Histories,* 75.

In 1959 I visited Murree, a hill station north of Rawalpindi, where the villagers had rights to graze their animals, to cut grass, to carry away dead trees, to lop trees that were more than 16 feet high, to cut one tree to meet the funeral expenses, and once in five years to take 315 cubic feet of wood for building purposes.[43] England, Magna Carta, seemed at the time far away.

In 1973 Chandi Prasad Bhatt hugged a tree, and saved it from the ax, thereby initiating the chipko movement that became a worldwide flashpoint of discussion on feminism, environment, and development. Apart from the drumming, the invocation of the sacred, the movement was also marked by a deep sense of history, recalling customary rights back to 1763. Women in fact were the repository of local tradition. "In the act of embracing the trees, therefore, they are acting not merely as women but as bearers of continuity with the past in a community threatened with fragmentation."[44] That continuity, we now can say, goes back to the Charters of Liberties. The ghost that haunted Europe—the commons—was full-bodied in India.

In southern Wales Alfred Russel Wallace's first job was in 1840 to survey lands in anticipation of railroads and enclosure. The powerful miners, the angry artisans, the sullen laborers, and resentful small farmers, resisted through nocturnal outlaw organizations known as Rebecca's Children. Its modern historian

43. Masudu Hasan, *Murree Guide* (Lahore: Pakistan Social Service Foundation, 1958), 39.

44. Vandana Shiva, *Staying Alive: Women, Ecology, and Development* (London: Zed Books, 1988).

writes that "an extramural nation took shape."[45] In later years Russel called enclosure an "all-embracing system of land-robbery."

Russel journeyed to the Amazon and the Orinoco, where he lived with indigenous peoples, and then departed for the Indonesian islands, searching for the bird of paradise. "I have lived with communities of savages in South America and in the East, who have no laws or law courts but the public opinion of the village freely expressed. . . . There are none of those wide distinctions, of education and ignorance, wealth and poverty, master and servant, which are the product of our civilization."[46]

Poverty and crime have accompanied the extension of commerce and wealth. "A great landholder may legally convert his whole property into a forest or a hunting-ground, and expel every human being who has hitherto lived upon it. In a thickly-populated country like England, where every acre has its owner and its occupier, this is a power of legally destroying his fellow-creatures." The system of land tenure originated at the Norman Conquest, when the whole land of the kingdom became vested in the Crown. Tenures with customary rights of commoning evolved from villeinage.[47]

Was there a golden age, a real age of *moglai*? The debate in India has been lively. The Gond people believed that when the

45. Gwyn A. Williams, *When Was Wales? A History of the Welsh* (London: Black Raven Press, 1985), 197.

46. Alfred Russel Wallace, *The Malay Archipelago, the Land of the Orang-utan and the Bird of Paradise* (London: Macmillan, 1872), 597.

47. Alfred Russel Wallace, *Land Nationalisation: Its Necessity and Its Aims* (London: Sonnenschein, 1892), 22.

government took the forest, an "age of darkness" commenced. Gandhi, as trained in English law, would have run across the phrase "prescription is a title acquired by a use, for time whereof the memory of man runneth not to the contrary." As one hill man of Dehra Dun put it, "the forests have belonged to us from time immemorial." And Russel, "mankind will have at length discovered that it was only required of them to develop the capacities of their higher nature, in order to convert the earth, which had so long been the theatre of their unbridled passions, and the scene of unimaginable misery, into as bright a paradise as ever haunted the dreams of seer or poet."[48]

48. Ross A. Slotten, *The Heretic in Darwin's Court: The Life of Alfred Russel Wallace* (New York: Columbia University Press, 2004).

CHAPTER EIGHT

Magna Carta and the U.S. Supreme Court

Right glad was he when he beheld her:
Stick after stick did Goody pull,
He stood behind a bush of elder,
Till she had filled her apron full.
When with her load she turned about,
The bye-road back again to take,
He started forward with a shout,
And sprang upon poor Goody Blake.

William Wordsworth, "Goody Blake
and Harry Gill" (1798)

If we were to summarize what we have found so far about Magna Carta and make a hasty march through the past, century by century, leading up to the Constitution of the United States, it might be as follows:

Created in the thirteenth century in the context of crusading as an armistice in civil war, the Charters of Liberties, both big and small, gradually became foundational to statute, law, and common right in the growth of English monarchy and the other constituents of the realm, such as church, town, family, and commons. At the dawn of modern capitalism in the sixteenth century, Magna Carta was ignored for two reasons. First, the centralized monarchy of the Tudors tended to monopolize force, whereas the Magna Carta tended to hedge the power of the king. Second, in the sixteenth century the commodity began to become the local, national, and imperial form of economic accumulation, replacing the many forms of commoning. But in the seventeenth century this changed, as Magna Carta took on its modern form—the protector of individual rights and free trade—just as private property (the legal form of the commodity) was reconciled during the English Revolution with mixed forms of political power. The change, however, required its severance from the Forest Charter.

Commoning persisted, adopting even to urban conditions, but commodity exchange and private property exploded in the rapacious greed of international trading that left tens of tens of thousands of fatalities in the racialized slave trade as human beings themselves became commodities in the eighteenth century. Commoners and slaves frequently crossed paths, but the emerging culture of white supremacy limited the possibilities to which Magna Carta was put, though it became part of the abolitionist movement in 1770 by the Fourth of July. The settler colonies of North America, which in the seventeenth century had embraced chapter 39 of Magna Carta, united in the 1770s using Magna Carta as an example of a charter of resistance and a declaration of independence. After the eighteenth-century slave risings in the Caribbean and the mainland colonies, Magna Carta was adopted to the federal Constitution without its commonist and abolitionist meanings. These nevertheless were kept alive at the same time by the English working class in its struggle against enclosure and the factory. In general, commoning persisted where the forest remained standing. The destruction of the woods, as we found in India's history, where it was a vast means of expropriation, left a cultural remnant of commoning even as the chartered basis receded. Its not being legal partly explains the "unrealistic" forms of the commons—primitive, romantic, childlike, cultural, artistic, utopian. In the United States Magna Carta was a foundational document to law and constitution, yet it also coexisted with the robbery of indigenous peoples' lands and the expansion of racial slavery. How was this paradox maintained?

An approach to answering the question may be possible if we examine a graph. The graph shows in chronological sequence, first, the number of U.S. Supreme Court cases citing Magna Carta and, second, the number of citations of Magna Carta in those cases. Three characteristics stand out. First is the salience of three cases that cited Magna Carta many, many times, far more than average. Second is the overall prevalence of Magna Carta in the Court's history. Third is the pattern of its absence during two periods of American history, the early republic and the twentieth century between the two world wars. I shall consider each of these attributes of the graph, bearing in mind that doing so adheres neither to chronological order nor to standard principles of legal reasoning.

First, then, the three cases that fairly jump out from the graph as startling pinnacles on a low horizon. The first such case is glaring indeed because it appears to hinge on the commons. *Martin v. Lessee of Waddell* (9 February 1842) settled a dispute over the oyster fisheries in Raritan Bay of eastern New Jersey. Roger B. Taney, a descendant of Maryland tobacco planters and slaveholders, was the chief justice and gave the opinion of the Court. He cited Magna Carta sixteen times.

The decision turned on the meaning of the letters patent from Charles II in 1664 to his brother James, Duke of York, granting him New Jersey, and the subsequent proprietors' surrender to the Crown (1702) of all the powers of government while retaining the rights of private property. Did the common right of piscary belong to the common people of England, or to the king as his property, or as part of his regalia, or was it held in trust by him for the people? There were questions about shellfish versus floating fish, and whether tidal mudflats are land or water. Taney decided the case against the private proprietors, just as he had decided the Charles River Bridge case (1837), upholding the principle of the "public interest" or "community rights" when it conflicted with the monopoly of private property. He argued that a common right of royal regalia became a public good with the transfer of sovereignty and independence of the United States.

Did Charles II have the right to make the grant to begin with? The right was claimed not by conquest but by discovery, for if by conquest, then the defeated Indians would retain their property, while right by discovery regarded the country as uninhabited, as waste and wild. Taney says that his right to do so "cannot at this day be questioned," the day in question running from the moment when the case first arose in 1836 to when it was decided in 1842. These were the days of the Trail of Tears, the forced removal of Cherokee, Chickasaw, Chocktaw, Creek, and Seminole nations from their lands. The conception of the commons enunciated by Taney was totally devoid of the experiences, practices, and ideas of the actual commoners. His notion of community rights, like that of the public, excluded indigenous peoples and

Figure 3. Graph showing citations of the Magna Carta in Supreme Court cases. Courtesy Phoebe Jane Ballard.

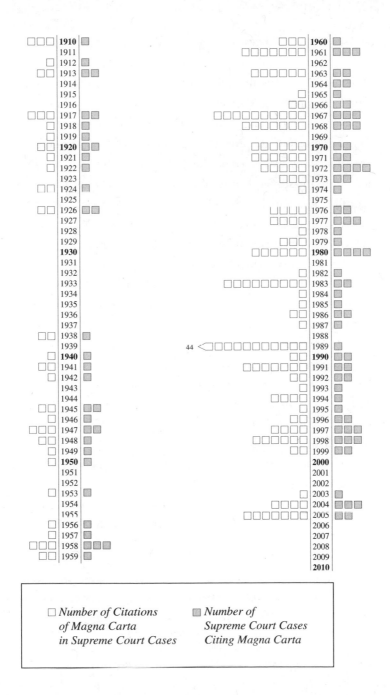

□ *Number of Citations*
   of Magna Carta
   in Supreme Court Cases

▩ *Number of*
   Supreme Court Cases
   Citing Magna Carta

African Americans alike.[1] The paradox of our graph—that the first frequent use of Magna Carta in the United States' judiciary concerned common rights but was devoted to the protection and expansion of private property—is solved once it is understood that the reality was based on the destruction of the native Americans and the subsequent legal fiction *(vacuum domicilium)*. Far from being anomalous in referring to common right, *Martin v. Lessee of Waddell* illustrates a central theme of American jurisprudence, its racist and genocidal presuppositions.

"The policy of England since Magna Charta for the last six hundred years has been carefully preserved, to secure the common right of piscary for the benefit of the public." In a 1918 case about Alaska fishing the Court affirmed, "Since Magna Charta . . . Crown grants of exclusive rights being expressly forbidden." The common right of piscary as well as the Charter of the Forest had been noticed by that court. In 1922 the Court noted that "[s]ince Magna Carta and the Charter of the Forest, the ownership of birds, fish and game . . . has been uniformly regarded . . . as a trust for the benefit of all the people in common." In 1920 the Court noted that "[w]ild game and the right of the people thereto have always been a 'touchy' subject with all English speaking people. It was of sufficient importance to be part of the Magna Charta and the 'Charter of the Forests *[sic]*.'"[2] The case is exceptional to the graph.

1. Bernard Steiner, *Life of Roger Brooke Taney* (Baltimore: Williams and Wilkins, 1922); and Carl Swisher, *Roger B. Taney* (New York: Macmillan, 1936).

2. *Alaska Pacific Fisheries v. United States* (9 December 1918). See also in *Appleby v. New York*, 1 June 1926; *McKee v. Gratz*, 13 November 1922; and *Missouri v. Holland*, 19 April 1920, which cited an Illinois case, *Parker v. People* (111 Illinois 581, 27 September 1884) in which Magna Carta was cited twenty-one times.

Now the second big Magna Carta case, *Hurtado v. California* (3 March 1884): it cited Magna Carta thirty-three times. In a case of murder Joseph Hurtado was indicted by a process of information rather than by grand jury. The majority opinion held that the due process of law clause of the Fourteenth Amendment did not require the states (California) to comply with the Fifth Amendment, which requires indictment by a grand jury. Hurtado was executed. Justice Harlan dissented, "There is nothing in Magna Carta, rightly considered as a broad charter of public right and law, which ought to exclude the best ideas of all systems and of every age; and as it was the characteristic principle of the common law to draw its inspiration from every fountain of justice, we are not to assume that the sources of its supply have been exhausted. On the contrary, we should expect that the new and various experiences of our own situation and system will mold and shape it into new and not less useful forms."

The third case citing Magna Carta numerous times was *Browning-Ferris Indus. v. Kelco Disposal* (26 June 1989); it mentioned the charter forty-four times. The sum of $51,146 was awarded in compensation, and $6 million in punitive damages, to a garbage disposal company in Burlington, Vermont. The case was partly argued over the three chapters in Magna Carta concerning *amercements* ("at the mercy") or discretionary fines. Were they part of criminal or civil law? Were the punitive damages excessive? These chapters of Magna Carta later affected the Declaration of Rights, and the prohibition of cruel and unusual punishment, which was incorporated into the Eighth Amendment to the U.S. Constitution. The principle against punitive excess and the doctrine of proportionality became guiding principles to punishment in general. In this case however, Justice Blackmun writing for the Court said that the Eighth Amendment did not apply.[3] The doctrine of proportionality says that the punishment should be proportionate to the crime, and it was the basis of legal reform movement led by Cesare Beccaria in the eighteenth century. We see that it has an origin in Magna Carta as well.

Magna Carta's principle of proportionality was cited often in the death penalty cases at the end of the twentieth century, for example in *Carmona v. Ward* (8 January 1979), *Rummel v. Estelle* (18 March 1980), *Solem v. Helm* (28 June 1983), *Spaziano v. Florida* (2 July 1984), *Walton v. Arizona* (27 June 1990), and *Harmelin v. Michigan* (27 June 1991). In the well-known *Furman* decision of 1972 that initiated a moratorium on the death penalty, Maitland's comment on excessive amercements was quoted: "very likely there was no clause in the Magna Carta more grateful to the mass of the people." The history of the provision led directly to the Eighth Amendment's prohibition of torture in the cruel and unusual punishment clause. The maintenance of a racial divide was upheld against reason and statistics in the case of *McCleskey v. Kemp* (22 April 1987); Justice Brennan, dissenting, quoted Magna Carta and suggested that the majority opinion feared "too much justice."

To summarize these salient cases: our procedure was to begin with an explanation of a graphic, yet each explanation quickly raises three powerful, contentious, subjects fundamental to the constitution of society. Magna Carta can be an active force in American jurisprudence, in particular, in issues of the commons ("a 'touchy' subject"), unlawful arrest, and the death penalty.

3. See for example *BMW of N. Am. v. Gore*, 20 May 1996; *United States v. Baj*, 22 June 1998; *State Farm Mut. Auto. Ins. Co. v. Campbell*, 7 April 2003.

Turning now to the second characteristic of the graph, the overall prevalence of Magna Carta, a time line showing the distribution of cases citing it across the years from 1790 to 2005, we note its mention by name in 195 cases of the U.S. Supreme Court over its 219-year history, a little less than once a year on average. The actual number of citations to Magna Carta is 407, or about two per case on average.

Its prevalence should not be surprising since the principles of Magna Carta appear in the provisions of the U.S. Constitution concerning the jury and habeas corpus. As the Constitution was amended, particularly by the Fifth (due process of law in federal cases), the Eighth (prohibition of cruel and unusual punishment), and the Fourteenth (due process of law in state cases), the authority of Magna Carta in American jurisprudence deepened. Its authority arose also in other symbolic forms. Representations of Magna Carta began to appear on the images of money in the rebellious colonies well before the Constitution (1787), even before the Declaration of Independence. Paul Revere included Magna Carta in his 1775 design for the Massachusetts seal. Law and money are essential to the modern state, the one protecting property, the other signifying value. Magna Carta backs up each. It *seems* to signify equity in exchange and equality under law. However, as Douglas Hay pointed out in *Albion's Fatal Tree,* substantial equality under law is impossible in a society of great inequality. Through a key phrase from chapter 39, as we'll see, Magna Carta became a legal instrument justifying the characteristic American forms of exploitation.

In *Ex parte Milligan* (3 April 1866) the Supreme Court named the sources of U.S. law as the Constitution, acts of Congress, Magna Carta, common law, and natural justice. The great charter's prevalence arises from the acknowledgment that it was an originating source of American law, or one of its "fountains," to use Justice Harlan's timeless image.

Magna Carta has often been used substantively as law; as a fountain it has watered many principles. This is perhaps clearest with respect to the jury. The jury is to consist of "twelve honest and impartial men of his neighborhood" (*Thompson v. Utah*, 25 April 1898). It is to be a "jury of vicinage" ([from the neighborhood]; *In re Palliser*, 19 May 1890); the jury is to consist of twelve people (*Williams v. Florida*, 22 June 1970); the grand jury is not become a tool of government (*United States v. Mara*, 22 January 1973); the right to a jury trial is affirmed (*United States v. Booker*, 12 January 2005; the trial is to be local (*National Equipment Rental, Ltd. v. Szukhent*, 6 January 1964); and the trial is to be speedy (*Klopfer v. North Carolina*, 13 March 1967).[4]

But it has been used in many other substantive issues. It was cited against imprisonment for debt (*Sturges v. Crowninshield*, 17 February 1817); it was cited to distinguish different kinds of writs (*Cassell v. Carroll*, 20 March 1826); it was cited in cases of mortmain, or possession in perpetuity (*Runyan v. Lessee of Coster*, 1 February 1840, *Perin v. Carey*, 25 February 1861); it was cited in a case of double jeopardy (*Ex parte Lange*, 30 January 1874); it was cited in opposition to using debt proceedings for purposes of oppression (*Den. Ex Dem. Murray v. Hoboken Land & Improv. Co.*, 19 Febru-

---

4. See also *Hyatt v. People*, 23 February 1903; *Hawaii v. Mankichi*, 1 June 1903; *Schick v. United States*, 31 May 1904; *Michaelson v. United States*, 20 October 1924; *Glasser v. United States*, 19 January 1942; and on speedy trials, see also *Moody v. Daggett*, 15 November 1976; and *Lafayette v. La. Power & Light Co.*, 4 October 1977.

ary 1856); it was cited in the limitation of the power of admiralty courts (*Jackson v. S. B. Magnolia,* 13 April 1858); it was cited in prohibition of a sheriff acting as magistrate (*S. v. Md.,* 21 April 1856); it was cited in a treason case (*Chambers v. Florida,* 12 February 1940); it was cited against compulsory self-incrimination (*Twining v. News Jersey,* 9 November 1908); it was cited in proceedings against deportation (*Fong Yue Ting v. United States,* 15 May 1893); it was cited in cases about the right to travel (*Kent v. Dulles,* 16 June 1958 and *Bell v. Maryland,* 22 June 1964); it was cited in a draft evasion case (*Kennedy v. Mendoza-Martinez,* 18 February 1963), in a case concerning the right to petition (*Adderley v. Florida,* 14 November 1966), in a case on legal imprisonment (*Smith v. Bennett,* 17 April 1961), in a welfare case (*Saenz v. Roe,* 17 May 1999), in a case against general warrants (*Minnesota v. Carter,* 1 December 1998), in a case about workplace hazards (*Collins v. City of Harker Heights,* 26 February 1992), in a case about abortion (*Planned Parenthood v. Casey,* 29 June 1992), and in a case concerning pornography (*A Book Named "John Cleland's Memoirs of a Woman of Pleasure" v. Attorney Gen. of Mass.,* 21 March 1966).

Its prevalence in American constitutional law is also ornamental, rhetorical, and ideological. "The interpreters of constitutional grants of power," wrote Thomas Cooley, the leading authority on constitutional law of the latter nineteenth century, were "the maxims of Magna Charta."[5] The Supreme Court cited Magna Carta decoratively, as a source of legal maxims (*Cummings v. Mo.,* 14 January 1867): "At least since Magna Charta

---

5. Thomas McIntyre Cooley, *A Treatise on the Constitutional Limitations Which Rest Upon the Legislative Power of the States of the American Union* (Boston: Little, Brown, 1868), 175.

some people have thought that to delay justice is to deny justice" (*Polizzi v. Cowles Magazines, Inc.*, 1 June 1953), or as a nugget of antiquarian interest (*Myers v. United States*, 25 October 1926): the phrase "'advice and consent' . . . comes down through Magna Charta." It was cited as ancient platitude (*Atchison, T. & S.F.R. Co, v. Matthews*, 17 April 1899): "If there is one place in our system of government where all should be in a position to have equal and exact justice done to them, it is a court of justice—a principle which I had supposed was as old as Magna Charta" or "the *fair application of law*, which purpose hearkens back to the Magna Carta" (*E. Enters. v. Apfel*, 25 June 1998). Magna Carta is frequently cited in the Court's scholarly footnotes.[6]

Magna Carta is often employed rhetorically. It is used as a figure of speech or as a synecdoche substituting one law for another. The following have been called "Magna Carta" by the Supreme Court—the Habeas Corpus Act of 1679 (*Ex parte Yerger*, 25 October 1869; *Perin v. Carey*, 22 February 1858; *In re Palliser*, 19 May 1890; *New York Foundling Hospital v. Gatti*, 3 December 1906 and 29 May 1973), inheritance law (*Jackson ex dem. St. John v. Chew*, 8 February 1827), the first ten amendments (*Kepner v. United States*, 31 May 1904), the U.S. Constitution (*Brig Army Warwick*, 10 March 1863), a commercial letter (*The St. Nicholas*, 21 March 1816), the 14th Amendment (*In re Winship*, 31 March 1970), the Clayton Antitrust Act (*Allen*

6. *The Chinese Exclusion Case*, 13 May 1889; *Howard v. Kentucky*, 2 January 1906; *United States v. Line Material*, 8 March 1948; *Clinton v. Jones*, 27 May 1997; *TXO Prod. Corp. v. Alliance Resources Corp.*, 25 June 1993; *O'Bannon v. Town Court Nursing Center*, 23 June 1980; *Lafayette v. La. Power & Light Co.*, 29 March 1978; and *Peyton v. Rowe*, 20 May 1968.

Bradley Co. v. Local Union No. 3 International Brotherhood of Electrical Workers, 18 June 1945), and the Sherman Antitrust Act. The rhetorical looseness threatens the legal coherence of the charters. To use Magna Carta as a metaphor, to mean "fundamental principle," for example, succeeds to the extent that its actual provisions are ignored.

Magna Carta has a continuing ethnic overtone in jurisprudence. The Supreme Court associated the Magna Carta with the nation as a family, an English family called the "parent country" (*Maxwell v. Dow,* 26 February 1900), which might also be called "the English race" possessing "peculiarly dear" privileges recorded in Magna Carta. "The people of this country brought with them to its shores the rights of Englishmen" as if there were no indigenous peoples, Africans, Irish, Jews, Hispanics, or Asians. Magna Carta was "their birthright" (*Beckwith v. Bean,* 6 January 1879). Charles Andrews, a leading professional historian of the nineteenth century, wrote for American high school and college students *A History of England* in 1903 in which he described "the career of a people, the greater part of whose history is our history." To him Magna Carta "was won by all classes of England acting together." By the 1960s this ethnocentrism was replaced by the trope of "the English-speaking world" (*Republic Steel v. Maddox,* 25 January 1965), or what we might call *anglophonophilia*. A teleological worldwide destiny awaited this imagined community formed "by descendants of Englishmen, who inherited the traditions of English law and history; but it was made for an undefined and expanding future, and for a people gathered and to be gathered from many nations and of many tongues" (*In re Oliver,* 8 March 1948; *McGautha v. California,* 3 May 1971).

Magna Carta is a source, a metaphor, an ethnic talisman, a scholarly sign. It has a contradictory position in American law. To be effective, ruling-class ideology must acknowledge those insistencies of the ruled that otherwise threaten alternatives to its overall rule. Law has long required the appearance of fairness and proportionality despite the emergency caprice of dictatorship (e.g., suspension of habeas corpus or Guantánamo) or the exercise of informal state terror (e.g., the Palmer raids or KKK). The difference expresses the odd relation of Magna Carta to American law—familiar *and* indifferent, obsessive *and* ornamental, fundamental *and* incidental. The Supreme Court adopted Magna Carta to the dominant institutions and social forces of the United States, private property, commerce, capitalism, slavery.

The key to understanding Magna Carta in the United States is private property. "Rights of personal liberty and of property . . . [are] the great principles of Magna Charta" (*Wilkinson v. Leland,* 23 February 1829). Blackstone stated that private property receives more protection in the Magna Carta than the Petition of Right (*Bates v. Brown,* 18 February 1867). "All the original States undertook to secure the inviolability of private property. This they did, either by extracting and adopting, in terms, the famous 39th article of Magna Charta" (*Reagan v. Farmer's Loan & Trust Co.,* 26 May 1894). "Every system of law provides that every man shall be protected in the enjoyment of his property, and that it shall not be taken from him without just compensation. The earliest constitution, in Magna Charta, guarantees that no freeman shall be disseized of his freehold but by the 'judgment of his peers or by the law of the land'" (*Carstairs v. Cochran,* 23 February

1904); "without the guaranty of 'due process' the right of private property cannot be said to exist" (*Ochoa v. Hernandez y Morales,* 16 June 1913).[7]

The United States began as a bourgeois republic and Magna Carta was to serve its purposes. During the Napoleonic Wars when danger on the high seas was great and the safety of neutral shipping insecure, the Supreme Court several times referred to that provision of Magna Carta that was designed to protect the interests of "merchant strangers."[8]

The United States was also a capitalist country. *United States v. Topco Assocs.* (29 March 1972) was frequently cited.[9] The case concerns a purchasing association for twenty-five supermarkets. "Antitrust laws in general, and the Sherman Act in particular, are the Magna Carta of free enterprise. They are as important to the preservation of economic freedom and our free-enterprise system as the Bill of Rights is to the protection of our fundamental personal freedoms. And the freedom guaranteed to each and every business, no matter how small, is the freedom to compete—to

7. See also *French v. Barber Asphalt Paving Co.,* 29 April 1901; *NLRB v. Stowe Spinning Co.,* 28 February 1949.

8. *Brown v. United States,* 2 March 1814; *The Frances,* 12 March 1814; *The Nereide,* 11 March 1815; *The St. Nicholas,* 21 March 1816.

9. *Flood v. Kuhn,* 19 June 1972; *United States v. Lovasco,* 3 October 1977; *Cal. Retail Liquor Dealers Ass'n. v. Midcal Aluminum,* 3 March 1980; *Cmty. Communications Co. v. Boulder,* 13 January 1982; *Associated General Contractors v. Cal. State Council of Carpenters,* 22 February 1983; *Mitsubishi Motors Corp. v. Soler Chrysler-Plymouth,* 2 July 1985; *Atl. Richfield Co. v. United States Petroleum Co.,* 14 May 1990; *Verizon Communs., Inc. v. Law Offices of Curtis V. Trinko, LLP,* 13 January 2004.

assert with vigor, imagination, devotion, and ingenuity whatever economic muscle it can muster."

The United States was a slave society as well. The due process clause of the Fifth Amendment was first used substantively by Taney in the Dred Scott decision. Does a prohibition against bringing slaves into a territory deprive a person of property without due process of law? Chief Justice Roger B. Taney ruled that a slave "had no rights which the white man was bound to respect." Taney argued that the due process clause of the Fifth Amendment applied to the "property" of the slave.[10] The dissent argued that this restriction of legislative power "was borrowed from Magna Charta; was brought to America by our ancestors, as part of their inherited liberties." (*Dred Scott v. Sandford,* 5 March 1857). The issue was the catalyst for civil war.

The Fourteenth Amendment, one of the legal fruits of the Civil War, reads, "No State shall make or enforce any law which shall abridge the privileges or immunities of citizens of the United States; nor shall any State deprive any person of life, liberty, or property, without due process of law; nor deny to any person within its jurisdiction the equal protection of the laws." This is the most decisive legal translation from Magna Carta to American law. In at least fifteen cases the Supreme Court explains how the phrase "due process of law" stems from the phrase "law of the land" (Edward III first used the latter expression to conclude chapter 39 in his 1354 confirmation of Magna Carta).[11] The pen-

---

10. Bernard Schwartz, *A History of the Supreme Court* (New York: Oxford University Press, 1993), 110.

11. 28 Edward III, c.1 (1354); *Livingston v. Moore,* 25 February 1833; *Webster v. Reid,* 7 March 1851; *Munn v. Ill.,* 1 March 1877; *Davidson v. New Orleans,*

chant for medievalism—an aesthetic response to industrial life, as well as a kind of make-believe—was an evasive avoidance of slavery.

The congressional debates on the Fourteenth Amendment often referred to the great charter, "To the people the declaration is: 'Take and hold this your certificate of status and of capacity, the Magna Charta of your rights and liberties." "Fairly construed these amendments may be said to rise to the dignity of a new Magna Charta." "This court considered due process in its historical setting, reviewed its development as a concept in Anglo-American law from the time of the Magna Carta until the time of the adoption of the Fourteenth Amendment and concluded that it was intended to be a flexible concept, responsive to thought and experience—experience which is reflected in a solid body of judicial opinion, all manifesting deep convictions to be unfolded" (*Barkus v. Illinois,* 30 March 1959).

Magna Carta was employed to maintain a central paradox of American law, namely, that persons were property. The due process clause of the Fifth Amendment was applied by the Fourteenth Amendment to the states. But instead of aiding the freed persons as intended, it became the means of encouraging a new type of slavery, through the expanding entity of the corporation. At first, Magna Carta was used to defend slave masters, then it was used to defend the robber barons of the gilded age. These

October 1877; *Sinking-Fund Cases,* October 1878; *Bugajewitz v. Adams,* 12 May 1913; *United Gas Public Service Co. v. Texas,* 14 February 1938; *Poe v. Ullman,* 19 June 1961; *In re Gault,* 15 May 1967; *Stovall v. Denno,* 12 June 1967; *Carafas v. LaVallee,* 20 May 1968; *Murray v. Carrier,* 21 January 1986; *Pac. Mut. Life Ins. Co. v. Haslip,* 4 March 1991; *Albright v. Oliver,* 24 January 1994.

American distortions of Magna Carta assisted the use of the English charter as an element of ideological continuity from the slave state to the corporate state.

The Slaughter-House Cases, 14 April 1873, were "a great landmark in American constitutional history." These decisions rejected the contention that the privileges and immunities clause of the Fourteenth Amendment protected the rights described in the Bill of Rights.[12] Carpetbag legislature granted monopoly to a New Orleans company for slaughtering livestock. Justice Campbell argued that the Fourteenth Amendment "enacted the principle of laissez-faire into the American constitution." Hence the courts could not defend the man of business and the slave at the same time. Laws that interfered with the free market violated the substantive due process. "In the name of federalism, the decision rendered national prosecution of crimes committed against blacks virtually impossible, and gave a green light to acts of terror where local officials either could not or would not enforce the law."[13] Bradley and Field dissented, contending that a person's calling or profession was his property, and their reasoning was to prevail subsequently. In the Granger cases, for example, corporate lawyers argued successfully against state regulation as a deprivation of property without due process of law.

12. Robert G. McCloskey, *The American Supreme Court* (Chicago: University of Chicago Press, 1960), 170; and Jeffrey Lustig, *Corporate Liberalism: The Origins of Modern American Political Theory, 1890–1920* (Berkeley: University of California Press, 1982), 90–93.

13. Eric Foner, *Reconstruction: America's Unfinished Revolution, 1863–1877* (New York: Harper and Row, 1988), 531.

At the end of the nineteenth century a narrow construction in civil rights cases and broad construction in corporate cases permitted the use of due process of law, that key notion of Magna Carta, on behalf of corporate capitalism, to maintain racism and intensify exploitation. During oral argument in the 1886 case *Santa Clara Co. v. Southern Pacific Railroad Company,* the chief justice said everyone on the Court believed the word "person" applied to corporations. The corporation, personified as a legal person, became the principal epiphenomenon of the capitalist class. Actual persons avoided liability while the fictive or corporate person gained privileges. The case of *Late Corp. of Church of Jesus Christ v. United States* (19 May 1890) denied "the right of the government to take from either individuals or corporations any property which they may rightfully have acquired. In the most arbitrary times such an act was recognized as pure tyranny, and it has been forbidden in England ever since Magna Charta, and in this country always. It is immaterial in what way the property was lawfully acquired, whether by labor in the ordinary avocations of life, by gift, or descent, or by making a profitable use of a franchise."[14]

Court deliberations over the *Income Tax Case* of 1895 made attack on communism explicit. Justice Field, a former pistol-packing knife-wielding Forty-Niner of the California gold rush, concurred, "The present assault upon capital is but the beginning. It will be but a stepping-stone to others, larger and more sweeping, till our political contests will become a war of the poor against

---

14. See also *Transportation Co. v. Chicago,* 3 March 1879; *Sinking Fund Cases,* 5 May 1879; *Spring Valley Water Works v. Schottler,* 4 February 1884; *Chicago v. Taylor,* 19 March 1888; and *Marx v. Hanthorn,* 6 March 1893.

the rich; a war constantly growing in intensity and bitterness." *Lochner v. New York* (1905) decided that a law setting a sixty-hour-maximum work week for bakery workers interfered with freedom of contract between master and employee. The due process clause of the Fourteenth Amendment was expanded to include the right to make contracts. If we were to omit the historic and legal steps in the reasoning from chapter 39 of Magna Carta to the Fifth Amendment and on from the Fourteenth to the state law limiting the hours of baking, we would find that a clause designed to remove oppression by the king was now used to oppress the baker. The legendary prayer of King John—for inflation from the penny loaf to the twelve-penny loaf—was at last realized. We find the same reasoning in subsequent cases. *The Child Labor Case* (1918) excluded Congress from making laws restricting child labor: it too should be left to the workings of laissez-faire. In *Adkins v. Children's Hospital* (1923) the Court struck down the minimum wage standard for adult women.[15]

Justice Hugo Black summed up the distorted transformation of the Fourteenth Amendment as follows, "It was aimed at restraining and checking the power of wealth and privilege. It was to be a charter of liberty for human rights against property rights. The transformation has been rapid and complete. It operates today to protect the rights of property to the detriment of the rights of man. It has become the Magna Charta of accumulated and organized capital" (*Adamson v. California,* 23 June 1947).[16]

---

15. Schwartz, *History of the Supreme Court,* 184–85.

16. Hugo Black quotes from Charles Collins, "The Corporations and the Twilight Zone," in *The Fourteenth Amendment and the States* (Boston: Little, Brown, 1912), passim.

Contemplating the history of Magna Carta seemed to give the Court courage to make changes of its own: "the words of Magna Charta stood for very different things at the time of the separation of the American colonies from what they represented originally." "Law is a social organism, and evolution operates in the sociological domain no less than in the biological. The vitality and therefore the validity of law is not arrested by the circumstance of its origin. What Magna Carta has become is very different indeed from the immediate objects of the barons of Runnymede" (*Green v. United States,* 31 March 1958).

The graph and time line of Supreme Court Magna Carta citations illustrate a third characteristic, namely, two large absences. It was hardly ever cited in the first two decades of U.S. history. It was mentioned once between 1927 and 1940, the period of the Great Depression. Yet the Magna Carta was often cited in cases at the end of the nineteenth century, from 1887 to 1903, and it was also frequently cited in cases during the second half of the twentieth century. But for eighty-one years no case mentioned it, whereas in forty-nine years it was cited more than once.

I do not think that the absences noted in the graph can be explained by logic internal to American law, whose paradoxes and contradictions pose problem after problem to direct reasoning. The first absence occurred as the American slave regime expanded across the South while the commercial North was asserting independence from English banking and commerce. The second absence reflects a period of revolutionary class conflict led by the Socialist Party, the Industrial Workers of the World, and the Communist Party, and this lapse requires us to find evidence outside the juridical domain, such as in the cultural representations of Magna Carta. So it is to these that we now turn.

CHAPTER NINE

Icon and Idol

Land tenure shall be on an equality basis, i.e., the land shall be distributed among the toilers in conformity with a labor standard or a
consumption standard, depending on local conditions. There shall be
absolutely no restriction on the forms of land tenure: household,
farm, communal, or cooperative.

Peasant Mandate on the Land, Izvestia, *Petrograd,*
19 August 1917

For a time during the twentieth century, the cultural development of Magna Carta led to its reification: it ceased to be an active constitutional force and became a symbol characterized by
ambiguity, mystery, and nonsense. It began to disappear as precise law. Without the steady discipline of legal interpretation and
amplification, its meanings were loosened, and by 1957 they
were actually inverted. It became an idol of the ruling class. It did
not start out that way.

At the end of the nineteenth century the progressive mayor of
Cleveland, Tom L. Johnson, made a pilgrimage to British cities;
his principal advisor wrote one book praising British municipal

policy and another book calling the city "the hope of democracy." Together, they organized a city center on a European model—courthouse, library, federal office building, train station, "to bring all classes most closely together."[1] The courthouse was finished under Mayor Newton Baker, a short, aristocratic man, who was apt to begin speeches with a Latin tag and was known as the "three cent" mayor—3¢ for streetcar fare, 3¢ dances, 3¢ ice cream cones, and 3¢ a pound for fish caught by city tugboats.[2]

One side of the courthouse faces the city, the opposite side faces Lake Erie. Inside the building an elegant, two-storied hall greets the visitor. Behind the balustrade within a large lunette on the second-floor wall is a crescent-shaped mural of the signing of Magna Carta. Completed in 1913, it shows detailed local knowledge of Runnymede. It stresses King John's reluctance to submit. The mural is a homage to the multitudes. The clouted shoon of plebeian England mull over the proceedings. Most prominent is the man propelling a river craft forward by pushing off on the sixteen-foot pole. No one—king or bishop, baron or clerk—could have assembled on the island Runnymede in the Thames without the labors of the ferrymen. He stands on a small platform on the back of the craft. He heaves his weight into the pole: he will strain on the tip of the pole with his arm and shoulders: he will push off from his right leg, his thighs and back going to work: thus the craft advances along the river, thanks to human power and grace.

1. Daniel T. Rodgers, *Atlantic Crossings: Social Politics in a Progressive Age* (Cambridge, MA: Harvard University Press, 1998), 139; and Frederick C. Howe, *The British City,* and *The City: The Hope of Democracy* (1905).

2. C. H. Cramer, *Newton D. Baker: A Biography* (Cleveland: World Publishing, 1961), 51.

Figure 4. Mural of Magna Carta in old Cuyahoga County courthouse, Cleveland, Ohio, by Frank Brangwyn. The Western Reserve Historical Society, Cleveland, Ohio.

The artist was Frank Brangwyn (1867–1956), born in Belgium to a hard-up Welsh family. Sleeping on the floor, eating bread and sugar, unable to pay for school, evicted from the family's rooms, later he remembered, "My poor father was a good man." "So, *why*—WHY should they turn out honest people from their homes because they can't pay their taxes. PHTH! POOH! DAMMIT! These sort of things are apt to make fellows like me see *red!*—make our blood boil—BOIL!" He loafed about the docks until the English craftsman and socialist William Morris took him as an apprentice. Later he said he got

started in mural painting, "and of course my working with Morris must have set things going in that direction also." In 1888 he ran away to sea. "His arms are covered with tattoo marks . . . all kinds of curious signs, including a large anchor."[3] The year he shipped out to Constantinople was the year of the East End dockers' strike.

To understand his approach to Magna Carta we need to put it in two contexts. One context is that of the city of Cleveland, which rested on the populist reforms of its mayor Tommy Johnson (he

3. William de Belleroche, *Brangwyn's Pilgrimage: The Life Story of an Artist* (London: Chapman and Hall, 1948), 28; and Philip Macer-Wright, *Brangwyn: A Study of Genius at Close Quarters* (London: Hutchinson, 1940), 29–33.

served four terms, 1901–9), and the other context is Brangwyn's notion of medievalism, which emphasized handicrafts, with the beauty and exercise of labor as taught by the pre-Raphaelite artists.

Cleveland was a labor town. The Cleveland Central Labor Union, formed in the 1880s, stated clearly the credo of socialists of those years. "The emancipation of the working class must be achieved by the working classes themselves, as no other class has any interest in improving their condition. In their hands rests the future of our free institutions, and it is their destiny to replace the present iniquitous social system by one based on equality and the nobility of all useful labor." The class struggle came to a pitch of extreme tension in the years preceding World War I. The longest strike, by the lake sailors, lasted from 1909 to 1912; their union joined the Industrial Workers of the World (IWW, who became known as the "Wobblies") in 1913, the year Frank Brangwyn completed his mural.[4]

The prewar period was one of scientific management in class relations characterized by the time-and-motion experts who centralized successive phases of fabrication, systematized distinct operations, provided detailed instruction and supervision, and tied the wage system to the system of command. Eugene Debs summarized the process, "the human must be reduced to a hand. . . . A thousand hands to one brain—the hands of workingman, the brain of a capitalist. A thousand dumb animals, in human form—a thousand slaves in fetters of ignorance, their heads having run to hands—all those owned and worked and fleeced by one stock-dealing, profit-mongering, capitalist. This is

4. Fred Thompson, *The Workers Who Built Cleveland* (Cleveland: Charles Kerr, 1987).

capitalism!"[5] The concept of human labor that reduced it to *a hand* was opposite to that of the socialists, communists, and anarchists of the prewar period who in intense class struggle fought for the emancipation of the whole body of labor.

The Brangwyn mural of Magna Carta at the old Cuyahoga county courthouse in Cleveland, Ohio, is a direct attempt to envision the unalienated thirteenth-century craftsmen dear to William Morris in gorgeous depiction of the class tension between a haughty royal and episcopal ruling class and a dignified multitude of workers during a moment of reflection. Here was a vision of anticapitalism.

The vision truthfully reflected the times. As war and then revolution threatened both the imperial geopolitical order and the stability of the laissez-faire capitalist mode, the representations of Magna Carta ceased to include the clouted shoon, the peasants and proletarians, or their allusions to a world of the commons. The Bolshevik mandate on the land (1917) as well as the *ejidos* of the Mexican Constitution (1912) showed that the world of the commons was not lost.

In contrast to Brangwyn's vividly colored Magna Carta, a year later Albert Herter (1871–1950) painted a Magna Carta mural in the Wisconsin Supreme Court in the capitol building at Madison. It illustrates an ethnic, familial, and patrimonial understanding of Magna Carta without the people or the working class. Herter was a successful businessman, a portrait painter of wealthy ladies, and the owner of a New York manufacturing

5. David Montgomery, *Workers' Control in America* (New York: Cambridge University Press, 1979), chap. 5.

Figure 5. Mural of Magna Carta in capitol building, Madison, Wisconsin, by Albert Herter. Wisconsin Historical Society.

company of elegant handwoven textiles and tapestries. His figures are slender, his colors are pale, his scenes are theatrical. The mural measures nine feet by eighteen feet six inches. Two boys, down stage left, peer over a shield with heraldic design at the tension between king and baron, listening intently. This is the

pedagogical interpretation of Magna Carta. They are looking up at the stage of the signing, just as schoolchildren touring the courtroom look up at the mural. Wearing green tights, a blonde-headed and rosy-cheeked adolescent boy sits on the platform in the foreground holding his dog. The artist's son served as the model for the boy, Christian Herter, later the secretary of state under Eisenhower.

The political rhetoric of English and American imperialism in the late nineteenth and early twentieth century developed the concept of Western civilization as a political and historical expression separate from the rest of the world.[6] In 1915 Nicholas Murray Butler, president of Columbia University, lectured the New York politicians in Albany on the seven hundredth anniversary of Runnymede. It was a gushing, pompous address linking race, blood, liberty, nationality, and personal effort. In his opening he refers to "the intermingling of the two bloods," Saxon and Norman, to form "the English-speaking race." Anglophonophilia again. This race sent "colonial offshoots of the parent stock" around the world. Boyd Barrington in his 1900 study of Magna Carta also referred to "the Anglo-Saxon race."[7] Kipling wrote lines meant to raise goose bumps on white skins:

> At Runnymede, at Runnymede,
> What say the reeds at Runnymede?
> The lissome reeds that give and take,
> That bend so far, but never break.
> They keep the sleepy Thames awake
> With tales of John at Runnymede.

6. Chris GoGwilt, "True West: The Changing Idea of the West from the 1880s to the 1920s," in *Enduring Western Civilization,* ed. Silvia Federici (London: Praeger, 1995), 38.

7. Nicholas Murray Butler, "Magna Carta, 1215–1915: An Address Delivered before the Constitutional Convention of the State of New York in the Assembly Chamber" (Albany, New York, 15 June 1915); Boyd C. Barrington, *The Magna Charta and Other Great Charters of England* (Philadelphia: W. J. Campbell, 1900).

In Palo Alto, California in 1916, a year after the seven hundredth anniversary of Magna Carta, and in the midst of war talk, Charles Weeks founded a poultry cooperative and named it Runnymede. At the chicken utopia of Runnymede each household possessed its separate water tank to irrigate the chard, kale, and cabbage that provided high-quality chicken feed. "We box ourselves in between walls," he wrote. "Why should men work long, weary hours in unhealthy places all the days of their lives for a mere subsistence?" he asked. Far from embodying the anti-enclosure principle found in the Charters of Liberties, he replaced free-range poultry farming with specially boxed chicken coops for feeding, perching, roosting, laying, and brooding. Its slogan was One Acre and Independence, and its ideology was provided by William Smythe, the founder of the Little Landers Movement, which sought "the conquest of waste places by promoting irrigation." Charles Weeks preached the arcadian gospel of fresh air, the great outdoors, and fresh chicken feed. He attracted more than a twelve hundred settlers to Runnymede. Many were single independent women or veterans recently returned from the First World War. The California Runnymede was not as innocent as it might appear from Charles Weeks's poultry pastoralism. Advocating the expulsion of Chinese laborers from California, Smythe shared in the prevalent racist codes of the day in which a name like Runnymede would not be lost to those thinking of themselves as Anglo-Saxon.[8]

8. Rudyard Kipling, "The Reeds of Runnymede," in *Rudyard Kipling: Complete Verse* (New York: Doubleday, 1988), 719; Charles Weeks, *Egg Farming in California* (San Francisco: Schwabacher-Frey Stationery, 1922); and Alan Michelson and Katherine Solomon, "Remnants of a Failed Utopia: Recon-

In January 1930 the National Trust in England acquired the meadow and island at Runnymede on the river Thames. Magna Carta had become a site of pilgrimage. J. W. Hamilton was the founder (1908) and secretary of the International Magna Carta Day Association, headquarters in St. Paul, Minnesota, which had representatives from Canada, Newfoundland, Australia, New Zealand, and South Africa, the "white" colonies, as well as the United States. It proposed that the third Sunday in June become "Magna Carta Sunday." In 1934 a pageant under the royal patronage of the Prince of Wales was held at Runnymede with five thousand actors, two hundred horses, and four elephants. In 1937 "the most famous meadow in the English-speaking world" was saved from the real estate developer. Rosarians named a perpetual hybrid the Magna Carta Rose, pink with a dash of carmine.[9]

In England Magna Carta had become a sacred cow. In September 1930 *Punch* satirized it: "That no one was to be put to death, save for some reason—(except the common People). That everyone should be free—(except the common People). . . . That the Barons should not be tried except by a special jury of other Barons

structing Runnymede's Agricultural Landscape," in *Shaping Communities: Perspectives in Vernacular Architecture,* ed. Carter L. Hudgins and Elizabeth Collins Cromley (Knoxville: University of Tennessee Press, 1997); Daniel Worster, *Rivers of Empire: Water, Aridity, and the Growth of the American West* (New York : Pantheon Books, 1985); and Robert V. Hine, *California's Utopian Colonies* (New Haven: Yale University Press, 1953), 144.

9. See articles in the *New York Times:* "All English-Speaking Lands Observing Magna Carta Day," 17 June 1928; "June Roses Add to Garden Beauty," 7 May 1933; "5,000 Actors, 200 Horses in Pageant of Runnymede," 11 March 1934; and "Runnymede Is Saved," 19 September 1937.

who would understand." It concluded "Magna Charter was therefore the chief cause of Democracy in England, and thus a *Good Thing* for everyone (except the common People)."[10] The satire was accompanied by an illustration of King John losing his clothes in the Wash (the Wash being the designation of the tidal waters on the eastern coast of England where King John had met his end).

If Magna Carta might have had its starch removed on one side of the Atlantic, on the other side it was becoming stiffer than ever, a pompous backdrop to a regime of white supremacy. The U.S. Supreme Court building in Washington DC was designed by Cass Gilbert and opened in 1935, when law and order needed such an awesome pile. Gilbert's design was a conscious allusion to the Roman empire. Gilbert was a friend of Benito Mussolini, who also sought to found his government in the grandeur of ancient Rome. Owing to that friendship, Gilbert was able to obtain the Siena marble for the decorative columns inside the building. The building was called the Marble Palace; Justice Stone found it "bombastically pretentious," and another justice wondered, "What are we supposed to do, ride in on nine elephants?"[11]

Gilbert designed it, but what workers built it? Bertolt Brecht, much impressed by the construction of the Moscow subway that year and much distressed by the Italian invasion of Ethiopia in 1935, mixed construction and destruction in his well-known "Question of a Literary Worker":

10. Walter Carruthers Sellar and Robert Julian Yeatman, *1066 and All That: A Memorable History of England* (New York: E. P. Dutton, 1931), 26.

11. Bernard Schwartz, *A History of the Supreme Court* (New York: Oxford University Press, 1993), 226.

Who built the seven gates of Thebes?
The books are filled with the names of kings.
Was it kings who hauled the craggy blocks of stone?
And Babylon, so many times destroyed,
Who built the city up each time? In which of Lima's houses,
The city glittering with gold, lived those who built it?
In the evening when the Chinese wall was finished
Where did the masons go? Imperial Rome
Is full of arcs of triumph. Who reared them up? Over whom
Did the Caesars triumph?[12]

The ornamental work on the Supreme Court included several references to the Magna Carta. The front doors were designed and forged by Irish immigrants, John Donnelly and his son. The friezes were designed by a German immigrant, Adolf Weinman, and carved by Italian immigrants, the Piccirilli brothers.

The bronze doors are almost eighteen feet high and weigh thirteen tons. In 1925 the stonecutters in the Donnellys' employ went on strike against the use of the pneumatic hammer to cut marble, "which they said caused numbness in the left hand."[13] The doors contain eight panels, each with a pair of standing male figures. The series of male couples in dialogue suggest access to a temple of graceful dialectics. One Greek, three Roman, three English, and one American episode tell the story of law—the *Iliad,* the praetor's edict, Julian and the scholar, Justinian's code, Magna Carta, the statute of Westminster, Coke and Charles I, and *Marbury v. Madison* (the 1803 case making the Supreme Court the ultimate arbiter of the Constitution). The Magna Carta panel is

12. Bertolt Brecht, *Selected Poems*, trans. H. R. Hayes (New York: Harcourt, 1947).

13. *New York Times,* 13 August 1925.

balletic, a graceful pas de deux. The doors, made by Irish Americans, opened into the highest chamber of law whose four walls were decorated by friezes carved by Italian Americans.

The four friezes of the courtroom, one on each side, were designed by Adolf Weinman (1870–1952) during 1931 and 1932. Each frieze is forty feet long and seven feet two inches high. The north and south friezes represent "a procession of Great Lawgivers of History"—depictions of Menes, Hammurabi, Moses, Solomon, Lycurgus, Solon, Draco, Confucius, Augustus, Justinian, Muhammad, Charlemagne, King John, Louis IX, Grotius, Blackstone, Marshall, and Napoleon. The conception of law represented by these figures is ecumenical and imperial. American jurisprudence had global ambition. Still, there were omissions, such as Hindu jurists. The friezes excluded the discussions about law in the Soviet Union, where a new era of human history, its advocates believed, was being formed. They excluded the Mexican Constitution. They excluded forms of customary law or unwritten traditional practices. The selection of "great lawgivers" is similar to that represented by the murals in the dome of the State Supreme Court of New York, an orientalist concept of Western law.[14]

King John stands out in several ways. He is the only one wearing armor. The chain mail hauberk (thousands of the interlaced links were cut into the marble) extends over his neck and hoods his head beneath an iron conical helm. His posture suggests resistance. We have a psychological portrait. The weathered look of a man recently on campaign, and the thin, tight-lipped mouth of a man who has met defeat and is unhappy about it. This is not

14. Taha Jaber al-Alwani, *Journal of Law and Religion* 1 (2000).

Figure 6. Panel from door of U.S. Supreme Court building, Washington DC: Edward Coke and James I. Photographed by Franz Jantzen, Collection of the Supreme Court of the United States.

a lawgiver but one who was compelled to accept the charter that his right hand clutches fiercely. In this age of dictators, his left hand too forms a fist. The figure is rendered with artistic subtlety and political prudence.

Giuseppe Piccirilli (1844–1910) was a marble worker from the Carrara quarry near Pisa who emigrated with his wife to the

Figure 7.   Panel from door of U.S. Supreme Court building, Washington DC: Archbishop Stephen Langton and King John. Photographed by Franz Jantzen, Collection of the Supreme Court of the United States.

United States in 1887, part of the great migration of Italians.[15] Giuseppe was a "redshirt," a militant follower of Garibaldi. He had six sons, Attilio, Furio, Ferruccio, Getulio, Masaniello, and Orazio, who collaborated on architectural sculptures. They were

15. Mari Tomasi, "The Italian Story in Vermont," *Vermont History* 28 (January 1960): 73–87.

descendants of centuries of craftsmen. The *quadratarii* (stonecutters) and the *marmorarii* (marble cutters) were among the trade guilds Constantine listed in a law of A.D. 337. The catacombs of Rome were first quarries before they became underground prisons. That was the past: the future lay before them. By 1890 they had established their own studio in the Bronx importing Italian marbles.[16]

In the period 1913–36 Magna Carta enjoyed solemn depictions in American halls of justice and "temples of sovereignty." It became an icon of little use to the legal proceedings of the Supreme Court but of vast and durable prominence in the architecture of government. In 1932 the Nebraska state capitol building opened. Lee Lawrie, America's foremost architectural sculptor, executed twenty-three relief panels on the four sides of its exterior. Called "The Spirit of the Law as Shown in Its History" the central panel on the south side depicts a tableau of standing bishop and baron, a kneeling monk, and a seated King John with a scroll in one hand and a sword in the other.[17] It is an image of stability, unity, monumentality, and completely without commons or commoner. The Mexican and Russian revolutions are dealt with by denial. Like the law, these murals conceal a truth about the charters of liberty.

The same year that Cass Gilbert's Supreme Court building opened with its Roman grandeur, a federal courthouse in Terre Haute, Indiana, was opened in the architectural style of art nou-

16. Josef Vincent Lombardo, *Attilio Piccirilli: Life of an American Sculptor* (New York: Pitman, 1944).

17. Francis Pio Ruggiero, *State Capitols: Temples of Sovereignty* (Milford, PA: Excelsior, 2002), 454.

Figure 8. Frieze in U.S. Supreme Court chambers: King John.
Photographed by Steve Petteway, Collection of the Supreme
Court of the United States.

veau. It too contains a mural of Magna Carta. The wall behind the judge's bench is covered by a triptych of the signing of Magna Carta painted by Frederick Webb Ross, of Shelbyville, Indiana. The visual energy concentrates in the center, on King John, on his hand, and the quill in it, about to scratch the scroll in front of him. He is surrounded by more than fifty people, many with their hands on their swords. "Through this Document Government Exists According to Law not Power," explains a cartouche in the central panel. The big difference between Magna Carta as presented in the 1935 Supreme Court and as presented in the mural in Terre Haute is that in the latter the king ratifies the law and in the former it is forced on him.

Runnymede was a public occasion in this Ross interpretation, like the courtroom, which the triptych decorates. The Stars and Stripes hangs from a pole to the left of the bench and atop the pole is a brass eagle with outstretched wings. Behind it one of the banners of the assembled army carries an image, too, of a golden eagle with open wings. The people are pleasant to look at—no cripples of war, no wounded, none sickly, nor underfed. They are back from the Crusades, several have the Jerusalem cross embroidered on their surcoats. Everything is both pretty and martial, friendly and white (no North Africans or Palestinians among them).[18] King John was known for his immense wardrobe; his footwear is attached by numerous delicate white straps.[19] He wears a golden girdle. The central figure of the left panel shows a slender young person of indeterminate gender, in

18. Milia Davenport, *The Book of Costume* (New York: Crown, 1948), 1:157.
19. Doreen Yarwood, *English Costume from the Second Century B.C. to 1972* (London: B. T. Batsford, 1972), 51.

Figure 9. Triptych mural of Magna Carta in federal courthouse, Terre Haute, Indiana, by Frederick Webb Ross. Martin Collection, Indiana Historical Society.

pink tunic with hip cocked, leg bent, in an attractive, sinuous posture. The tone is gay rather than bellicose.

The legal establishment of the United States has liked to control these memorializations. During the cold war it linked monotheism, militarism, and Magna Carta. In God We Trust was declared the national motto in 1957 and was also placed on American paper money. In that year the American Bar Association (ABA) opened a memorial to Magna Carta at Runnymede, surrounded by a landscape dense with ruling-class symbolism. The architect of the graceful rotunda was Edward Maufe, an Establishment figure who designed country houses and tasteful churches and college buildings, whose pastel interiors of pink, mauve, and cream helped set interwar taste in England in a style called "modernity with manners." In the center of the rotunda is a plinth. On it is a five-pointed star within a blue circle, a mark of identification of the U.S. Air Force, an insignia with no significance in English heraldry or semiotics.

The queen was present and the speeches were broadcast on the BBC. Prince Philip rode up to the ceremony on his horse from a polo match. Five thousand dignitaries came for the "rites" upon the "hallowed ground," to hear Smythe Gambrell, past president of the American Bar Association, speak on how each "man is a creature of divine will" and how the truths of Magna Carta "are universal and eternal." "There flows within our veins a common blood line, commingling Celt and Saxon, Dane and Norman, Pict and Scot." A "temple" was dedicated, "a shrine," or "an altar," where "all mankind may worship."[20]

The next speaker was Lord Evershed, master of the rolls, who concluded his remarks by saying the burden of leadership "under God of the free peoples of the earth" now rested on American shoulders. After Lord Evershed came Charles Rhyne, the ABA's incoming president, the legal counsel to President Eisenhower, and the person who had suggested the Magna Carta memorial in the first place. He explained the meaning of the expression FREEDOM UNDER LAW carved in the Portland stone. This truth, he asserted, "has made mighty nations of both Britain and America," adding that it is the truth against "the alien tyranny of Communism." But in fact, it inverted the meaning of Magna Carta that Stubbs, the

20. These speeches are printed in *Journal of the American Bar Association* (October 1957): 900–907.

Figure 10. Memorial rotunda at Runnymede, by Edward Maufe. Photo by the author.

Victorian constitutional historian, expressed as "the King is, and shall be, below the law." The cold war turned the meaning upside down. Moreover, the commons is not at all alien to Magna Carta. Artistic symbols can conceal the truth in the twentieth century just as impressionism in the nineteenth century expunged from historical memory the haunting nightmare of the Paris Commune.[21]

The Right Honorable Sir Hartley Shawcross, QC, MP, concluded the speeches with some upper-class, irrational, quasi-druidic mysteries centered in an enclosure that includes an oak tree planted by the Duke of Gloucester, another by the prime minister of India in 1994. In the same year Her Royal Highness Queen Elizabeth II planted an oak there. In 1987 John O. Marsh Jr., secretary of the U.S. Army, had planted a young oakling with

21. Albert Boime, *Art and the French Commune: Imagining Paris after War and Revolution* (Princeton: Princeton University Press, 1995).

Figure 11.   Plinth at center of
rotunda, Runnymede. Photo by
the author.

Figure 12.   Text engraved on
plinth, Runnymede. Photo by
the author.

soil that had been brought from Jamestown, Virginia, "the first
permanent settlement in the new world." The Egham and
Thorpe Royal Agricultural and Horticultural Association, having found a great oak recently cut down that had been young in
1215, made a plaque out of some of it and presented the plaque
to the American Bar Association.

The oak grew in the neighboring Windsor Forest, once a
place where men in blackface poached deer and held mock
courts to protect their customs. In actuality it stood its ground for
so long because it belonged to a commons and was protected by
a system of commoning that had included seasonal festivals such
as May Day. Charles S. Rhyne attempted to abolish this too: in
the same year he propounded the Runnymede monument, he

also proposed that May Day be replaced by Law Day, and in 1958 Eisenhower duly made the change of May Day to Law Day in the United States.[22] One of the origins of English racism, the Waltham Black Act, was provoked in 1722 within this same forest. In 1957 Rosa Parks in Montgomery, Alabama, and the third-world nations in Bandung, Indonesia, began to challenge the racist consequences of white supremacy. Just as the Jamestown earth spread by the U.S. Army on English soil conceals the genocide of conquest, so the ABA monument conceals the commonist origin of Magna Carta and inverts its political meaning. Symbols are treacherous means of communication.

In June 2005 while rendering the Supreme Court's majority decision in the case of *Van Orden v. Perry,* Chief Justice Rehnquist found himself gazing up at the marble frieze ("Great Lawgivers of History") surrounding the four walls of the courtroom. He explained that the seven-foot figure of Moses and some legible Hebrew letters on a tablet he held did not violate the constitutional principle of separation of church and state. Likewise, a graven monolith, six feet high and three and a half wide, on which was inscribed an abridged version of the King James translation of Exodus 20:6–17 (the Ten Commandments) might be placed on the lawn of the Texas capitol without violating the Constitution. Justice Souter dissented from this opinion. He said that the Texas monolith of the Ten Commandments was "not a work of art."[23] Perhaps he made an aesthetic contrast between the exalted vision of lawgivers on the courtroom's marble friezes and the graven

22. James Podgers, obituary for Charles S. Rhyne, *Journal of the American Bar Association* (October 2003).

23. *Van Orden v. Perry,* 27 June 2005.

tablets whose design stems from the 1956 remake of Cecil B. De-Mille's film *The Ten Commandments,* with Charlton Heston playing Moses.

The same day the Court heard arguments about another Ten Commandments case, *McCreary County v. ACLU.* The proponents of courthouse displays of the Ten Commandments sought to allay the Supreme Court's concern that government not appear to establish religion by including with the framed image of the Ten Commandments eight other framed documents, namely, Magna Carta, the Declaration of Independence, the Bill of Rights, the lyrics of "The Star-Spangled Banner," the Mayflower Compact, the national motto, the preamble to the Kentucky Constitution, and a picture of Lady Justice. Souter wrote the majority opinion ordering the removal of display–"The Foundation of American Law and Government Display"—from the hallway of a Kentucky courtroom.[24] But what exactly is Magna Carta supposed to add? It too is a document presupposing monotheism, a document of the state in the form of church and king. It is an argument of this chapter that most people are unfamiliar with Magna Carta because a careful reading of both Charters of Liberties reveals their presupposition of the commons and shows up as a whitewash the tale of a Magna Carta extolling individualism, private property, laissez-faire and English civilization. Hence, the importance of its iconic representations. These, the icons, then become idols, and idols, even venerable ones, may intoxicate and destroy, as a "lord of the flies."

Souter wrote the Court's opinion. It objected to the "lack of a demonstrated analytical or historical connection" between the

24. *McCreary County v. ACLU,* 27 June 2005.

Ten Commandments and the other documents. The divine imperatives of the Decalogue and the Declaration of Independence have no connection because the former derives its sanction from Yahweh while the latter derives it "from the consent of the governed." Furthermore, Souter was baffled by the omission of the Fourteenth Amendment, "the most significant structural provision adopted since the original framing." He continued, "and it is not less baffling to leave out the original Constitution of 1787 while quoting the 1215 Magna Carta even to the point of its declaration that 'fish weirs shall be removed from the Thames.'"

CHAPTER TEN

This Land Was Made by You and Me

And fiercely by the arm he took her,
And by the arm he held her fast,
And fiercely by the arm he shook her,
And cried, "I've caught you then at last!"
Then Goody, who had nothing said,
Her bundle from her lap let fall;
And kneeling on the sticks, she pray'd
To God that is the judge of all.
        William Wordsworth, "Goody Blake
        and Harry Gill" (1798)

Justice Souter smiles at the fish weirs of the river Thames as if to say, How ridiculous in our own day and age to display a document eight centuries old concerning a river some thousands of miles away with its medieval practices that scarcely anyone, apart from a handful of scholars and one or two locals, pretends to understand! The abstract reasoners of the Court might be equally likely to smile at a dispute in New Jersey's Raritan Bay over its oyster beds. Yet, as we've seen, though the case of *Martin v. Lessee of Waddell* (1842) seems to be about commoning, its assumptions depended upon the genocide of Indians and the robbery of lands.

The Thames is thousands of miles away from the U.S. Supreme Court. Nevertheless one of its meadows, Runnymede, is depicted in more than one building of the American government. It is depicted in Frank Brangwyn's homage to Magna Carta in the Cuyahoga County Courthouse: the feet of King John rest among the yellow irises typical of the meadows of the river Thames. Brangwyn knew the river well, having once lived (as his master, William Morris, did) in Hammersmith. The ferryman propels a punt, a vessel whose origin lies in the fenlands of East Anglia during the Middle Ages, when it was an essential craft for quietly navigating the marshes and reeds. The fowlers, fishermen, and reed cutters of the English fens and Norfolk broads lost access to their many common rights just as the punt was becoming a vehicle of courtship and amusement during Edwardian times (the Thames Punt Sailing Club was formed in 1897).

The commons is a touchy subject in America. We must probe both it and another tender subject, communism, as their relationship has been subject of a coverup. The idolatry of Magna Carta effectively shut off debate about both. And yet the idea of the commons (and the recognition of its many practices) persisted in the twentieth century through cooperation of English and American socialists, through the expansive ideals of Italian American anarchism, through the Spanish civil war evident especially at Guernica, and it reemerged in the crisis of 1940 despite the repression associated with Fascism and the Great Depression. We must scratch beneath the surface of the murals and representations of Magna Carta.

While Brangwyn was apprenticed to William Morris, the master was reading *Progress and Poverty* (1879) by the American Henry George (1839–97), who was visiting England and Ireland at the time, offering his critique of commercial values, his determination to right the wrong of poverty, and his notion of a common good based on the common ownership of land. He clearly stated the problem, "private property in land is a bold, bare, enormous wrong, like that of chattel slavery," and he clearly stated the solution, *"We must make land common property."* Echoing Winstanley, the English Chartists, and the cry of Indians across the American plains he declaimed, "the equal right of all men to the use of land is as clear as their equal right to breathe the air— it is a right proclaimed by the fact of their existence."[1]

George was himself a poor boy from Philadelphia who never got beyond seventh grade in school. He shipped out as a cabin boy to San Francisco and got his education before the mast and then at the printer's stone. He had a gendered conception of the productivity of labor that expressed itself in planetary evocations of useful activity—garnering grain in California, swinging the lariat in the pampa of La Plata, digging ore in Comstock, chasing whales in the Arctic, picking coffee beans in Honduras, making toys in the Hartz mountains, and so forth. His theory of wages left much to be desired. George wrote, "If I devote my labor to gathering birds eggs or picking wild berries, the eggs or berries I thus get are my wages." Unlike Marx who found his communist starting point in the commons of the Moselle peasantry

---

1. Henry George, *Progress and Plenty* (New York: Schalkenbach Foundation, 1985), 328–30; E. P. Thompson, *William Morris: Romantic to Revolutionary,* 2nd ed. (New York: Pantheon, 1977), 269.

of his childhood, or Engels who wrote a neglected manifesto on the German *Mark* or commons, Henry George does not deal with the actuality of berry picking. The duplicity of the wage form (hiding the origins of profit, interest, and rent) was unknown to his definition. Marx soon discovered that it was the bosses who pluck ripe berries out of the bodies of their wage slaves.

Socialism indeed is a grand and noble idea, but the means of realizing the idea cannot rely on commoners whom George considers to be beyond the pale: black savages, red Indians, Bedouin Arabs, or Flathead squaws who he believed characterized the country, or as the tramps, drunks, and criminals who he believed characterized the urban proletariat. Such racist class composition is equally distant from the primitive communism that Frank Cushing (1857–1900 ethnologist) began to find in 1879 among the Zuni, whose pueblos in New Mexico seemed to him "the long-sought social utopia," or the industrial anticapitalism proposed by urban militants whose agitation in 1886 for a reduced working day exploded at Haymarket Square, Chicago.[2]

Yet Henry George's history acknowledged the survival of laws and customs based on equal shares. "Underneath, and side by side with the feudal system, a more primitive organization, based on the common rights of the cultivators, took root or revived, and has left its traces all over Europe." It allots equal shares to cultivated ground and common use of uncultivated ground. But these residuals "have lost their meaning," he noted.

2. Frank Hamilton Cushing, *My Adventures in Zuñi* (1882–83; repr. Palmer Lake, CO: Filter Press, 1967); and James Green, *Death in the Haymarket* (New York: Pantheon, 2006).

The Thames is, after all, just a river, as commoners are just rogues and vagabonds, and the privatizers may once again smile.

George propounded a history of privatization going back to Egypt and Moses, advancing through Greece and Rome to the German forests, and then to the Italian city-states. The common law is the will of the landowner. "They were belted barons led by a mitered archbishop who curbed the Plantagenet [monarchy] with Magna Charta; it was the middle class who broke the pride of the Stuarts; but a mere aristocracy of wealth will never struggle while it can hope to bribe a tyrant." This contradiction permitted a rough nationalism. "It was the strength born of Magna Charta that won Crécy and Agincourt," referring to English victories over the French. Racial and ethnic essentialism was part of the dominant ideology in this era of rampant Anglo-Saxon imperialism.

There were problems with Henry George's conception of the working class's composition, with his conception of the commons, and with his history of Magna Carta that are not found in William Morris, who in 1882 crossed "the river of fire," casting his lot with the working class. In the following year Morris joined the Social Democratic Federation and began both his socialist lectures and public appearances at Speakers' Corner in Hyde Park. "In England what may be called the chronic rebellion of the Foresters, which produced such an impression on the minds of the people, that it has given birth to the ballad epic known by the name of its mythical hero, Robin Hood. Resistance to authority and contempt of the 'Rights of Property' are the leading ideas in this rough but noble poetry." And it was true enough, as no figure in English history embodies the notions of reparations and redistributive justice as persistently as Robin

Hood, whose real-life prototype did indeed roam the forests of the English midlands at the time of Magna Carta.[3]

Morris reminds us that it was not only a myth of robbing from the rich to give to the poor that persists. The praxis of the working class maintains the notion of the commons in the following practices, symbols, and experiences: "The poor remains of the old tribal liberties, the folk-motes, the meetings round the shire-oak, the trial by compurgation, all these customs which imply the equality of freemen, would have faded into mere symbols and traditions of the past if it had not been for the irrepressible life and labour of the people, of those who really did the work of society in the teeth of the arbitrary authority of the feudal hierarchy."[4]

Such were the thoughts of Brangwyn's teacher. They took wing to Chicago, the heart of industrial America, where Carl Sandburg (1878–1967) paid tribute amidst the destruction of the Great War.[5]

> You never lied to us, William Morris, you loved the shape of
> those stones piled and carved for you to dream over and
> wonder because workmen got joy of life into them,
> Workmen in aprons singing while they hammered, and pray-
> ing, and putting their songs and prayers into the walls and
> roofs, the bastions and cornerstones and gargoyles—all
> their children and kisses of women and wheat and roses
> growing.

3. J. C. Holt, *Robin Hood* (New York: Thames and Hudson, 1982).

4. William Morris, "Art and Industry in the Fourteenth Century" (1890), in *Art and Society: Lectures and Essays by William Morris,* ed. Gary Zabel (Boston: George's Hill, 1993), 158, 166.

5. Carl Sandburg, "Salvage," from *Chicago Poems* (New York: Henry Holt, 1915).

No condescending smiles over *folk-motes* here, just the gratitude of comrades. Roger Baldwin, the founder of the American Civil Liberties Union, liked to trace his family lineage to the time of William the Conqueror. After World War I he was part of a Greenwich Village scene with other radicals and reformers— John Reed, Scott Nearing, Kate Richards O'Hare, Emma Goldman. "Those individuals placed great emphasis on what might unfold in England. . . . In 1918 the Fabian socialist Sidney Webb drafted clause four of the Labour Party constitution: 'to secure for the producers by hand or by brain the full fruits of their industry, and the most equitable distribution thereof that may be possible, upon the basis of the common ownership of the means of production.'" This is not George's common ownership of land or Morris's equality of freemen; it became parliamentary socialism. In the April 1922 issue of *World Tomorrow* Roger Baldwin wrote, "We admit that no ideal of social and intellectual freedom can be real for any great number, until we are rid of this competitive struggle for property. We readily accept in theory the ethics of a communist society, 'to each according to his need, from each according to his ability.'"[6] Could this be reconciled with self-emancipation?

Brangwyn was commissioned after the war to do murals for the Coronation Room of the House of Lords. His work was rejected twice. The first time his images of the war were too strong. The second time his lush colorful organic leafy fruity green veggie Morris-like designs of the empire were rejected as being insufficiently imperial. "The joke of the whole of this House of

6. Robert C. Cottrell, *Roger Nash Baldwin and the American Civil Liberties Union* (New York: Columbia University Press, 2000), 129.

Lords' business is—the Lords turned down my work on the grounds that the treatment suggested in no degree our Empire. Ha! Ha!" he scoffed. Two years later he took on the job at Rockefeller Center from which Diego Rivera was dismissed, and Brangwyn executed four dull panels depicting humankind's technological progress culminating in a panel of Jesus preaching. His Cleveland mural of 1913 was vibrant and vital, alive with the working-class spirit of self-emancipation. He fell victim to the fright that the Russian Revolution of 1917 gave to other British imperialists and American capitalists. He accepted what once he scoffed at. His murals of Rockefeller Center are such that the color looks like crud, the visages are hideous cartoons, the drawing garish in the pulp style. Times had changed.

In England a colossal change in the source of hydrocarbon energy took place between the nineteenth and twentieth centuries, from wood to coal. Where industrialization in India meant famine and destruction of forest, where in America it meant the urban jungle of slaughterhouse and factory, in England it caused an increase by fivefold in the numbers of people sent underground into the pits. The number of miners employed in English coal mines grew from 214,000 in 1854 to 1,248,224 in 1920. The actual commons and the commons of the imaginary changed. The English writer D. H. Lawrence illustrates the problem. His father, a coal miner, passed on to the son his love of flowers, knowledge of the fauna of the English midlands, and his labors in the garden allotments of the mining village. "To me, as a child and a young man, it was the Old England of the forest and agricultural past."

The commons is the setting from the first poem of his *Collected Poems,* "The Wild Common." Is the commons an actual place of cooperation, or is it a notion of the nation, part of the patriot game? In 1915 Lawrènce attempted an answer in his story *England, My England*. It was a ruthless riposte to the chauvinism of William Ernest Henley, whose poem "England, My England" was a patriotic recruiting verse.

> What have I done for you,
> England, my England?
> What is there I would not do,
> England, my own?

Lawrence opens the story with a fellow who loves the dances and customs of old England, "He was working on the edge of the common, beyond the small brook that ran in the dip at the bottom of the garden, carrying the garden path in continuation from the plank bridge on to the common." He becomes a dropout, rejecting capitalist values of getting and accruing. The war destroyed the commons as figured in the English countryside. Lawrence never found the commons in England, nor in the emerging revolutionary alternative of the Bolsheviks. Only in America did he begin to find an agreeable approximation among the New Mexico pueblos of the Indians.[7]

In the last chapter we noted that Runnymede, the cooperative poultry farm established in 1916 on San Francisco Bay, illustrated some of the racialist undertones found in the cultural representations of Magna Carta. While it is true that aspects of it were cooperative (the marketing or a clubhouse for instance) and while it was more successful than the other short-lived colonies of the Little Landers, we should place its founding, like its nam-

---

7. David Worthen, *D. H. Lawrence: The Life of an Outsider* (London: Allen Lane, 2005), 315.

ing, firmly in the context of its time, a time of revolutionary class struggle associated with the political movement of the Industrial Workers of the World and the ubiquitous feature of the Western labor market, the casual migratory worker. In words that might have been taken from a Stanford professor or a Sacramento politician, Charles Weeks, Runnymede's founder, intoned, "We pass our fellow men on the highways of life with their roll on their back restlessly wandering, listless, unkempt, bored, no purpose, no will dragging out an existence." Yet much purpose was expressed in the Wheatland hop riot of 1913 in northern California when 2,800 men, women, and children, among them Hindus and Japanese, struck for water. They started work at four in the morning in heat of 105 degrees. Their employer privatized the water. Four people were killed (including a Puerto Rican and an English boy). It was a turning point in the California class struggle. The trials of the strike's Wobbly leaders dragged on for several years in which the political principles of Magna Carta were violated during the year of its anniversary— no torture, the jury, habeas corpus, and due process. Thorstein Veblen summarized the demands in a 1918 report to the state legislature that could hardly express more succinctly the political and the economic principles of the Charters of Liberties: "freedom from illegal restraint" and "proper board and lodging."[8]

Frank Brangwyn's mural has led us to a consideration of the commons as understood by English followers of Henry George and American followers of William Morris. Their ideas were

8. Carleton H. Parker, "The California Casual and His Revolt," *Quarterly Journal of Economics* 30, no. 1 (November 1915). Joyce Kornbluh, ed., *Rebel Voices, an I.W.W. Anthology* (Ann Arbor: University of Michigan Press, [1964]).

hammered by the experience of World War I and the Russian Revolution, retaining some form in the notion of state socialism found in the British Labour Party. Looking now beneath the surface of things in the artwork of the U.S. Supreme Court, we find a similar transition from generous expansiveness of the social imagination before the war to bleak repression and colorless spirit afterward.

No notion of the commons is to be found among the sculptures of the U.S. Supreme Court. Yet the Piccirilli brothers were subtle artists. They must have had something of a sense of humor, otherwise why put a dermoid cyst over the left eye of King John? If the commons was not in the sculptures, it was among the sculptors. Their Bronx studio was a center of artistic life. Their studio resembled a Renaissance master's *bottega* "with its mountains of marble and granite, its antique busts and plaster reproductions of Greek and Roman art," to quote a visitor to the studio in 1919.[9] Here the brothers and their many assistants worked. The helpers did the roughing-out work while faces, hands, drapery were left to the brothers. On Saturday afternoons the workers came down with paper hats made from newspapers against the studio's dust and ate off a huge rectangular marble slab along with visitors from an immigrant culture that included defrocked priests, musicians, patrons, educators, and anarchists.

Anarchists? In the hundred Italian language anarchist newspapers in America we have evidence of the very strong pedagogical tradition going back to Renaissance humanism. Their

9. W. M. Berger, *Scribner's Magazine,* quoted by Don Mitchell in *The Lie of the Land: Migrant Workers and the California Landscape* (Minneapolis: University of Minnesota Press, 1996), chap. 2.

commitment was to bring art to the people. The inquiring, open-minded spirit of the anticapitalist, anti-imperialist movement is summarized in the credo of Bartolomeo Vanzetti, "I am and will be until the last instant (unless I should discover that I am in error) an anarchist-communist, because I believe that communism is the most humane form of social contract, because I know that only with liberty can man rise, become noble and complete."[10] Less known as an Italian American anarchist was Onorio Ruotolo (arriving in the United States from Cervinara, Italy in 1908), who collaborated with Arturo Giovanitti (the great Wobbly poet and organizer victimized in the Lawrence strike of 1912) on a Italian American magazine called *Il Fuoco,* and then on another journal of socioliterary subjects, *Minosse,* before joining Piccirilli in founding the Leonardo da Vinci Art School on 16th Street in 1923. His sculptures in the first decades of the century such as "Hunger," "The Drunkard," and "The Condemned" (a Sing Sing death row prisoner) evince a powerful social conscience (they have been called "sermons in stone") and exemplify the ideals of equality and human dignity of Italian American artists, "the beautiful idea," as they called anarchism.[11]

Such sermons were silenced by the 1919 Palmer raids, one of those repressive spasms against the common people that have periodically convulsed the republic from the Alien and Sedition Act (1798) to the McCarthy era. H. L. Mencken accused the Department of Justice of maintaining "a system of espionage altogether

10. Paul Avrich, *Sacco and Vanzetti: The Anarchist Background* (Princeton: Princeton University Press, 1991), 45.

11. Francis Winwar, ed., *Ruotolo: Man and Artist* (New York: Liveright Corporation, 1949).

without precedent in American history, and not often matched in the history of Russia, Austria, and Italy. It has, as a matter of daily routine, hounded men and women in cynical violation of their constitutional rights, invaded the sanctuary of domicile, manufactured evidence against the innocent, flooded the land with *agents provocateurs,* raised neighbor against neighbor, filled the public press with inflammatory lies, and fostered all the worst poltrooneries of sneaking and malicious wretches."[12] The church, fascism, and gangersterism further gagged the anticapitalists.[13] The liberties of Magna Carta—no torture, habeas corpus, due process of law, trial by jury—and the principles of the Forest Charter—subsistence, no enclosure, neighborhood, travel, and reparations—began to disappear.

In his youth Jerry Capa got to know both men well and at the end of his life he wrote a memoir about them. The boy remembered Ruotolo as "a large, spirited man with exaggerated gestures" who lived near Union Square.[14] Ruotolo moderated his anarchist politics, disavowed his friendship with Carlo Tresca and Arturo Giovanitti, and yet went on to work for the Amalgamated Clothing Workers. Well into the 1930s he wrote the poem "In Union Square Park" with no trace of the apostate's bitterness and kept a clear-eyed sense of the possibility of the brotherhood of man even within the imperial city. Union Square was an oasis for the vanquished, the survivors, the destitute, the disappointed, the

12. Quoted in Avrich, *Sacco and Vanzetti,* 176.

13. Philip Cannistraro and Gerald Meyer, eds., *The Lost World of Italian American Radicalism* (Westport, CT: Praeger, 2003), 2.

14. Bill Carrol and Mary Shelley Carroll, "The Piccirilli Studio," *Bronx County Historical Society Journal* (1999): 1–12.

lost, and rebellious. Embracing lovers, snoring drunks, thin poets, long-haired artists, dog walkers, the loquacious, the learned, the Good Humor man with his ice cream and the comrades with their "new heresies and old utopia."[15] Why was there no crime?

> Perhaps because that oasis, an island
> Ill known and ill famed,
> Lost and forgotten
> In the heart of the boundless city
> Swarming with greedy and grasping beings,
> Is a true, integral democracy:
> So that the wandering pilgrims
> Of all ages and all races,
> Of all faiths and all ideals,
> Like its hundred varicolored doves,
> Find a place of refuge, outlet, and peace
> In Union Square.
>
> Little park, with no other laws
> Than free and brotherly tolerance
> And mutual respect
> For the civil liberties of all!

Just two blocks away from Union Square the anarchist tribune Carlo Tresca was assassinated in 1943. Two years later the Piccirilli studio closed. The tradition of civic freedom and urban commoning at Union Square persisted and it became the common meeting ground for New Yorkers in lower Manhattan on 11 September 2001 until Mayor Giuliani shut it down.

15. Martino Marazzi, *Voices of Italian America: A History of Early Italian American Literature with a Critical Anthology* (Teaneck, NJ: Farleigh Dickinson University Press, 2004), 242–53.

Beneath the surface of those marble sculptures of the Supreme Court is a story of Italian American immigrants that takes us from the anarchist quarries of Italy to similar quarries in Vermont. The "beautiful idea" that they brought with them was snuffed out just as its proponents met assassination. The idea certainly did not call for a solution from the state. This was true also of the struggle for the commons within the antifascist movement in the Spanish civil war of 1936. Several million workers collectivized the land, meeting in village assemblies, drawing on several generations of anarchists, inspired by the Ferrer schools. In the countryside of Aragon and Catalonia, it also drew upon "the collectivist legacy of traditional Spanish village society."[16]

Led by Colonel von Richthofen of the Condor Legion, the German Luftwaffe dropped thermite incendiary bombs on the Basque village of Guernica on 26 April 1937. The attack occurred on market day. Animals and people were slaughtered. It was an urban firestorm, an inferno, anticipating the bombing of Dresden, London, Hamburg, Tokyo, Hiroshima, and Nagasaki.

The first vice president of the United States, an improbable observer, helps us to understand the significance of the destruction. As a student of republics, John Adams traveled to the Basque country and was astonished. The Basque have "never known a landless class, either slave or villein." Well before the regicides of modern European revolutions, "one of the privileges they have most insisted on, is not to have a king," Adams wrote.[17] The seamless

16. Murray Bookchin, *The Spanish Anarchists: The Heroic Years, 1868–1936* (San Francisco: AK Press, 1998).

17. John Adams, *A Defense of the Constitutions of the United States of America* (1786), in *The Works of John Adams* (Boston: Little, Brown, 1851), 4:310–13.

woolen beret became the symbol of Basque social equality. As a political style, the beret made its way through the Basque refugees to France, from France to the Resistance, from the Resistance to beatniks in the metropolis, to Che Guevara, and to the Black Panthers.

The liberties of the Basques were traditionally renewed at an oak standing on ground in Guernica. The liberties derive from the *fueros* or charters of the eleventh through the thirteenth centuries. They are similar to the Magna Carta—providing jurisdiction, defining customs, delineating tenures, documenting pasturage rights. The Castilian king swore at Guernica that he and his successors would maintain the "fueros, customs, franchises, and liberties" of the land.[18] The charters began as an orally transmitted code of uses and customs. The details of commoning varied from valley to valley, village to village, but clearly indicated a precommodity regime.[19]

An episode of covering up Picasso's *Guernica* at the United Nations building in New York just prior to the U.S. bombing campaign and invasion of Iraq was emblematic of the state's anxiety about symbolic production.[20] The American secretary of state was not the first to try to cover up the Guernica story. Colonel Richthofen himself tried to hide it. Conservatives of England, Spain, and Germany hoped to hide the story, but the intrepid journalist George Steer revealed the truth, showing that the town was a center of Basque liberties and the location of the oak where local

18. William T. Strong, "The Fueros of Northern Spain," *Political Science Quarterly* 8, no. 2 (June 1893): 326.

19. José Peirats, *Anarchists in the Spanish Revolution* (London: Freedom Press, 1990).

20. Iain Boal, T. J. Clark, Joseph Matthews, and Michael Watts, *Afflicted Powers: Capital and Spectacle in a New Age of War* (New York: Verso, 2005).

assemblies had met for centuries.[21] Picasso began *Guernica* on May Day 1937 and exhibited it a month later at the Paris World's Fair.

To cover up his mural, therefore, was more than a deliberate attempt to destroy the memory of civilian bombing; it struck at a location that presented the most durable, actual alternative to monarchy and capitalism found in Europe and, as such, a place of constitutional interest to John Adams as well. Behind *Guernica* was the commons. The story of Guernica thus returns us to the Middle Ages and the Charters of Liberties. The most influential medievalist of the twentieth century, Marc Bloch (1886–1944), documented the medieval commons right through the ancien régime. His major work, *Feudal Society,* published in 1940, concluded with the "right of resistance," the germ of which was already present in the Oaths of Strasbourg (843) and in the pact between Charles the Bald and his vassals (846), resounded in the thirteenth and fourteenth centuries in a multitude of texts beginning with England's Great Charter of 1215, whose originality "consisted in the emphasis it placed on an agreement capable of binding the rulers."[22] Captured by the Nazis after the fall of France, Bloch died in a Nazi camp.

21. George Steer, *The Tree of Gernika* (London: Hodder and Stoughton, 1938); and Nicholas Rankin, *Telegram from Guernica: The Extraordinary Life of George Steer, War Correspondent* (London: Faber and Faber, 2003).

22. "What do we really mean by *document* if it is not a 'track,' as it were— the mark, perceptible to the senses, which some phenomenon, in itself inaccessible, has left behind?" Marc Bloch asked in *The Historian's Craft,* trans. Peter Putnam (Manchester: Manchester University Press, 1954), 55; see also *Les caractères originaux de l'histoire rurale française* (1931); and *Feudal Society,* vol. 2, *Social Classes and Political Organisation,* trans. L. A. Manyon (Chicago: University of Chicago Press, 1964), 452.

The Spanish civil war drew upon international solidarities among workers in the socialist, communist, and anarchist movements. Some of its power and depth arose also from that of the Basques whose independence and pride went back to the Middle Ages, untouched by that era's feudalism. Hence communists with a small *c* might refer to a continuity in the commons of eight centuries, while Communists with a big *C* concealed this with rigid notions of progress.

In 1939 Jack Lindsay and Edgell Rickword wrote a *Handbook of Freedom* for English soldiers to take into battle. It referred to the Great Charter on the second line. "The freedom we possess had to be won by centuries of endeavour, as the land itself was wrested from forest and swamp."[23] However, since many of the freedoms were *in* and *of* the forest, the possession of freedom depended on the preservation of the forest rather than on its destruction. The Soviet Union signed a nonaggression pact with Germany in August 1939 and did not enter the war until 1941. England was alone after France fell in June 1940. What did little *c* communism mean, big *C* Communists might ask? With indiscriminate bombardment beginning, what was the meaning of common welfare? Blood, sweat, tears became common: what else? These were the brooding questions of the day that brought forth a crescendo of answers in 1940, answers that delved deep into the past, to Magna Carta again.

As Americans sat back in their easy chairs on Sunday afternoon, 4 February 1940, to listen to the radio before another week at the treadmill began, they found themselves listening to the

23. *Handbook of Freedom: A Record of English Democracy Through Twelve Centuries* (London: Lawrence and Wishart, 1939), vii.

music of the German exile Kurt Weill, the erstwhile collaborator of Bertolt Brecht, and to the easygoing Hoosier lingo of Maxwell Anderson, the playwright from Indiana, as this unlikely duo played out a drama of medieval English history, *The Ballad of Magna Carta.*

Columbia Broadcasting System commissioned them to create a show for the Sunday afternoon radio program called *The Pursuit of Happiness.* It was aired only a month after Paul Robeson welcomed the New Year, performing the sensational "Ballad for Americans" on the same program. Designed to be sung by high school and college glee clubs, *The Ballad of Magna Carta* was enlisted in the war against Hitler. "Resistance to tyranny is obedience to God," it concluded.[24]

> King John of England was an old man in twelve hundred fifteen;
> He had reigned long and unjustly
> And both the Nobles and the Common People were enraged
> And desperate during those last years of his life.

Herbert Butterfield would call the view that translated *liber homo* as "the common people" a superstition, just as conservatives in the seventeenth century called such notions bad scholarship. Butterfield proposed a providential version of English history ("the belief that we were God's Chosen People") that depended upon deliberately misconstruing Magna Carta. "His-

---

24. Maxwell Anderson and Kurt Weill, *The Ballad of Magna Carta: Cantata for Solo Voices and Mixed Chorus* (New York: Chappell, 1940); Ronald Sanders, *The Days Grow Short: The Life and Music of Kurt Weill* (Los Angeles: Silman-James, 1991); and Ronald Taylor, *Kurt Weill: Composer in a Divided World* (Boston: Northeastern University Press, 1992).

tory itself may in certain ways become a superstition, and particularly when cataclysm is upon us."[25]

Dona Torr (1883–1957), who did much to set the tone of relative intellectual freedom for which the British Communist Party was known, observed in 1940, "Millions who stood outside history have become makers of history." She referred specifically to India and China. Nevertheless, she was not free of dogmatism: "It is not through some memory of a former state of complete equality and equal shares that the tradition of democracy with a material or communal basis subsists, but through the conjunction of equal rights and unequal shares operating within a class society, in which inequality increases with wealth."[26] As if to second her, Christopher Hill (1912–2003 English Marxist historian) wrote that the golden age lies in the future, not the past.

Hill's essay *The English Revolution, 1640* was written for the soldiers going into battle and the civilians who suffered the Blitz. It brought Milton and Winstanley to the cause of human agency. "Winstanley's communist idea was in one sense backward-looking, since it arose from the village community which capitalism was already disintegrating," yet Winstanley did not look only to the past; he also glimpsed a future in which "wheresoever there is a people united by common community of livelihood into oneness it will be the strongest land in the

25. Herbert Butterfield, *The Englishman and His History* (Cambridge: Cambridge University Press, 1945), 81–82.

26. Dona Torr, *Marxism, Nationality and War* (London: Lawrence and Wishart, 1940), D. K. Renton, "The History Woman," *The Socialist Review* 224 (November 1998): 19.

world, for there they will be as one man to defend their inheritance.' "[27]

This was the "breakthrough" that E. P. Thompson (1924–93 English socialist humanist) said was so decisive to him as a student and soldier in 1940. The same breakthrough led to the formation of the Communist Party's History Group after the war and shaped the English social history of the end of the twentieth century, social history with the constitution left out.

Back in 1940 *The Ballad of Magna Carta* continued,

> He laid taxes without warrant and without mercy,
> He punished without trial,
> And he loaded favorites with riches and honors.
> It was he who invented the practice of pulling a tooth a day
>   to extort money from wealthy Jews.

Anti-Semitism was strong. Torture was widely used by John's castellans to enforce the taxation of the Jews. A Jew of Bristol had seven teeth extracted, one each day, until he consented to pay the sum demanded by King John. Jews were massacred in London in 1189. Usury was forbidden to Christian princes. Magna Carta's chapter 10 stated that the heir to anyone indebted to a Jew shall not owe interest.[28]

> You shall punish no Freeman without fair trial;
> You shall lay no tax
> Not in general use;

27. Christopher Hill, *The English Revolution, 1640* (London: Lawrence and Wishart, 1968), 62.

28. William Sharp McKechnie, *Magna Carta: A Commentary on the Great Charter of King John* (Glasgow J. Macklehose and Sons, 1914), 228.

You shall use no torture on Christians and Jews.
And he held out a copy of "Magna Carta."

Weill and Anderson did not take an anarchist, or communist, or socialist position on the land question (and with it the status of the old commons) but they could not avoid it entirely,

And he wrote on parchment with the goose quill in his hand,
And he signed away the right of Kings to take away our land;
He signed away the right of Kings to take your teeth and eyes,
And Kings since that time are cut down to normal human size.

What was the commons? In 1940 the answers were several and deep: we have mentioned reflections of Dona Torr and Christopher Hill. Here we add four others: C. Day Lewis (1904–72 Anglo-Irish writer) seemed to withdraw into an aesthetic retreat translating Virgil's *Georgics* but there he found "That veteran . . . / Who made a kitchen-garden by the Galaesus / On derelict land." That is the commons of waste. In 1940 Henry Miller (1891–1980 American writer) cried, "The earth is not a lair, neither is it a prison. The earth is a Paradise, the only one we will ever know. We will realize it the moment we open our eyes. We don't have to make it a Paradise—it is one. We have only to make ourselves fit to inhabit it."[29] That is the American commons. In May 1940 Vir-

29. Henry Miller, *The Air-Conditioned Nightmare* (New York: New Directions, 1945–47), 25; C. Day Lewis, *The Georgics of Virgil* (London: Jonathan Cape, 1940), 11; Virginia Woolf, "The Leaning Tower," a paper read to the Workers' Educational Association, Brighton, May 1940, in *Collected Essays* (London: Hogarth Press, 1966), 2:162–81; and C. L. R. James, "Revolution and the Negro, in *C. L. R. James and Revolutionary Marxism: Selected Writings of C. L. R. James, 1939–1949*, ed. Scott McLemee and Paul Le Blanc (Atlantic Highlands, NJ: Humanities Press, 1994).

ginia Woolf (1882–1941 writer and humanist) asked, "are we not commoners, outsiders?" The end of class society had to become the basis of that compensation of the man's loss of his machine, the loss of his gun, his imprisonment within patriarchy. "We must make happiness," she concluded. The feminist commons. A few months earlier C. L. R. James (1901–89 West Indian Marxist) had written, "What we as Marxists have to see is the tremendous role played by Negroes in the transformation of Western civilization from feudalism to capitalism." The pan-African commons.

> And the difference, dear listener, between the now and then
> Is just that we're resentful of a government by men;
> We sit secure behind our doors,
> Our teeth are never drawn,
> Because the Nobles drew that day the teeth of old King John.
> Yes, they drew that day the teeth of old King John and since
>   that fateful hour
> It is not treasonous to chafe at governmental pow'r;
> No longer do men bow their necks
> . And humbly kiss the rod.
> Resistance to Tyrants is obedience to God.

I wonder whether the Dust Bowl composer Woody Guthrie (1912–67) listened to the radio that afternoon. A couple weeks later he wrote a song putting the idea of the commons square into the nation's memory from Oklahoma, where dispossession had been tricky, violent, and oily. He composed it as an alternative to the complacency of Irving Berlin's "God Bless America."[30] Here is the song with two of its suppressed stanzas.

---

30. Elizabeth Partridge, *This Land Was Made for You and Me: The Life and Songs of Woody Guthrie* (New York: Viking, 2002), 85.

This land is your land, this land is my land
From California to the New York Island,
From the Redwood Forest, to the Gulf Stream waters,
This land was made for you and me

Was a big high wall there that tried to stop me
A sign was painted said: PRIVATE PROPERTY,
But on the back side it didn't say nothing—
This land was made for you and me

One bright sunny morning in the shadow of the steeple
By the relief office I saw my people—
As they stood hungry, I stood there wondering if
This land was made for you and me

Woody Guthrie was hitchhiking around, an expropriated man, looking hungrily at the land with the simple yearning that has since made his song an anthem of the people. Its conclusion expressed the sense of entitlement of the New Deal, this land was made *for* you and me. A sense of reparation making it a little less "white" might be expressed with a little modification more consistent with the spirit of the Charters of Liberties, this land was made *by* you and me.

CHAPTER ELEVEN

The Constitution of the Commons

And the self-proclaimed planners who try to enclose the world have
Seized and taken away the free, innocent future from my mind.
Still, something will be enacted,
Something that will darken me and the girls
And, even though unable to seize hold of our minds,
Will in the end expropriate our bodies.
In order to protect our remaining land,
We gather together our minds,
Somewhere on Earth, a place that is not enclosed
Will make us live absolutely.

Yoshimoto Taka'aki, "The Earth Is Being Enclosed" (1951),
translated by Manuel Yang

Magnae Chartae Libertatum Angliae, or "The Great Charters of
the Liberties of England," as Coke or Blackstone named them,
have occupied the first page of the law books of England ever
since law books were printed. They stipulated restraints upon the
royal realm: they provided subsistence in the common realm. We

are taught that these are archaic relics of feudalism, or we are taught that they are peculiarities of the English. I have argued that the reliquary leads to the idol and the idol destroys what it purports to preserve. As for the peculiarities of the English the practice of commoning is always local, and thus apparently peculiar (in Roman times the *peculium,* indeed, was the slave's bit of land).

How do these principles relate to the constitution of the United States? In *Federalist Paper* no. 10 James Madison expressed his alarm at the violence of faction caused by "the various and unequal division of property. Those who hold, and those who are without property, have ever formed distinct interests in society," he stated. Madison wrote from, for, and to the propertied class. The constitution was to harmonize the different types of property—landed, manufacturing, mercantile, and banking. Madison argued directly against "theoretic politicians" who sought "an equal division of property, or for any other improper or wicked project." If, as he explained, the U.S. Constitution was founded for the propertied, we must infer that the constitution of the unpropertied was left to a later time.

Those without property were not homogeneous either, and for purposes of understanding the Great Charters of Liberties in America I group the whole class of those without private property into four forces or vectors that comprise the historical composition of the working class. Each force is the result of historical agency; each has been produced through active struggle of considerable duration. These unpropertied vectors have constituted (in all but name) the ecology, the infrastructure, the economy, and the community. They are the salt of the earth.

First in point of time, as in point of foundation, is the labor that has preserved or conserved by mixed commoning modes of production in fishing, hunting, and horticulture the ecological characteristics of the continent. The forest, the tomato, and corn are not gifts of nature but products of indigenous culture by the first Americans. "Their vast land conserved by them through ten thousand years," as Phil Deloria wrote.[1]

Second in temporal sequence as well as in economic importance are the hewers of wood and drawers of water whose labors drained the swamps and felled the forests that prepared the fields for the agrarian infrastructure and the production of commodities. This proletarian labor was the work of the African American slaves.

Third, the factory proletarians, the immigrant workers in mine and manufactures—so often male breadwinners—the citizen workers, whose cooperative labor built American industry.

Fourth are those who carry out the invisible labors of reproduction to keep body and soul together, raise the young, nurse infants, give birth to future generation. Reproduction precedes social production. Touch the women, touch the rock.

Has the salt lost its savor? I propose to answer this through the mnemonics of four epitomes: the sacred hoop, the battering ram, Article 7(a), and the jury box. These are symbolic and heuristic categories and as such simplified (each reader will come up with exceptions or overlaps, such as the women stitching in the sweatshops or with back bent in the plantation fields, the Chinese immigrants hewing the railways through the Rockies, the Mohawks erecting the skyscrapers, the African Americans suffering "niggermation" in the auto plants). I write them partly as

1. Philip J. Deloria, *Playing Indian* (New Haven: Yale University Press, 1998), 236.

economic categories of class composition, partly as constituents to our social constitution, partly as essentialist identities maintained by racist and sexist divides, and partly as specific differences in struggle—genocidal conquest, racial enslavement, economic exploitation, and gender oppression.

Whether the salt has lost its savor remains to be found as the latent commonages of North America are manifested. Commoning as associated with Indians, African Americans, industrial workers, and women has on occasion alluded to Magna Carta, so we have a double task—to reveal how commoning has been exercised in the American past and what Magna Carta has meant. We can uncover in that history the five principles of Magna Carta's commons, namely, anti-enclosure, reparations, subsistence, neighborhood, and travel.

THE SACRED HOOP

Philip J. Deloria wrote, "Someday this country will revise its constitution, its laws, in terms of human beings, instead of property." Indigenous constitutional genesis has happened before: the Iroquois gave both the federal principle of Madison's constitution and the primitive communism of the Marxist heritage. Deloria continues, "If Red Power is to be a power in this country it is because it is ideological. . . . What is the ultimate value of a man's life? That is the question." The first peoples of America have a moral authority far in excess of numbers, an authority deriving not from priority but from the ecological commons whose material memory was maintained by a spiritual notion, the sacred hoop. Black Elk, a survivor of massacre, prayed in 1931 to the Great Spirit, "At the center of this sacred hoop you have said that I should make the tree bloom. . . . Here, old, I stand, and the tree is withered. . . . It may be that some little root of the sacred tree still lives. . . . O make my people live!" When Edmund Wilson traveled across the country in 1930 to record the distresses of capitalism, an old-timer told him, "The Indian's religion and government are the same thing and they fit him like a glove—whereas our laws don't fit us anywhere—not our religion either!"[2]

"This law is important; it may justly come to be regarded as an Indian Magna Carta," wrote the *New York Times* referring to the Indian Reorganization Act of 1934.[3] The act reversed the Dawes Act of 1887, restored tribal ownership of surplus lands; it provided credit to businesses and some home rule. John Collier (1884–1968), the New Deal's Commissioner of Indian Affairs, a reader of William Morris and Prince Kropotkin, explained the idealist project, "our design is to plow up the Indian soul, to make the Indian again the master of his own mind." John Collier admired the *ejido,* the Gaelic revival, the mutualism of Kropotkin, the "red Atlantis" of the New Mexico pueblo that he visited in 1922.

Against the landgrabs of the early nineteenth century, Tecumseh had said in 1810, "The way, and the only way, to check and stop this evil is for all the Redmen to unite in claiming a common and equal right in the land, as it was at first and should be yet; for it was never divided, but belongs to all for the use of each." Before

2. Edmund Wilson, *The American Jitters; a Year of the Slump* (New York: C. Scribner's Sons, 1932), 199–206. See Alfred A. Cave, *Prophets of the Great Spirit: Native American Revitalization Movements in Eastern North America* (Lincoln: University of Nebraska Press, 2006).

3. Frank Ernest Hill, "A New Pattern of Life for the Indian," *New York Times,* 14 July 1935.

him Joseph Brant had called for "a dish with one spoon," or a federation of tribes to share common lands. From the old Wintu woman of California ("we don't chop down trees. We only use dead wood") to Sitting Bull ("nor will I have the whites cutting our timber along the rivers, more especially the oak," he vowed), the sacred relation to the earth has been mocked or adulated.

The land was stolen *and* it was privatized. The project of assimilation or the project of genocide was expressed by Thomas Jefferson who in 1801 began to anticipate the termination of their history. That history depended on common land. The Indian Removal Act of 1830 led to the Trail of Tears forcing the Cherokees, the Chickasaws, the Choctaws, the Creek, and the Seminole nations—the Five Civilized Tribes—to evacuate their lands and remove to Oklahoma. These five nations retained most of what is now eastern Oklahoma as communal. Roxanne Dunbar Ortiz in her study of land tenure systems of New Mexico explained how the community land grant of the Spanish included common pasture lands and preserved the system of pueblo communalism in water irrigation and riparian rights.[4]

Senator Henry L. Dawes of Massachusetts led the next attack. "They have got as far as they can go, because they own their land in common. It is Henry George's system, and under that there is no enterprise to make your home any better than that of your neighbors. There is no selfishness, which is at the bottom of civilization." The Commission of Indian Affairs would define citizenship and allotments. The Dawes Act of 1887 destroyed the common lands of Oklahoma's indigenous peoples, turning them

---

4. Roxanne Dunbar-Ortiz, *Roots of Resistance: Land Tenure in New Mexico, 1680–1980* (Los Angeles: American Indian Studies Center, UCLA, 1980), 5.

into either individual private allotments for the Indians or surplus to be sold to the whites, in a "saturnalia of exploitation."[5]

"If we had our own way we would be living with lands in common, and we would have these prairies all open, and our little bunches of cattle, and would have bands of deer that would jump up from the herd of every hollow, and flocks of turkeys running up every hillside," testified Pleasant Porter of Oklahoma, speaking the language of pannage, chiminage, assarts, and so on.

The Indian experience with treaties was an experience of betrayal, bad faith, and lies. Those who signed them were called "earth eaters." Russell Means, an Oglala Sioux of Pine Ridge, learned from his grandfather, "I see the white man chop down a tree without a prayer, without a fast, without any kind of reverence. And here the tree can tell him how to live." He took his stand with "the Treaty" (the 1868 Fort Laramie Treaty) that preserved the prairie commons to the Sioux unless ceded by three-fourths of the adult males.[6]

The development of American anarchism coincided with the Indian wars and the way of life sustained on the plains, the lakes, and the forests. Joseph Labadie (1850–1933) fished, hunted, cooked, and slept with the Pottawatomie of Michigan until he was fourteen. He remembered, "equality in economic conditions made the neighborhood kin."[7] He became Michigan's most well-known labor agitator, trade unionist, anticapitalist.

5. Henry L. Dawes, "The Indian Territory," *The Independent* 52 (October 1900); Angie Debo, *And Still the Waters Run: The Betrayal of the Five Civilized Tribes* (Princeton: Princeton University Press, 1940), 5.

6. Roxanne Dunbar-Ortiz, *The Great Sioux Nation: Sitting in Judgment on America* (Berkeley: Moon Books, 1977), 44.

7. Carlotta R. Anderson, *All-American Anarchist: Joseph A. Labadie and the Labor Movement* (Wayne State, 1998), 33.

The anti-enclosure struggles of native Americans are fundamental to the ecology and landscape of American history. The management of the sheep herds of the Long Trail on the eastern slopes of the Sierra Nevada "record the progress," in the words of Mary Austin, "from nomadism to the commonwealth."[8] The sacred hoop surrounds the open commons. It is the first principle of the commons acknowledged in Magna Carta.

THE BATTERING RAM

The second force constituting American society is African American slavery. Frederick Douglass said in 1854, "Let the engine of the Magna Carta beat against the Jericho walls of slavery, and no seven days blowing of ram's horn would be necessary." Douglass had returned from touring England and Ireland, where his knowledge of Magna Carta as a living document of struggle was refreshed by the English working-class movement known as Chartism, which opposed child labor and prison construction in favor of land redistribution, female suffrage, and the ten-hour day. In Ireland he became acquainted with the dire consequence of monoculture and privatization—famine.

Two years earlier William Goodell expressed the abolitionists' revolutionary nature in terms of Magna Carta as he knew it, that is, without the Forest Charter. "Ours is an advanced period in the struggle for human freedom. It is not to the contest of the barons against an unlimited autocrat that we are summoned—nor to the struggle of the middle classes against the barons. . . . The

8. Mary Austin, *The Flock* (Boston: Houghton Mifflin, 1906), 72.

demands of liberty strike deeper, now, and reach the ground tier of their humanity, hid under the rubbish of centuries of degradation—classes who have scarcely been thought of as human and to whom no Magna Carta . . . have brought even a tithe or foretaste of their promised blessings."[9] The "ground tier" of humanity is the equivalent to the commoners.

How could the legal engine of Magna Carta—the battering ram—bring down the walls of slavery? The Massachusetts abolitionist Lysander Spooner based his arguments on English history, which included "the writ of habeas corpus (the essential principle of which . . . is to deny the right of property in man) and the trial by jury."[10] Spooner showed that the Fugitive Slave Acts of 1793 and 1850 denied the fugitive the petition of habeas corpus or trial by jury. In the struggle the legal action of the petition of habeas corpus—have the body—was accompanied by direct action to take the body from the clutches of the slave catchers. More than sixty separate legal and extralegal attempts had been counted to recapture fugitives by 1852. Thus in 1851, as abolitionist lawyers were in court discussing the grounds of a second habeas petition in the case of the fugitive slave Shadrach Minkins, a crowd of abolitionists entered the court and took the body and person of Shadrach Minkins, "plucked as a brand from the burning," conveying him to freedom in Montreal.[11]

9. William Goodell, *Slavery and Anti-Slavery: A History of Great Struggle in Both Hemispheres* (New York: W. Harned, 1852).

10. Lysander Spooner, *The Unconstitutionality of Slavery* (Boston: B. Marsh, 1845–47).

11. Gary Collins, *Shadrach Minkins: From Fugitive Slave to Citizen* (Cambridge, MA: Harvard University Press, 1997), 52.

When General William Tecumseh Sherman issued his fifteenth field order on 16 January 1865 (coincidentally, fifty-four years before Martin Luther King Jr.'s birthday), it provided resources for the freedman, "forty acres and a mule." The forty-acre plots however became the basis not of individualist yeomen's farms but of something resembling common field systems in which household strips were dispersed to share in different land uses (pasture, fishing, hunting, horticulture). This experience in actual commoning was the background to the Fourteenth Amendment.[12]

The Civil War was compared to the barons' war against King John, and "a rich and perpetual product" was the result: in the former, Magna Carta, in the latter, Fourteenth Amendment. They are "blazed on the forehead of constitutional liberty." References to Magna Carta were plentiful in Congress during debates concerning the Thirteenth, Fourteenth, and Fifteenth Amendments, especially the Fourteenth.[13] The ability to walk the streets, the ability to use public transport, to be a witness in a trial, to be a juryman, these were examples of the "common rights" recognized by the Fourteenth Amendment and the Magna Carta. During Reconstruction the principles of Magna Carta expanded. When Reconstruction came to an end those principles were perverted with the New Orleans slaughterhouse cases of 1877.

Ella Baker, the indispensable civil rights organizer of the mid-twentieth century, grew up in North Carolina, where the exchange of goods and services through a large network of mutual

12. Julie Saville, *The Work of Reconstruction: From Slave to Wage Laborer in South Carolina, 1860–1870* (New York: Cambridge University Press, 1994), 38.

13. The Reconstruction amendments' debates.

aid included collective purchase and use of expensive farm equipment. She internalized values of the commons as a child and as an adult realized them in the formation of the Young Negroes Cooperative League in which "all power rests in the hands of the rank and file," as she wrote in 1935. She anticipated "the day when the soil and all of its resources will be reclaimed by its rightful owners—the working masses of the world."[14] Passage from the nadir to the zenith was made possible by the commons.

Frederick Douglass referred to Magna Carta in the context of a debate organized by the Cincinnati Ladies' Anti-Slavery Sewing Circle in which he argued that slavery was unconstitutional, against the position taken by Lucy Stone that the U.S. Constitution was a slaveholder's document.[15] The unity of legal writ and direct action has been a characteristic of the African American freedom struggle. Hence the "engine" in Frederick Douglass's powerful image. From Granville Sharp and Thomas Lewis to Lysander Spooner and Shadrach Minkins, then to Dr. Martin Luther King Jr., direct action, taking the body from the slave ship, taking the person from the courtroom, marching to Selma, Alabama, has gone on in the juridical context of higher law.

From the Atlantic struggle to abolish slavery through the Civil War to the paramilitary racist terrorism that followed Reconstruction, the battering ram of African American experience leads

14. Barbara Ransby, *Ella Baker and the Black Freedom Movement: A Radical Democratic Vision* (Chapel Hill: University of North Carolina Press, 2003), 37, 82–83, 86.

15. John W. Blassingame, ed., *The Frederick Douglass Papers. Series One: Speeches, Debates, and Interviews,* vol. 2 *(1847–54)* (New Haven: Yale University Press, 1982), 467.

to reparations, the second principle of Magna Carta found in its several provisions for the return of expropriated forest lands.

ARTICLE 7(A)

Proletarian labor is the source of value. The proletarian, by definition, does not own the means of production. Yet he must use them. By the same token, he may misuse, abuse, or refuse them. Lacking also the means of reproduction, he must subsist upon what his wages could purchase. From these fundamentals of the capitalist economic system, the collective workers' weapons became the picket, the strike, and the boycott, or not selling, not working, not buying.

Samuel Gompers, a London Jewish cigar maker, and John L. Lewis, a coal miner and son of Welsh immigrants, were the most powerful labor leaders at the end of the nineteenth century and the first half of the twentieth. Gompers helped found the American Federation of Labor (AFL) and Lewis founded the Congress of Industrial Organizations (CIO). Both were active organizers of unions, campaigners on behalf of workers' rights, and lobbyists of government. They were reformers rather than revolutionaries, and both attained significant legislation on behalf of labor from the U.S. Congress; they compared it to Magna Carta. Yet that legislation was contradictory.

The Sherman Antitrust Act of 1890, although intended to restrain monopoly capitalism, was turned upside down by the courts and used against the working class to enjoin workers from striking, picketing, and boycotting in restraint of trade. Hundreds of court injunctions were issued by federal and state judges. Eugene Debs said that such court orders, not the U.S. Army, broke the unions after the Pullman strike of 1894. Felix Frankfurter wrote, "The heart of the problem is the power, for all practical purposes, of a single judge to issue orders, to interpret them, to declare disobedience, and to sentence."[16] One man was judge, jury, and jailer, giving new meaning to the term "monopoly capitalism."

In November 1914 after a decade of struggle Congress passed the Clayton Antitrust Act, which seemed to restore the legality of the strike, the picket, and the boycott. "In no other country in the world," Samuel Gompers wrote, "is there an enunciation of fundamental principles comparable to the incisive, virile statement" at the heart of the law. He said, "The declaratory legislation, *The labor of a human being is not a commodity or article of commerce,* is the Industrial Magna Carta upon which the working people will rear their structure of individual freedom."[17]

John L. Lewis, the president of the United Mine Workers of America, testified to the Finance Committee of the U.S. Senate in the fall of 1932, reading a report that "was the birth certificate of Section Seven(a), popularly known as Labor's Magna Carta." The NRA, or National Recovery Act, became law in June 1933. Its article 7(a) said, "employees shall have the right to organize and bargain collectively through representatives of their own choosing." After the Supreme Court struck it down in *Schecter v. U.S.* (27 May 1935), Congress passed the Wagner Act restoring article 7(a). This swift response reflected the power of the working

16. Felix Frankfurter and Nathaniel Green, *The Labor Injunction* (New York: Macmillan, 1930), 190.

17. Samuel Gompers, "The Charter of Industrial Freedom," *American Federationist* 21, no. 11 (November 1914): 957–74.

class, led by the miners. In 1932 Josephine Roche reached an extraordinary agreement with the Colorado lignite coal owners in "a declaration of principles that sounds like an industrial Magna Carta." In October 1933 the UMWA reached agreement with the bituminous coal owners. "A Magna Carta of human rights underground has been written," said the *New York Times.*[18] The coal miners of America told one another, "the President wants you to join the union."[19] The miners were joined by industrial workers everywhere. A turning point came in 1934 with the general strikes of the San Francisco dockers, the Minneapolis teamsters, and the Toledo Auto-Lite employees.

Samuel Gompers's Magna Carta did not treat labor as a commodity while John L. Lewis's did. We know Magna Carta has no chapter declaring that labor is or is not a commodity. Instead, it forbids the king or his servants from taking what belongs to commoners. The means of production and reproduction are collective and the goal of Magna Carta was to limit the king's access to them. Article 7(a), on the contrary, helped to bring labor, in the words of one critic, into the "regulatory ambit of the administrative state."[20] Incisive as the statement is in challenging the legal distortions of the antitrust act, it also flew in the face of the real-

18. Louis Stark, "A Woman Unravels an Industrial Knot," *New York Times,* 7 February 1932; Malcolm Ross, "Lifting the Coal Miner Out of the Murk," *New York Times,* 1 October 1933.

19. Saul Alinsky, *John L. Lewis, an Unauthorized Biography* (New York: Putnam, 1949), 65–66.

20. Christopher Tomlins, *The State and the Unions: Labor Relations, Law, and the Organized Labor Movement in America, 1880–1960* (New York: Cambridge University Press, 1985).

ity of union organizers in the era of the mass worker who had to make the "virile statement" a reality from the Lawrence textile mills to the Colorado mines to the bindle stiffs of the great plains. Furthermore its virility depended on the reproduction of workers in America, which was accomplished either by immigration or the unpaid, invisible labor of housework.

. In Indiana in the early 1930s there was a back-to-the-land movement, and then, once on the land, a resumption of commoning: pasturing a cow, cutting wood, planting gardens, collecting berries or walnuts and hickory nuts in season with the tolerance of private property owners.[21] In Terre Haute, Indiana, visiting miners helped form a union at the Columbia Enameling and Stamping Company, and its members struck in March 1935. Community commissaries were organized. In July they led a "labor holiday," or general strike (the workers pulled the clocks off the walls and overturned the bosses' desks). Martial law was declared and the city occupied by the National Guard. Responding to the prohibition of public speaking, the Socialist Norman Thomas referred to the city worthies as "a lot of Hoosier Hitlers."

Labor's Magna Carta needed the force of the workers in motion. The force was evident in the murals of Terre Haute, Indiana. We have commented on the mural of Frederick Webb Ross, finished in a WPA courthouse in September 1935. In April 1935 another, powerful, mural was chalked on the walls of the junior high school with as direct an analysis of class struggle as could be found—a multiracial troop of Boy Scouts (think of "The Law of the Jungle") leveling their rifles upon the fat, trembling,

21. Ralph D. Gray, ed., *Indiana History: A Book of Readings* (Bloomington: Indiana University Press, 1994), 343–49.

Figure 13.   Diamond-wearing capitalists from mural in Terre Haute junior high school, by Gilbert Wilson. Martin Collection, Indiana Historical Society.

diamond-wearing capitalists—as well as a deep tribute to the knowledge and labor of Indiana's farmers and scientists. At the three walls' center the brown-skinned hands of a sky deity nurture a seedling. People in the Midwest knew that maize came from the Mayas. On the mural the artist had written, "You can no more prevent the revolution from coming than you can prevent the growth of new life over the face of the earth each spring," until the school board covered it up with a flag. The artist, Gilbert Wilson, admired the Mexican Revolution and was influenced by David Siqueiros.[22] The two murals are in a sort of dialogue interrupted by the general strike. They are there to this day.

22. Edward K. Spann and Graeme Reid, "The Terre Haute Murals of Gilbert Wilson," *Traces of Indiana and Midwestern History* (winter 2002).

The New Deal embodied not new values, as FDR said in his message to Congress on 8 June 1934, but "a recovery of the old and sacred possessive rights for which mankind has constantly struggled—homes, livelihood, and individual security." These were "values lost in the course of our economic development and expansion": given the upside-down meaning of the terms, economic development and expansion depended precisely on destruction of the commons. During the New Deal the federal government responded to demands of the mass worker both for increasing the value of the working class and for taking a hand in its reproduction. The experience led many to think that the government could replace many of the functions that commoning had historically fulfilled.

The Report of the Committee on Economic Security (1935) aimed primarily at "the assurance of an adequate income to each human being in childhood, youth, middle age, or old age—in sickness or in health."[23] The Social Security Act and Aid to Families with Dependent Children were designed to accomplish this at a time when the term welfare meant the good life, not a grudging handout. Social Security resembles Magna Carta's provision on behalf of a widow's reasonable estovers of common. The first U.S. Social Security check was issued on 30 January 1940, a few days before *The Ballad of Magna Carta.*

---

23. *The Report of the Committee on Economic Security and Other Basic Documents Relating to the Development of the Social Security Act,* 50th anniversary ed. (Washington DC: National Conference on Social Welfare, 1985). See also Linda Gordon, *Pitied But Not Entitled: Single Mothers and the History of Welfare, 1890–1935* (New York: Free Press, 1994).

Thanks to the valiant experience of unionized industrial workers, the New Deal in article 7(a) of the Wagner Act paved the way for legislation that set out social and economic rights for security against want. The principle of subsistence for all has a derivation in the numerous usufructs named in Magna Carta.

THE JURY BOX

In 1927 more than half of the United States did not permit women to serve as jurors. The state had typed women as persons whose assistance in the administration of justice was unneeded by the community. Women were "insisting that the ballot [and] the jury box are as much a part of woman's duty to her children as the stew-pan and feather duster." Wistfully they rued the day in 1215 when the rumpus between King John and the English people did not provide jury service by men and women.[24] Pauli Murray—who had refused to sit in the back of the bus in 1940, who raised money for black sharecroppers, who opposed capital punishment—campaigned against Jim Crow and Jane Crow. She led the fight for the inclusion of women in jury pools.[25] Yet in the United States it was not until 1975 and *Taylor v. Louisiana* that the Supreme Court ruled that gender as a means of discrimination in drawing the jury pool was in violation of the due

24. Burnita Shelton Matthews, "The Woman Juror," *Women Lawyers' Journal* 15, no. 2 (April 1927); and Gretchen Ritter, "Jury Service and Women's Citizenship Before and After the Nineteenth Amendment," *Law and History Review* 20, no. 3 (autumn 2002): 479–515.

25. Linda K. Kerber, *No Constitutional Right to Be Ladies: Women and the Obligations of Citizenship* (New York: Hill and Wang, 1998), chap. 4.

process clause of the Fourteenth Amendment. The impartial jury became the jury drawn impartially.

For women, jury service raises the issue of what it means to be a *peer* (as in "a jury of one's peers")—whether this is a formal legal status, or something deeper and more substantive, that speaks to the way that women bring their lived experiences to the exercise of their civic duties. Women could speak truth or render a verdict (according to its Latin etymology, speak the truth). The article on the jury in the *Oxford English Dictionary* quotes an important passage from Pollock and Maitland's history of law:

> The question to be addressed to [the jury] may take many different forms: it may or may not be one which has arisen in the course of litigation; it may be a question of fact or a question of law, or again what we should now-a-days call a question of mixed fact and law. What are the customs of your district? What rights has the king in your district? Name all the land-owners of your district and say how much land each of them has.

Long recognized in English law, women's jury service had provided a jury of matrons to determine pregnancy and in some cases rape. Women sought to practice in the only place within the constitutional system where popular sovereignty exists without the intermediation of representatives, namely the jury, with roots in the neighborhood. We should see the jury in relation to other popular forums such as the assembly, the conventicle, the council, the soviet, the powwow, the *encuentro*.

In the Middle Ages the jury was central to the regulation of the commons: it appointed officials such as pindars or rangers, reeves and haywards, it adjudicated disputes, it allocated strips, it assisted in the rotation of crops. In the eighteenth century its power to set a price on stolen property mollified the rigors of capital statutes. John Adams said its duty was to find a verdict according to its "own best Understanding, Judgment and Conscience, tho in Direct opposition to the direction of the court." And in 1735 Peter Zenger persuaded a jury to override established law that truth was not a defense against the charge of seditious libel. The jury was the one place, in monarchy and republic alike, where the people governed.

In 1917 Jane Addams, founder of Hull House in Chicago as well as the first president of the Women's International League for Peace and Freedom, wrote, "The very breakdown exhibited by the present war reinforces the pacifists' contention that there is need of an international charter—a Magna Charta indeed—of international rights, to be issued by the nations great and small, with large provisions for economic freedom." She felt "it is unspeakably stupid that the nations should have failed to create an international organization."[26] Her call for planetary Magna Carta originated in the microworld of the immigrant neighborhood of the mass worker, where she saw the cooperative ethic at work.

The violence of the state is restrained by jury, by prohibition of torture, by habeas corpus, and by the due process of law: these are accomplishments of commoners. Their derivations include the system of *compurgation,* where trial was conducted by witnesses on behalf of the defendant. The restraints are designed to enforce a neighborly justice, relations between power and the

---

26. Jean Bethke Elshtain, ed., *The Jane Addams Reader* (New York: Basic Books, 2002), 355. I thank Tom Chisholm for drawing my attention to this source.

people is in the open. These are also characteristics of the commoning experiences.

The rules of coverture meant women were not recognized in law as persons. They had no presence in the public realm. Yet this was often the opposite of reality, visible at the Tenement Museum on Manhattan's Lower East Side, where photographs, letters, journals, government reports, and memories of the tour guides testify that the street was the public realm of the unpropertied, or the urban commonage—the location of laundry, the place of commerce and street peddlers, the scene of courtship, children's playground, beauty salon, outdoor parlor for housewives. Nursery, charity, orphanage, poorhouse, almshouse—these were social services of the neighborhood, which together with schools, bands, baths, gyms, reading rooms, galleries, and orchestras made city civilization.

Between the tenement room and the street were transitional architectural elements, the fire escape, the stoop, and the sidewalk. Jane Jacobs considers the *sidewalk* the center of urban civilization, the place where the self-activity of the neighborhood can flourish despite the plans of utopian busybodies. It is opposed to the enclosed turf; it combines privacy and makes the presence of strangers an asset. Here is where the grapevine of informal communication grows. The "web of reputation, gossip, approval, disapproval and sanctions" filters out dullness and barbarism.[27]

In 1910 a proposed "Women's Charter" by the Women's Liberal Federation in England called for equal pay with men, free

27. Jane Jacobs, *The Death and Life of Great American Cities* (New York: Random House, 1961), 35.

milk and playrooms for children, and public baths for all. Virginia Woolf quoted her father, the eminent Victorian Leslie Stephen, "Whenever you see a board up with 'Trespassers will be prosecuted,' trespass at once." She recommended the practice. After the war there will be "no more classes and shall we stand, without hedges between us, on the common ground?" In the United States writing *Common Human Needs* (1945), Charlotte Towle anticipated victory on the battlefield, argued that the idea of the dignity of man will be won or lost in the postwar days, in "democracy's conviction regarding its responsibility for human welfare."[28]

John Arden, a playwright from Barnsley, Yorkshire, was commissioned by the City of London to write a play for the seven hundred fiftieth anniversary of Magna Carta. It was publicly performed on 14 June 1965 at the Mermaid Theatre, Puddle Dock, London. He called his play *Left-Handed Liberty.* Arden approaches Magna Carta as a conflict of gender. The groom customarily offered the left hand to the bride in a morganatic marriage, in which the spouse of a lower rank was not entitled to a share in the other's possessions. King John's mother, the aged Eleanor of Aquitaine, advises him to wear his most treasured jewel on his left hand. She is described as "the old black witchcraft queen," associating her with the heresies of Albi that pope and king had such trouble crushing, for the Albigensians called for equality between men and women.

28. Antoinette Burton, *Burdens of History* (Chapel Hill: University of North Carolina Press, 1994), 5; Claire Hirshfield, "Fractured Faith," *Gender and History* 2, no. 2 (summer 1950): 192; Charlotte Towle, *Common Human Needs* (Washington DC: National Association of Social Workers, 1945), 1.

Lady de Vesci: "I am a free woman, indeed, a noblewoman—
if you can establish a court of noble ladies of equivalent rank, I
daresay they will be prepared to hear your cause against me, and
to pronounce a verdict in accordance with the evidence," alluding to chapter 39 and the provision that judgment is to be by the
peers of the accused. It works both ways: it works ambidex-
trously as a means to restrain kingly power and, equally well, as
a means to release wifely desire. Left-handed liberty blows back
at the authority of the husband.

The final scene of the play has the actor playing King John di-
vest himself of sword, crown, and mantle, to stand naked of the
clothing of authority, in order to justify his existence. "Because
this play concerns Magna Carta, and Magna Carta only, the lady
is peripheral. . . . Yet nevertheless she exists." He then addresses
the audience directly: "You cannot remodel it. Never let that be
said of this parchment—I warn you! And as you have all come
here in some sort of celebratory and congratulatory frame of
mind, I will also give a warning to the parchment itself: 'Woe
unto you when all men speak well of you.'"

The struggle to seat women in the jury box brings to justice the
ancient democracy of neighborhood such as we've found in the
informal gathering of local women in Tudor times who stopped
the price gouging of fuel to the amplification of the collective of
tenement women who embodied Jane Addam's internationalism
of peace and freedom, and in a major principle of Magna Carta.

THE BORDER

To become manifest, the commonages latent in American history
need an outside catalyst, hence the importance of the border.

Armed resistance to the government's division of tribal land in Oklahoma erupted in 1901 under the leadership of Chitto Harjo, or Crazy Snake. "I am telling you now about what was done since 1492," he said in the oil town of Tulsa. He wanted to submit the case to international arbitration. And after the debacle of the siege of Wounded Knee in 1973 the American Indian movement, far from being defeated, extended its range to indigenous people throughout the two American continents. When Article 27 of the Mexican Constitution, the last vestige of the village *ejidos* or common land, was repealed in preparation for NAFTA (1994), the reaction arose from the indigenous people in defense of the forest commons. As their lands were lost they migrated north.

The Pan-African Congress meeting in London in 1921 concluded with a manifesto, "A Declaration to the World," that demanded among other things "the ancient common ownership of the Land and its natural fruits and defense against the unrestrained greed of invested capital."[29] Governments in wartime promise soldiers the earth. The Atlantic Charter (1941) specified four freedoms (freedom of speech, freedom of worship, freedom from want, freedom from fear). A British Labour Party conference resolution of 1942 was designed to commit the party to decolonization: "in all colonial areas, in Africa and elsewhere, where the primitive systems of communal land tenure exist, these systems should be maintained and land should be declared inalienable by private sale or purchase. All natural resources

---

29. J. Ayodele Langley, *Pan-Africanism and Nationalism in West Africa, 1900–1945: A Study in Ideology and Social Classes* (Oxford: Clarendon Press, 1973), 76–77.

should be declared public property and be developed under public ownership." Churchill later wrote that the Atlantic Charter was not "applicable to coloured races in colonial empires."[30]

Eleanor Roosevelt in her 1948 speech to the General Assembly of the United Nations, urging adoption of the Universal Declaration of Human Rights, expressed the hope that it would take its place alongside the Magna Carta and the Bill of Rights. When the UN Human Rights Commission began its work on the Declaration of Human Rights, W. E. B. DuBois was leading the forces to intervene on behalf of the colonized people of the world. DuBois challenged to their faces the American authors of the Bretton Woods agreements (1944) establishing the International Monetary Fund and the World Bank: "seven hundred fifty millions of people, a third of mankind, live in colonies. Cheap labor and materials are basic to postwar industry and finances. Was this matter mentioned in any form at Bretton Woods?"[31]

In 1955 a congress of the people met at Kliptown, "a multiracial village on a scrap of veld a few miles southwest of Johannesburg," to write a charter of freedom. It was read aloud in English, Sesotho, and Xhosa. "The people have been robbed of their birthright to land, liberty, and peace. The national wealth shall be *restored* to the people. The land shall be *redivided* amongst those who work it." In the village community there was no such

30. Penny Von Eschen, *Race against Empire: Black Americans and Anticolonialism, 1937–1957* (Ithaca: Cornell University Press, 1997), 25.

31. Allida M. Black, *Courage in a Dangerous World: The Political Writings of Eleanor Roosevelt* (New York: Columbia University Press, 1999), 10; David Levering Lewis, *W. E. B. DuBois: The Fight for Equality and the American Century, 1919–1963* (New York: Henry Holt, 2000), 504.

thing as individual land ownership. The land belonged to the people. Farming was based on joint efforts and shared labor; exchange was based on reciprocity and mutualism. "We believe that in the long run the special contribution to the world by Africa will be in this field of human relationship."[32]

Nelson Mandela was sentenced to life imprisonment at the Rivonia trial of 1964 but not before saying from the dock, "The Magna Carta, the Petition of Rights, and the Bill of Rights, are documents which are held in veneration by democrats throughout the world." Mandela was attracted "by the idea of a classless society, an attraction which springs in part from Marxist reading and, in part, from my admiration of the structure and organization of early African societies in this country. The land, then the main means of production, belonged to the tribe. There were no rich or poor and there was no exploitation."

The International Covenant on Economic, Social and Cultural Rights (1966) refers directly to the Atlantic Charter and the ideal of free human beings enjoying freedom from want and freedom from fear. These were precisely the freedoms George W. Bush omitted in his speech of late September 2001 launching the "war on terror." Subsequent events ripped to shreds chapter after chapter of Magna Carta.

The path this chapter suggests—to manifest the commonages in a constitution just as once the propertied regime James Madison described organized itself a constitution—is a path already

32. In England the New Left welcomed the Kliptown Charter as "one of the finest documents produced by any political movement anywhere since the days of the British Chartists." John Rex, "Africa's National Congresses," *The New Reasoner: A Quarterly Journal of Socialist Humanism,* no.2 (autumn 1957): 64.

familiar to Bolivians under Evo Morales. Discussion has begun for a constituent assembly to draft a new constitution including indigenous values, the most fundamental of which is the *Ayllu,* or the commons. *¡Sí, se puede!* The principle of open travel is explicitly stated in Magna Carta's chapters 41 and 42 as pertaining to merchants and the trade of commodities. In our age the principle must be applied to the direct circulation of experiences across the border—pan-African, indigenous, revolutionary, or constitutional.

CHAPTER TWELVE

Conclusion

The Daughters of Memory Shall Become the Daughters of Inspiration.
William Blake, Milton (*1808*)

A missing charter preceded Magna Carta. In 1235 the chronicler Roger Wendover wrote that Archbishop Stephen Langton discovered a charter in 1213 of "antient liberties" from the time of Henry I. Langton informed the barons that this charter could be the means "by which (if they pleased) they might re-establish their ancient liberties." And this led them to swear an oath to "contend for those liberties even to death itself." The charter of liberty sealed at Runnymede was the result. The commoning vectors in our recent past have referred to Magna Carta as ancient liberty.

The connection between lost liberties and a missing charter is recurrent, indeed; to those who look at history merely as a fable, it may seem to be just a trope or figure, to be used, for instance, in plotting a story about Robin Hood; it becomes a miraculous seal of legitimacy and right. The trope expresses reverence for the written word. It might be taken as a substitute for that which it records, the superiority of the signifier over the signified. If the charter were restored, would it not restore also the past? In America the Bill of Rights performs an analogous function. In the colony of Connecticut the English governor attempted to assert control by taking back a charter granted by Charles II in 1662, but in concealing the charter in a thousand-year-old oak, the colonists believed they were preserving their independence.

The "laws and customs" of the miners in the Forest of Dean originated in the thirteenth century but were not written down until 1610 as the Book of Denis. By the nineteenth century, as privatization and enclosure provoked resistance, the Book of Denis was reissued. A spokesman for the royal authorities spoke more truly than perhaps he knew when he described the Book of Denis as "that little book which they consider their Magna Carta." Warren James, one of the commoners of the forest, put no great stock in books or charters. When push came to shove he indulged in no such talk of charters or rights: "With a face of the most imperturbable gravity he produced as the voucher of his privilege, an enormous pick axe."[1] He and thousands of others cut down the fences and he was transported for his pains.

Thomas Walsingham was the *scriptorarius* at St. Albans during the Peasants' Revolt of 1381, the massive uprising that proposed the classic riddle of equality,

---

1. Chris Fisher, *Custom, Work and Market Capitalism: The Forest of Dean Colliers, 1788–1888* (London: Croom Helm, 1981), 38. A hundred years later Edna Healey, growing up in the forest purlieus amid its druidical stones and trees, remembered a nickname at school for any obstreperous child, "Chopper James." Edna Healey, introduction to Fay Godwin, *The Secret Forest of Dean* (London: Redcliffe Press, 1986).

When Adam delved and Eve span,
Who was then the Gentleman?

The exactions on the peasantry, as well as their expropriations, were recorded. When the St. Albans insurgents attacked, Walsingham, the records keeper, handed over the documents, which the people then burned. "These did nothing to satisfy the unruly populace; no, they demanded a certain ancient charter confirming the liberties of the villeins, with capital letters, one of gold and the other of azure; and without that, they asserted, they would not be satisfied with promises."[2] Decorated capital letters in fact appeared on royal charters: Gold at that time originated in West Africa. Azure was a blue pigment made from Persian lapis lazuli. Walsingham assumed peasants were illiterate but they were only being prudent (these were times when it was dangerous to be "found with an inkwell").[3]

The Charters of Liberties quickly acquired the aura of power, the glamour of color, and the solemnity of religion. The king swore an oath to the charters. "So help me God, I will keep all these things inviolate, as I am a man, as I am a Christian, as I am a knight, and as I am a king crowned and anointed." If the charters were violated, a sentence of excommunication and anathema was passed when, in Blackstone's words, "the prelates cast down their tapers extinguished and smoking with this execration, 'so may all that incur this sentence be extinguished and stink in hell.'" In Oc-

2. Thomas Walsingham, *Gesta abbatum monasterii Sancti Albani,* ed. Henry Thomas Riley, Rolls Series 28 (London: Longmans, Green, 1869).
3. Steven Justice, *Writing and Rebellion: England in 1381* (Berkeley: University of California Press, 1994), 256–57.

tober 1297 Edward I confirmed the charters as both common law and statute law. The purpose was to replenish his military after its defeat in Scotland at the hand of William Wallace a month earlier, on 11 September 1297. To the aura, glamour, solemnity, of the Charters of Liberties I add the coincidence of dates, in order to elude the iron sequence of links in the chain of *khronos,* one year after another—on and on.

Is law part of the ideological superstructure and exclusive to particular historical epochs? Or are there immutable principles of law discovered through history and thenceforth forever valid? *Jus cogens,* or compelling law, is a body of higher law of overriding importance to the international community. It prohibits genocide, torture, slavery. Since 1215 the charters have had their day, and night, beginning with 11 September 1217. They were *British* law after 11 September 1297. They opposed privatization of the commons and called for reparations to the oppressed in the Levellers' petition of 11 September 1648, when Oliver Cromwell and the English bourgeoisie began to detach the Forest Charter from Magna Carta. The Charters of Liberties were separated and detached with the aid of the reimposition of slavery and the English slave trade after the *asiento* of 11 September 1713. With the "war on terror" following 11 September 2001, midnight approached for the Charters of Liberties with warrantless wiretapping, imprisonment without charges, capricious enforcement of law, and transoceanic tortures. The "war on terror" silenced the worldwide discussion about reparations then taking place in Durban, South Africa. And it silenced the worldwide discussion about another possible world taking place in Genoa, Italy.

The methodology of diplomatics over the centuries has left the legal or constitutional fate of the commons to the vagaries of parchment, the faults of copyists, the attention of rodents, the mysteries of archives. It was not until the 1930s that medievalists began to employ the techniques of fieldwork to the examination of the past.[4] The specialized diplomatics of the Enlightenment were no longer the only scholarly means of knowledge of the commons. Philology, dialects, folklore, direct observation, oral history, and above all, fieldwork at the site of commoning, characterized social history. It is one of the roots of history from below. Yet somehow during the efflorescence of the social history during the last third of the twentieth century the constitutional issues were mislaid. Not until the 1990s and the movement to reclaim the commons has the issue returned, thanks to the struggles of the indigenous peoples of America, and thanks to the Zapatistas.

Full discussion of the commons is hampered by two abbreviated categories of thought that have become spasmodic intellectual tics. One goes back to the 1790s and arose against the romantic movement; the other developed against the communist movement of the twentieth century. The first scorned utopia and the second denounced totalitarianism; one became the condescending term for all that is foolish, the other the pompous designation for all that is hideous. Yet under the circumstances of actually existing commons, they were irrelevant. Still, the attitudes conveniently colonized the mind and shut off debate where it needed to begin.

Writing in 1968, E. P. Thompson reached back to the 1790s and to William Wordsworth in order to understand the cultural sub-

---

4. C. S. Orwin and C. S. Orwin, *The Open Fields* (Oxford: Clarendon Press, 1938).

ordination of class by class in England. He found in Wordsworth "an affirmation of the worth of the common man, a statement of faith enduring through perplexity and shock in universal brotherhood." The common man in this reading was husband, father, he was continent of mind and possessed a sense of right even in the midst of strife. This was what was left over after the Terror against the revolutionary claims of égalité. Thompson comments further, "the equality of worth of the common man . . . lay in moral and spiritual attributes, developed through experiences of labor, suffering, and through primary human relationships."[5] The common man has been separated from the common woman, and from the common land. Homo sapiens had become *homo .oeconomicus.*

The twentieth-century radical and revolutionary tradition stayed away from that Magna Carta, whose accretions of Anglo-Saxon racism had attached themselves to the dominant interpretation during the nineteenth century. Thus John Cornford, the passionately brilliant young Communist student who was to die with the International Brigades in Spain, scorned the Victorian medievalist Stubbs at Cambridge University, in these words: "the illusions of capitalist democracy are read back into the past as far as Magna Carta."[6] An exception to this neglect might be found in some strands of the anarchist tradition in which the village commune was praised. Pyotr Kropotkin studied the French Revolution, finding that the peasants' resistance to the theft of common lands was the basis of the endemic *émeutes* of the countryside

5. E. P. Thompson, *The Romantics: England in a Revolutionary Age* (New York: New Press, 1997), 11–13.

6. John Cornford, "Notes on the Teaching of History at Cambridge," in *Collected Writings,* ed. Jonathan Galassi (Manchester: Carcaent, 1976), 77.

essential to the revolutionary process. Toward the end of his life Marx wrote comrades in Russian that, yes, the *mir* (the village community of czarist Russia) could become the basis of the communist transformation of society.[7]

Otherwise, the theme of the commons remained alienated from the long line of restraints on state power. We certainly need them, technical as they may seem. Magna Carta is required to open the secret state. Magna Carta is needed for the prisoners in Guantánamo Bay. Magna Carta is needed for the prisoners who have been rendered to torture chambers in other countries. Furthermore Magna Carta is needed to condemn torture altogether; its prohibition is part of the tradition of chapter 39. That same chapter of Magna Carta acknowledges a form of justice that depended on peers and the neighborhood and that we recognize as trial by jury. Due process of law must be returned to its roots in the neighborhood. These four restraints are in dire need of recovery, threatened as they have been by the "war on terror." This book shows that they cannot succeed without the accompanying principles of commoning: anti-enclosure, neighborhood, travel, subsistence, and reparation. A major illusion of capitalist democracy is value for value, or the exchange of equivalents. It is illusory because both the organization of reproduction and labor markets and the organization of production and surplus value depend on those letters of blood and fire that referred both to written law and to the practice of state terror and violence. In full

---

7. Petr Kropotkin, *The Great French Revolution,* trans. N. F. Dryhurst (New York: Vanguard Press, 1929); and Teodor Shanin, ed., *Late Marx and the Russian Road: Marx and "the Peripheries of Capitalism"* (New York: Monthly Review Press, 1983).

cognizance of both charters we must recover more: we want the letters of azure and gold.

During the Great Depression the idea of the commons expressed desires of subsistence, community, and cooperation without encumbrances of the rule of law or due process of law. This is why in the early twentieth century such opposites as the revitalization of decadent bourgeois society or the critique of commerce and industrial capitalism might appeal to the commons even at the risk of fascist and right-wing agrarian programs. Just as it became all misty in the folkish fog of fascism, the commons lost its actual connection with the actualities of nurturance. If anything, subsistence seemed to arise from the state, either as the cradle-to-the-grave welfare policy of Great Britain, the New Deal legislation of the United States, the promises of the five-year plans in the Soviet Union, or National Socialism.

Aspirations of the commons nevertheless survived, even as estovers or housebote did. A modest, unpretentious memorial can be found at Runnymede with apparently nothing to do with Magna Carta. Two oral historians produced a book on sale at the Magna Carta tearoom of "the life stories of twenty-two ordinary people of Runnymede." It provides a microscopic view into the twentieth-century British working class. So many of the individuals were born before or during World War I, so many suffered from childhood diseases, some were orphaned, others fostered children left homeless. Ernie Holland had a "bad war," and he could not stop shaking and weeping for decades afterward. Rose Vincent said, "Life seemed one long catastrophe." Many worked in the empire or overseas—Burma, North Africa, Spain, Australia, New Zealand, Ireland, Naples, Poland,

Canada. Many worked during the postwar engineering boom, at Vickers, building Spitfires, Wellingtons, and other weapons of war. Although there is one reference to a communal water well, the commoning experienced by this testimony was either of an emergency kind—survival during the Battle of Britain, in which the self-activity of ordinary people discovered sharing—or it was indirect and a result of the postwar welfare state. Time after time the happiest moment, the "luckiest," was the acquisition of a council flat. Housing was a fulfillment of the demand of the Diggers in 1649. Of the twenty-two people, fourteen were widows and they have their estovers, by which I simply mean that they do not lack fuel, shelter, and nurturance.[8]

Lord Justice Laws of a British high court in November 2000 referred to Magna Carta's chapter 42, declaring that exile without due process of law is prohibited. (In Palestine this would be called the "right of return.") The case was this. The United States made a secret 1966 deal with the British government to purchase Diego Garcia, one of the islands forming part of the Chagos Archipelago in the Indian Ocean, for the price of a discounted nuclear submarine. Its thousands of inhabitants were tricked or terrorized into exile. Swept of people, it acquired a military base from which U.S. aircraft took off to bomb Afghanistan.[9]

About two hundred years earlier, the first British embassy to Afghanistan made its way across the Indus River to Peshawar in

---

8. Ray Ward and Jean Simpson, *Harvest of Lives: The Life Stories of Twenty-two Ordinary People of Runnymede Spanning almost One Hundred Years* (Surrey: R. and H. Ward Systems, 2003).

9. John Pilger, *Freedom Next Time* (London: Bantam Press, 2006); and *The Guardian,* 29 May 2006.

1808. Leading it was Mountstuart Elphinstone, a twenty-nine-year-old soldier and scholar, his mind trained in the heady enlightened days of 1791 Edinburgh, who carried with him a copy of the Roman historian Tacitus. The young ambassador mulled over the observations of Tacitus on the commoning practices of central Europe in the first century. The land in Afghanistan was more equally divided than anywhere else he knew of, and that equality was preserved by the democratic constitution (as Elphinstone put it) and the custom of the *waish* or periodic land redistribution.[10] The passage in Tacitus poses difficulty but it is not a philological problem of translation or one of textual integrity; it lies in the reader's ability to recognize the level of historical reality, or commoning. Shortly after publishing *Das Kapital* (1867), Marx came across the same passage. In an extraordinary letter to Engels he pointed out how the passage had been mistranslated by the brothers Grimm and then exclaimed with the pride of a homeboy, remembering his father's words to him as a child, how the old Germanic system of commoning survived "right in *my own* neighbourhood."[11]

"Common" has a multitude of meanings—common land, common rights, common people, common sense. In 1598 John Manwood published *A Treatise and Discourse of the Lawes of the Forrest* in which he attempted to answer the question, "what Common is, and whereof named Common."

10. Mountstuart Elphinstone, *An Account of the Kingdom of Caubul* (London: Longman, Rees, Orme, Brown, and J. Murray, 1815), 2:16–18.

11. The disputed passage in Tacitus is from chap. 26 of his *Germania*. Marx to Engels, 25 March 1868, in Karl Marx and Frederick Engels, *Selected Correspondence,* trans. I. Lasker, ed. S. Ryazanskaya (Moscow: Progress Publishers, 1965), 201.

> It taketh the name of Common, a Communitate, of communitie, participation, or fellowship, because that most commonly, where men have common of pasture for the feeding of their beastes or cattell, many mens cattell do use to feedde there together.

A hundred and fifteen years later a fourth edition, "corrected and enlarged," was published in which this passage was rendered without the term "fellowship."[12] In this way the textual codification of commoning was misrendered and diminished. The meanings imprinted in text were subject to further closure in the removal of a powerful term of sharing, agency, and equality.

To speak of the commons as if it were a natural resource is misleading at best and dangerous at worst—the commons is an activity and, if anything, it expresses relationships in society that are inseparable from relations to nature. It might be better to keep the word as a verb, an activity, rather than as a noun, a substantive. But this too is a trap. Capitalists and the World Bank would like us to employ commoning as a means to socialize poverty and hence to privatize wealth. The commoning of the past, our forebears' previous labor, survives as a legacy in the form of *capital* and this too must be reclaimed as part of our constitution. Chapter 61 giving liberty to the *communa totius terrae* provides the right of resistance to the reality of a planet of slums, gated communities, and terror without end.

Three propositions leap forth concerning the mass, the ideas, and the willingness to contribute to that planetary common. One: there are more proletarians, both relatively and absolutely, on the

---

12. John Manwood, *A Treatise and Discourse of the Lawes of the Forrest* (1598; New York: Garland, 1978); and *Manwood's Treatise of the Forest Laws,* ed. William Nelson ([London]: Printed by E. Nutt for B. Lintott, 1717), 84.

face of the earth now than ever before in history, so even as the conservatives trumpet "the end of history," the class that can abolish all classes is a democratic possibility. Two: there are active movements of human commoning and worldwide demands to share wealth and safeguard common resources on every continent, from movements of urban gardening to transcontinental oil swaps, efforts of actual autonomous communism. Three: there is a militant movement that wages war against American imperialism. These propositions demand that we be up and doing, as left to themselves they spell defeat or disaster. The Charters of Liberties do not call for regrets or nostalgia, and certainly not for restoration of medievalism. Of course it is not our duty to fulfill *their* promise, though they remain ready, as this book has tried to indicate, to help us to fulfill *ours*.

APPENDIX

The Great Charters of the Liberties of England; or, Magna Carta and the Charter of the Forest

MAGNA CARTA

Three versions of Magna Carta are important in this study, that of 1215, that of 1217, and that of 1225. The earliest has sixty-three chapters, and this is the one whose English translation is appended here, with one significant emendation from the 1217 version. The addition is in chapter 7 concerning the widow's estovers. As Maitland says "substantially it is in 1217 that the charter takes its final form," and the charter of 1225 is the Magna Carta of future times. The clause regarding estovers in the common remains in the 1225 text, despite the omission of other chapters appearing in the 1215 version, thus giving it fewer chapters (forty-seven in 1217, thirty-seven in 1225). Clauses marked [*] were omitted in all later reissues of the charter. In the charter itself the clauses are unnumbered, and the text reads continuously.

JOHN, by the grace of God King of England, Lord of Ireland, Duke of Normandy and Aquitaine, and Count of Anjou, to his archbishops, bishops, abbots, earls, barons, justices, foresters, sheriffs, stewards, servants, and to all his officials and loyal subjects, Greeting.

KNOW THAT BEFORE GOD, for the health of our soul and those of our ancestors and heirs, to the honour of God, the exaltation of the holy Church, and the better ordering of our kingdom, at the advice of our reverend fathers Stephen, archbishop of Canterbury, primate of all England, and cardinal of the holy Roman Church, Henry archbishop of Dublin, William bishop of London, Peter bishop of Winchester, Jocelin bishop of Bath and Glastonbury, Hugh bishop of Lincoln, Walter bishop of Worcester, William bishop of Coventry, Benedict bishop of Rochester, Master Pandulf subdeacon and member of the papal household, Brother Aymeric master of the knighthood of the Temple in England, William Marshal earl of Pembroke, William earl of Salisbury, William earl of Warren, William earl of Arundel, Alan de Galloway constable of Scotland, Warin Fitz Gerald, Peter Fitz Herbert, Hubert de Burgh seneschal of Poitou, Hugh de Neville, Matthew Fitz Herbert, Thomas Basset, Alan Basset, Philip Daubeny, Robert de Roppeley, John Marshal, John Fitz Hugh, and other loyal subjects:

[1] FIRST, THAT WE HAVE GRANTED TO GOD, and by this present charter have confirmed for us and our heirs in perpetuity, that the English Church shall be free, and shall have its rights undiminished, and its liberties unimpaired. That we wish this so to be observed, appears from the fact that of our own free will, before the outbreak of the present dispute between us and our barons, we granted and confirmed by charter the freedom of the Church's elections—a right reckoned to be of the greatest necessity and importance to it—and caused this to be confirmed by

Pope Innocent III. This freedom we shall observe ourselves, and desire to be observed in good faith by our heirs in perpetuity.

TO ALL FREE MEN OF OUR KINGDOM we have also granted, for us and our heirs for ever, all the liberties written out below, to have and to keep for them and their heirs, of us and our heirs:

[2] If any earl, baron, or other person that holds lands directly of the Crown, for military service, shall die, and at his death his heir shall be of full age and owe a 'relief', the heir shall have his inheritance on payment of the ancient scale of 'relief'. That is to say, the heir or heirs of an earl shall pay £100 for the entire earl's barony, the heir or heirs of a knight 100s. at most for the entire knight's 'fee', and any man that owes less shall pay less, in accordance with the ancient usage of 'fees'

[3] But if the heir of such a person is under age and a ward, when he comes of age he shall have his inheritance without 'relief' or fine.

[4] The guardian of the land of an heir who is under age shall take from it only reasonable revenues, customary dues, and feudal services. He shall do this without destruction or damage to men or property. If we have given the guardianship of the land to a sheriff, or to any person answerable to us for the revenues, and he commits destruction or damage, we will exact compensation from him, and the land shall be entrusted to two worthy and prudent men of the same 'fee', who shall be answerable to us for the revenues, or to the person to whom we have assigned them. If we have given or sold to anyone the guardianship of such land, and he causes destruction or damage, he shall lose the guardianship of it, and it shall be handed over to two worthy and prudent men of the same 'fee', who shall be similarly answerable to us.

[5] For so long as a guardian has guardianship of such land, he shall maintain the houses, parks, fish preserves, ponds, mills, and everything else pertaining to it, from the revenues of the land itself. When the heir comes of age, he shall restore the whole land to him, stocked with plough teams and such implements of husbandry as the season demands and the revenues from the land can reasonably bear.

[6] Heirs may be given in marriage, but not to someone of lower social standing. Before a marriage takes place, it shall be made known to the heir's next-of-kin.

[7] At her husband's death, a widow may have her marriage portion and inheritance at once and without trouble. She shall pay nothing for her dower, marriage portion, or any inheritance that she and her husband held jointly on the day of his death. She may remain in her husband's house for forty days after his death, and within this period her dower shall be assigned to her, *and she shall have meanwhile her reasonable estover in the common. There shall be assigned to her for her dower a third of all her husband's land which was his in his lifetime, unless a smaller share was given her at the church door.* [1217 and 1225] *No widow shall be forced to marry so long as she wishes to live without a husband, provided that she gives security not to marry without our consent if she holds of us, or without the consent of her lord if she holds of another.*

[8] No widow shall be compelled to marry, so long as she wishes to remain without a husband. But she must give security that she will not marry without royal consent, if she holds her lands of the Crown, or without the consent of whatever other lord she may hold them of.

[9] Neither we nor our officials will seize any land or rent in

payment of a debt, so long as the debtor has movable goods sufficient to discharge the debt. A debtor's sureties shall not be distrained upon so long as the debtor himself can discharge his debt. If, for lack of means, the debtor is unable to discharge his debt, his sureties shall be answerable for it. If they so desire, they may have the debtor's lands and rents until they have received satisfaction for the debt that they paid for him, unless the debtor can show that he has settled his obligations to them.

[* 10] If anyone who has borrowed a sum of money from Jews dies before the debt has been repaid, his heir shall pay no interest on the debt for so long as he remains under age, irrespective of whom he holds his lands. If such a debt falls into the hands of the Crown, it will take nothing except the principal sum specified in the bond.

[* 11] If a man dies owing money to Jews, his wife may have her dower and pay nothing towards the debt from it. If he leaves children that are under age, their needs may also be provided for on a scale appropriate to the size of his holding of lands. The debt is to be paid out of the residue, reserving the service due to his feudal lords. Debts owed to persons other than Jews are to be dealt with similarly.

[* 12] No 'scutage' or 'aid' may be levied in our kingdom without its general consent, unless it is for the ransom of our person, to make our eldest son a knight, and once to marry our eldest daughter. For these purposes only a reasonable 'aid' may be levied. 'Aids' from the city of London are to be treated similarly.

[13] The city of London shall enjoy all its ancient liberties and free customs, both by land and by water. We also will and grant that all other cities, boroughs, towns, and ports shall enjoy all their liberties and free customs.

[* 14] To obtain the general consent of the realm for the assessment of an 'aid'—except in the three cases specified above—or a
'scutage', we will cause the archbishops, bishops, abbots, earls, and
greater barons to be summoned individually by letter. To those
who hold lands directly of us we will cause a general summons to
be issued, through the sheriffs and other officials, to come together
on a fixed day (of which at least forty days notice shall be given)
and at a fixed place. In all letters of summons, the cause of the summons will be stated. When a summons has been issued, the business appointed for the day shall go forward in accordance with the
resolution of those present, even if not all those who were summoned have appeared.

[* 15] In future we will allow no one to levy an 'aid' from his
free men, except to ransom his person, to make his eldest son a
knight, and (once) to marry his eldest daughter. For these purposes only a reasonable 'aid' may be levied.

[16] No man shall be forced to perform more service for a
knight's 'fee', or other free holding of land, than is due from it.

[17] Ordinary lawsuits shall not follow the royal court around,
but shall be held in a fixed place.

[18] Inquests of *novel disseisin, mort d'ancestor,* and *darrein presentment* shall be taken only in their proper county court. We
ourselves, or in our absence abroad our chief justice, will send
two justices to each county four times a year, and these justices,
with four knights of the county elected by the county itself, shall
hold the assizes in the county court, on the day and in the place
where the court meets.

[19] If any assizes cannot be taken on the day of the county
court, as many knights and freeholders shall afterwards remain
behind, of those who have attended the court, as will suffice for

the administration of justice, having regard to the volume of business to be done.

[20] For a trivial offence, a free man shall be fined only in proportion to the degree of his offence, and for a serious offence correspondingly, but not so heavily as to deprive him of his livelihood. In the same way, a merchant shall be spared his merchandise, and a husbandman the implements of his husbandry, if they fall upon the mercy of a royal court. None of these fines shall be imposed except by the assessment on oath of reputable men of the neighbourhood.

[21] Earls and barons shall be fined only by their equals, and in proportion to the gravity of their offence.

[22] A fine imposed upon the lay property of a clerk in holy orders shall be assessed upon the same principles, without reference to the value of his ecclesiastical benefice.

[23] No town or person shall be forced to build bridges over rivers except those with an ancient obligation to do so.

[24] No sheriff, constable, coroners, or other royal officials are to hold lawsuits that should be held by the royal justices.

[* 25] Every county, hundred, wapentake [a subdivision of the shire], and tithing shall remain at its ancient rent, without increase, except the royal demesne manors.

[26] If at the death of a man who holds a lay 'fee' of the Crown, a sheriff or royal official produces royal letters patent of summons for a debt due to the Crown, it shall be lawful for them to seize and list movable goods found in the lay 'fee' of the dead man to the value of the debt, as assessed by worthy men. Nothing shall be removed until the whole debt is paid, when the residue shall be given over to the executors to carry out the dead man's will. If no debt is due to the Crown, all the movable goods

shall be regarded as the property of the dead man, except the reasonable shares of his wife and children.

[* 27] If a free man dies intestate, his movable goods are to be distributed by his next-of-kin and friends, under the supervision of the Church. The rights of his debtors are to be preserved.

[28] No constable or other royal official shall take corn or other movable goods from any man without immediate payment, unless the seller voluntarily offers postponement of this.

[29] No constable may compel a knight to pay money for castle-guard if the knight is willing to undertake the guard in person, or with reasonable excuse to supply some other fit man to do it. A knight taken or sent on military service shall be excused from castle-guard for the period of this service.

[30] No sheriff, royal official, or other person shall take horses or carts for transport from any free man, without his consent.

[31] Neither we nor any royal official will take wood for our castle, or for any other purpose, without the consent of the owner.

[32] We will not keep the lands of people convicted of felony in our hand for longer than a year and a day, after which they shall be returned to the lords of the 'fees' concerned.

[33] All fish-weirs shall be removed from the Thames, the Medway, and throughout the whole of England, except on the sea coast.

[34] The writ called *precipe* shall not in future be issued to anyone in respect of any holding of land, if a free man could thereby be deprived of the right of trial in his own lord's court.

[35] There shall be standard measures of wine, ale, and corn (the London quarter), throughout the kingdom. There shall also be a standard width of dyed cloth, russett, and haberject, namely two ells within the selvedges. Weights are to be standardised similarly.

[36] In future nothing shall be paid or accepted for the issue of

a writ of inquisition of life or limbs. It shall be given gratis, and not refused.

[37] If a man holds land of the Crown by 'fee-farm', 'socage', or 'burgage', and also holds land of someone else for knight's service, we will not have guardianship of his heir, nor of the land that belongs to the other person's 'fee', by virtue of the 'fee-farm', 'socage', or 'burgage', unless the 'fee-farm' owes knight's service. We will not have the guardianship of a man's heir, or of land that he holds of someone else, by reason of any small property that he may hold of the Crown for a service of knives, arrows, or the like.

[38] In future no official shall place a man on trial upon his own unsupported statement, without producing credible witnesses to the truth of it.

[39] No free man shall be seized or imprisoned, or stripped of his rights or possessions, or outlawed or exiled, or deprived of his standing in any other way, nor will we proceed with force against him, or send others to do so, except by the lawful judgement of his equals or by the law of the land.

[40] To no one will we sell, to no one deny or delay right or justice.

[41] All merchants may enter or leave England unharmed and without fear, and may stay or travel within it, by land or water, for purposes of trade, free from all illegal exactions, in accordance with ancient and lawful customs. This, however, does not apply in time of war to merchants from a country that is at war with us. Any such merchants found in our country at the outbreak of war shall be detained without injury to their persons or property, until we or our chief justice have discovered how our own merchants are being treated in the country at war with us. If our own merchants are safe they shall be safe too.

[* 42] In future it shall be lawful for any man to leave and return to our kingdom unharmed and without fear, by land or water, preserving his allegiance to us, except in time of war, for some short period, for the common benefit of the realm. People that have been imprisoned or outlawed in accordance with the law of the land, people from a country that is at war with us, and merchants—who shall be dealt with as stated above—are excepted from this provision.

[43] If a man holds lands of any 'escheat' such as the 'honour' of Wallingford, Nottingham, Boulogne, Lancaster, or of other 'escheats' in our hand that are baronies, at his death his heir shall give us only the 'relief' and service that he would have made to the baron, had the barony been in the baron's hand. We will hold the 'escheat' in the same manner as the baron held it.

[44] People who live outside the forest need not in future appear before the royal justices of the forest in answer to general summonses, unless they are actually involved in proceedings or are sureties for someone who has been seized for a forest offence.

[* 45] We will appoint as justices, constables, sheriffs, or other officials, only men that know the law of the realm and are minded to keep it well.

[46] All barons who have founded abbeys, and have charters of English kings or ancient tenure as evidence of this, may have guardianship of them when there is no abbot, as is their due.

[47] All forests that have been created in our reign shall at once be disafforested. River-banks that have been enclosed in our reign shall be treated similarly.

[* 48] All evil customs relating to forests and warrens, foresters, warreners, sheriffs and their servants, or river-banks and their wardens, are at once to be investigated in every county

by twelve sworn knights of the county, and within forty days of their enquiry the evil customs are to be abolished completely and irrevocably. But we, or our chief justice if we are not in England, are first to be informed.

[* 49] We will at once return all hostages and charters delivered up to us by Englishmen as security for peace or for loyal service.

[* 50] We will remove completely from their offices the kinsmen of Gerard de Athée, and in future they shall hold no offices in England. The people in question are Engelard de Cigogné, Peter, Guy, and Andrew de Chanceaux, Guy de Cigogné, Geoffrey de Martigny and his brothers, Philip Marc and his brothers, with Geoffrey his nephew, and all their followers.

[* 51] As soon as peace is restored, we will remove from the kingdom all the foreign knights, bowmen, their attendants, and the mercenaries that have come to it, to its harm, with horses and arms.

[* 52] To any man whom we have deprived or dispossessed of lands, castles, liberties, or rights, without the lawful judgement of his equals, we will at once restore these. In cases of dispute the matter shall be resolved by the judgement of the twenty-five barons referred to below in the clause for securing the peace [§ 61]. In cases, however, where a man was deprived or dispossessed of something without the lawful judgement of his equals by our father King Henry or our brother King Richard, and it remains in our hands or is held by others under our warranty, we shall have respite for the period commonly allowed to Crusaders, unless a lawsuit had been begun, or an enquiry had been made at our order, before we took the Cross as a Crusader. On our return from the Crusade, or if we abandon it, we will at once render justice in full.

[* 53] We shall have similar respite in rendering justice in connetion with forests that are to be disafforested, or to remain forests, when these were first afforested by our father Henry or our brother Richard; with the guardianship of lands in another person's 'fee', when we have hitherto had this by virtue of a 'fee' held of us for knight's service by a third party; and with abbeys founded in another person's 'fee', in which the lord of the 'fee' claims to own a right. On our return from the Crusade, or if we abandon it, we will at once do full justice to complaints about these matters.

[54] No one shall be arrested or imprisoned on the appeal of a woman for the death of any person except her husband.

[* 55] All fines that have been given to us unjustly and against the law of the land, and all fines that we have exacted unjustly, shall be entirely remitted or the matter decided by a majority judgement of the twenty-five barons referred to below in the clause for securing the peace [§ 61] together with Stephen, archbishop of Canterbury, if he can be present, and such others as he wishes to bring with him. If the archbishop cannot be present, proceedings shall continue without him, provided that if any of the twenty-five barons has been involved in a similar suit himself, his judgement shall be set aside, and someone else chosen and sworn in his place, as a substitute for the single occasion, by the rest of the twenty-five.

[56] If we have deprived or dispossessed any Welshmen of lands, liberties, or anything else in England or in Wales, without the lawful judgement of their equals, these are at once to be returned to them. A dispute on this point shall be determined in the Marches by the judgement of equals. English law shall apply to holdings of land in England, Welsh law to those in Wales, and the

law of the Marches to those in the Marches. The Welsh shall treat us and ours in the same way.

[* 57] In cases where a Welshman was deprived or dispossessed of anything, without the lawful judgement of his equals, by our father King Henry or our brother King Richard, and it remains in our hands or is held by others under our warranty, we shall have respite for the period commonly allowed to Crusaders, unless a lawsuit had been begun, or an enquiry had been made at our order, before we took the Cross as a Crusader. But on our return from the Crusade, or if we abandon it, we will at once do full justice according to the laws of Wales and the said regions.

[* 58] We will at once return the son of Llywelyn, all Welsh hostages, and the charters delivered to us as security for the peace.

[* 59] With regard to the return of the sisters and hostages of Alexander, king of Scotland, his liberties and his rights, we will treat him in the same way as our other barons of England, unless it appears from the charters that we hold from his father William, formerly king of Scotland, that he should be treated otherwise. This matter shall be resolved by the judgement of his equals in our court.

[60] All these customs and liberties that we have granted shall be observed in our kingdom in so far as concerns our own relations with our subjects. Let all men of our kingdom, whether clergy or laymen, observe them similarly in their relations with their own men.

[* 61] SINCE WE HAVE GRANTED ALL THESE THINGS for God, for the better ordering of our kingdom, and to allay the discord that has arisen between us and our barons, and since we desire that they shall be enjoyed in their entirety, with lasting

strength, for ever, we give and grant to the barons the following security:

The barons shall elect twenty-five of their number to keep, and cause to be observed with all their might, the peace and liberties granted and confirmed to them by this charter.

If we, our chief justice, our officials, or any of our servants offend in any respect against any man, or transgress any of the articles of the peace or of this security, and the offence is made known to four of the said twenty-five barons, they shall come to us—or in our absence from the kingdom to the chief justice—to declare it and claim immediate redress. If we, or in our absence abroad the chief justice, make no redress within forty days, reckoning from the day on which the offence was declared to us or to him, the four barons shall refer the matter to the rest of the twenty-five barons, who may distrain upon and assail us in every way possible, with the support of the whole community of the land, by seizing our castles, lands, possessions, or anything else saving only our own person and those of the queen and our children, until they have secured such redress as they have determined upon. Having secured the redress, they may then resume their normal obedience to us.

Any man who so desires may take an oath to obey the commands of the twenty-five barons for the achievement of these ends, and to join with them in assailing us to the utmost of his power. We give public and free permission to take this oath to any man who so desires, and at no time will we prohibit any man from taking it. Indeed, we will compel any of our subjects who are unwilling to take it to swear it at our command.

If one of the twenty-five barons dies or leaves the country, or is prevented in any other way from discharging his duties, the rest of them shall choose another baron in his place, at their discretion, who shall be duly sworn in as they were.

In the event of disagreement among the twenty-five barons on any matter referred to them for decision, the verdict of the majority present shall have the same validity as a unanimous verdict of the whole twenty-five, whether these were all present or some of those summoned were unwilling or unable to appear.

The twenty-five barons shall swear to obey all the above articles faithfully, and shall cause them to be obeyed by others to the best of their power.

We will not seek to procure from anyone, either by our own efforts or those of a third party, anything by which any part of these concessions or liberties might be revoked or diminished. Should such a thing be procured, it shall be null and void and we will at no time make use of it, either ourselves or through a third party.

[* 62] We have remitted and pardoned fully to all men any ill-will, hurt, or grudges that have arisen between us and our subjects, whether clergy or laymen, since the beginning of the dispute. We have in addition remitted fully, and for our own part have also pardoned, to all clergy and laymen any offences committed as a result of the said dispute between Easter in the sixteenth year of our reign [i.e., 1215] and the restoration of peace.

In addition we have caused letters patent to be made for the barons, bearing witness to this security and to the concessions set out above, over the seals of Stephen archbishop of Canterbury, Henry archbishop of Dublin, the other bishops named above, and Master Pandulf.

[* 63] IT IS ACCORDINGLY OUR WISH AND COMMAND that the English Church shall be free, and that men in our kingdom shall have and keep all these liberties, rights, and concessions, well and

peaceably in their fulness and entirety for them and their heirs, of us and our heirs, in all things and all places for ever.

THE GREAT CHARTER OF THE FOREST

The following is a 1680 translation of *The Great Charter of the Forest* from 1225, confirmed by Edward I in 1299. This translation has been chosen not only because it has the authority of being used by Edward Coke in his fourth *Institute of the Laws of England* (1642). Its seventeenth-century spelling and capitalization along with the archaisms will, it is hoped, cause the work of semantic comprehension to lead to an interest in the recovery of the commoning practices subsequently lost in smoother versions.

Henry, by the Grace of God, King of England, Lord of Ireland, Duke of Normandy and Guyan, and Earl of Anjou, to all Archbishops, Bishops, Abbots, Priors, Earls, Barons, Sheriffs, Provosts, Officers, and to all Bailiffs, and other our Faithful Subjects, who shall see this present Charter, greetings. Know ye, That We, unto the Honour of Almighty god, and for the Salvation of our souls of our Progenitors and Successors Kings of England, to the advancement of Holy Church, and amendment of our Realm, of our meer and free will have given and granted to all Archbishops, Bishops, Abbots, Priors, Earls, Barons, and to all Freemen of this our Realm, these Liberties following, to be kept in our Kingdom of England for ever.

[1] We will, that all Forests, which King Henry our Grandfather afforested, shall be view'd by good and lawfull men; and if he hath afforested any other Wood, more than his own Demesne, by which the Owner of the Wood hath damage, it shall be forthwith disafforested; and if he hath afforested his own Wood, then

it shall remain Forest: saving the Common of Herbage, and of other things in the same Forest, to them who before were accustomed to have the same.

[2] Men that dwell out of the Forest, from henceforth shall not come before the Justices of our Forest by common Summons, except they be impleaded there, or be Sureties for some others that were Attached for the Forest.

[3] All Woods that have been made Forest by King Richard our Uncle, or by King John our Father, until our first Coronation, shall be forthwith, disafforested, unless it be our Demesne Wood.

[4] All Archbishops, Bishops, Abbots, Priors, Earls, Barons, Knights, and other Freeholders, who have their Woods in Forests, shall have their Woods as they had them at the first Coronation of Henry our Grandfather, so that they shall be quit for ever of all Purprestures, Wastes, and Asserts [assarts], made in those Woods, after that time until the beginning of the second year of our Coronation: And those who from henceforth do make Purpresture without our License, or Waste, or Assert in the same, shall answer unto us for the same Wastes, Purprestures, and Asserts.

[5] Our Rangers shall go through the Forests to make range, as it hath been accustomed at the time of the First Coronation of King Henry our Grandfather, and not otherwise.

[6] The Enquiry or view of Lawing of Dogs within our Forest, shall be made from henceforth, when the Range is made, that is to say, from three year to three year, and then it shall be done by the view and testimony of lawful men, and not otherwise. And he whose Dog is not lawed, and so found, shall pay for his amercement three shillings. And from henceforth no Ox shall be taken for lawing of Dogs. And such lawing shall be done by the Assise commonly used, that is to say, that three claws of the forefoot shall be cut off by

the skin. But from henceforth such lawing of Dogs shall not be, but in places where it hath been accustomed from the time of the first Coronation of the aforesaid King Henry our Grandfather.

[7] No Forester or Bedle from henceforth shall make Scotal, or gather Garb or Oates, or any Corn, Lamb, or Pig; nor shall make any Gathering, but the Sight, and upon the Oath of the Twelve Rangers, when they shall make their Range. So many Foresters shall be assigned to the Keeping of the Forests, as reasonably shall seem sufficient for the Keeping of the same.

[8] No Swanimote from henceforth shall be kept within this our Realm, but thrice in the Year; viz. In the Beginning of Fifteen Dayes afore Michaelmass, when that our Gest-takers, or Walkers of our Woods come together, to take Agistment in our Demesne Woods; and about the Feast of Saint Martin, in the Winter, when our Gest-takers shall receive our Pawnage. And to these two Swanimotes, shall come together our Foresters, Verderors, Gest-takers, and none other by Distress. And the Third Swanimote shall be kept in the Beginning of Fifteen Dayes before the Feast of Saint John Baptists, when that our Gest-takers do meet to Hunt our Deer. And at this Swanimote shall meet our Foresters, Verderors, and none other by Distress. Moreover, every Forty Dayes through the Year our Foresters and Verderors shall meet, to see the Attachments of the Forest, as well for Greenhue, as for Hunting, by the Presentment of the same Forester, and before them Attached. And the said Swanimotes shall not be kept, but within the Counties wherein they have used to be kept.

[9] Every Free-Man may Agist his own Wood within Our Forest, at his Pleasure, and shall take his Pawnage. Also, We do grant, That every Free-Man may drive his Swine freely; without Impediment, through our Demesne Woods, to Agist them in their

own Woods, or where else they will. And if the Swine of any Free-Man lie one Night without our Forest, there shall be no Occasion taken thereof, whereby he may lose any thing of his own.

[10] No Man from henceforth shall lose either Life, or Member, for Killing of Our Deer: But if a Man be Taken, and Convict for Taking of Our Venison, he shall make a Grievous Fine, if he have any thing whereof. And if he have nothing to lose, he shall be Imprisoned a Year, and a Day: And after the Year and the Day is expired, if he can find sufficient Sureties, he shall be Delivered; and if not, he shall Abjure the Realm of England.

[11] Whatsoever Archbishop, Bishop, Earl, or Baron, coming to Us at Our Commandment, passing by our Forest; it shall be Lawful for him to Take and Kill one or two of our Deer, by View of our Forester, if he be present; or else he shall cause one to blow a Horn for him, that he seem not to Steal Our Deer. And they shall do so likewise in their Return from Us, as it is aforesaid.

[12] Every Free-Man from henceforth, without Danger, shall make in his own Wood, or in his Land, or in his Water, which he hath within Our Forest; Mills, Springs, Pools, Marsh-Pits, Dikes, or Earable Ground, without inclosing that Earable Ground; so that it be not to the Annoyance of any of his Neighbours.

[13] Every Free-Man shall have within his own Woods Ayries of Hawkes, Sparrow-Hawkes, Falcons, Eagles, and Herons; and shall have also the Honey that is found within his Woods.

[14] No Forester from henceforth, who is not Forester in Fee, paying to Us Ferm for his Bailywick, shall take any Chiminage, or Toll within his Bailywick: But a Forester in Fee, paying Us Ferm for his Bailywick, shall take Chiminage; that is to say, for Carriage by Cart, the Half-Year Two Pence, and for another Half-Year Two Pence: for an Horse that beareth Loads, every

Half-Year an Half-Penny; and by another Half-Year, an Half-Penny. And but of those only that come as Merchants through his Bailywick by License, to buy Bushes, Timber, Bark, Cole; and to sell it again at their Pleasure. But for none other Carriage by Cart Chiminage shall be taken. Nor Chiminage shall not be taken, but in such Places only where it hath been used to be. Those who bear upon their Backs Brushment, Bark, or Coal to sell, though it be their Living, shall pay no Chiminage to our Forester, except they take it within our Demesne Woods.

[15] All that be Our-Law'd for the Forest only, since the time of King Henry our Grand-Father, until our first Coronation, shall come to our Peace without Lett, and shall find to us Sureties, That from henceforth they shall not Trespass unto us, within our forest.

[16] No Constable, Castellani, or Bailiff, shall hold Plea of Forest, neither for Greenhue nor Venison, but every Forester in Fee shall make Attachments for Pleas of Forest, as well for Greenhue, as Venison; and shall present them to the Verderors of the Provinces. And when they be Inrolled and Inclosed under the Seals of the Verderors; they shall be presented to our Chief Justices of our Forest; when they shall come into those Parts, to hold the Pleas of the Forest, and before them they shall be determined. And these Liberties of the Forest, we have granted to all Men; Archbishops, Bishops, Abbots, Priors, Earls, Barons, Knights, and to other Persons, as well Spiritual, as Temporal, Templars, Hospitallers, their Liberties and free Customes, as well within the Forest, as without, and in Warrens, and other places, which they had. All these Liberties and Customes, We, &c. as it is in the End of MAGNA CHARTA, and We do confirm and ratify these gifts, &c. as you may see there too is specified, &c.

GLOSSARY

The following definitions depend on the *OED* or the *Oxford New English Dictionary on Historical Principles,* on Raymond Williams, *Keywords: A Vocabulary of Culture and Society* (New York: Oxford University Press, 1976), Ambrose Bierce, *The Devil's Dictionary* (New York: Dover, 1958), Captain Grose, *Classical Dictionary of the Vulgar Tongue,* 3rd edition (1796), and on Iain Boal's glossary in *The Battle of Seattle: The New Challenge to Capitalist Globalization,* ed. Eddie Yuen, Daniel Burton Rose, and George Katsiaficas (New York: Soft Skull Press, 2001). To several medieval archaisms I've added a modern amplification, abbreviated mod. amp.

AFFOREST. To convert into a forest or hunting ground; Henry II afforested many woods and wooded wastes. Essentially, a juridical process or type of management, rather than an act of planting.

AGISTMENT. The action of opening a forest for a specified time to livestock; "the common of herbage" (Manwood, *Treatise and Discourse of the Lawes of the Forrest* [1598]). Free range is a restricted mod. amp.; milk, bacon, and beef are an expanded mod. amp.

AMERCEMENTS. The infliction of a penalty left to the "mercy" of the inflictor, generally milder than a fixed fine.

ANGLOPHONOPHILIA. Literally, love of an English speaker (anglophone + philia); the mask that formerly disguised a predisposition of white supremacy.

ASIENTO. The license or contract granted by the Treaty of Utrecht (1713) for allowing the subjects of Great Britain to import African slaves into Spanish America.

ASSART. A piece of forest land converted to arable by grubbing up trees and brushwood; the action of doing so. Urban squats qualify as a mod. amp.

BALKS. A strip of ground left unplowed as a boundary line between two plowed portions; as an area at the end of the furrow in which to turn the plow and its team of oxen. Covetous men plow up "the common balks and walks."

BLACKING. The action of applying some substance to color something black. In the eighteenth century blacking became a means by which poachers and commoners disguised their individual identity while expressing sympathy with African slaves, sailors, and pirates.

BRANKS. A torture instrument applied to women said to be scolds. It consists of an iron framework enclosing the head with a sharp metal bit or gag that enters the mouth and restrains the tongue.

CABAL. A small group or clique of persons whose exact identity is disputed and who intrigue secretly for sinister purpose. Five aristocratic Whigs during Charles II's reign provide the acronym, Clifford, Arlington, Buckingham, Ashley, and Lauderdale. Like the conspiracy, its existence is doubted by historians, skeptics, and innocents.

CARTBOTE. An allowance of wood to a tenant for making and repairing carts, a definition suggesting that it is in the gift of the landlord rather than a right, custom, or entitlement. Public transport is one form of the mod. amp.

CAMPING. Besides sleeping outdoors or under tents, camping has meant contending or fighting, as well as an early form of football, such as a game of 1840 cited in the *OED* between the English counties Norfolk vs. Suffolk on Diss common with three hundred on a side; it lasted fourteen hours with several fatalities.

CHATTELS. Moveable possessions, property, goods, money; originally from Norman French appearing in the thirteenth-century vernacular, deriving from cattle or livestock as property. The *OED* comments on the two meanings, cattle and money, that "the history is better understood by treating the word as a historical whole."

CHIMINAGE. A toll formerly paid for passage through a forest, and expressly regulated to favor commoners by the Forest Charter. Mod. amp. = public transport.

CLOUTED SHOON. Patched shoes or shoes whose soles are studded with nails; expressing both poverty and outdoor work on rough ground requiring traction. Name for common people, like redneck, *bras nus,* sansculotte, blue-collar, or **hand** (q.v.).

COMMODITY. Something useful and something for sale. Also, female private parts, a meaning overlooked in Karl Marx's otherwise indispensable disquisition in *Das Kapital,* but more than hinted at in the Bastard's long speech in Shakespeare's *King John.*

COMMON LAW. The body of law derived from the accumulated weight of past judicial decisions, as distinct from law deriving from legislative **statute** (q.v.) or from the customs of a trade, locality, or commons.

COMMONS. From the quaint village commons to the cosmic commons of the electromagnetic spectrum, from the medieval subsistence economy to the general intellect, no term has been simultaneously so ignored and so contentious, so comic and tragic as this cognate of communism. It has provided the universal horizon upon which as Rousseau noted, the privatizer, the commodifier, and the capitalist have intruded with ever-increasing savagery. From monastic times it meant the allowance of victuals. Captain Grose provides an antidote to the theoretical meanings: he says it refers either to Parliament or to "the necessary house" (toilet).

COMMUNISM. With a little *c* it is the theory of society that both vests all property in the community and organizes labor for the common benefit of all. "From each according to his capacity, to each according to his needs." During the 1840s, the decade of the Irish potato famine, it was the "specter haunting Europe." The Irishman Bronterre O'Brien wrote the history of the Babeuf Conspiracy (1797), named after the first theorist of communism whose early experience was the defense of peasants' common rights.

COMMUNISM. With a big *C* it refers to the political party of the twentieth century whose ideology sought the overthrow of capitalism by proletarian revolution.

COMPURGATION. The process of clearing a person of an accusation by the oaths or testimony of others, "oath helpers." Local or class solidarity is a mod. amp.

CONSTITUTION. The political notion arising between 1689 and 1789 that a written document (U.S.A.) or documents (U.K.) could express and prescribe the principles of government of the body politic. It has other meanings, such as (1) the arrangement of parts to make a whole; (2) temperament of mind; (3) vitality and strength of body, all of which are much needed to augment the political notion. It can go nowhere until it includes *economic* relations.

COPPICE. Wood or thicket consisting of small trees grown for the purpose of periodical cutting.

COPYHOLD. A kind of ancient English land tenure, in contrast to the freeholder, held "at the will of the lord according to the custom of the manor" or by "immemorial custom." Valuable part of this tenure were the common or customary rights held by custom. In the era preceding photocopying machines it was held in the memory of most senior citizens.

COURT LEET. An annual or semiannual local court of record held in a hundred (a medieval administrative unit) or manor before the lord or steward and attended by all the residents of the district for administering common affairs. Neighborhood assemblies from Bolivia to Oaxaca are mod. amps.

DIGGERS. A section of the Levellers who in 1649 began to dig and plant the commons with parsnips, carrots, and beans. Hippies with the same name three centuries later added marijuana to the program. "You noble Diggers all, stand up now, stand up now."

DIPLOMATICS. Of or pertaining to official documents and charters; of the nature of official papers connected with international relations; of the pouch wherein such papers are transmitted.

DISAFFOREST. To exempt from the operation of the forest law; to reduce from the legal state of forest to ordinary land. See **afforest**. A mod. amp. is to return to commons.

DIVISION OF LABOR. Adam Smith gave it two meanings, (1) regional, national, or global specialization of production; and (2) the specialization of tasks within the workshop such as described in the famous example of pin manufacture. The former produces for the export sector leading to monoculture, the latter fractionates work so that it will be obediently and best done by the "stupid" worker, to use his description.

DRIFTS. Acts of driving of cattle within the forest to one place on a particular day to determine ownership, accompanied by hoots and hollers against the blowhards trumpeting the **tragedy of the commons** (q.v.).

DUE PROCESS OF LAW. Filling out the correct forms correctly, or to quote *Black's Law Dictionary,* "the conduct of legal proceedings according to established rules for the protection of private rights." In history of Magna Carta the phrase replaced "law of the land" (chapter 39), whose agrarian meaning necessarily included the commons. Thus, due process and commoning inhere.

EJIDO. Land distributed by the state to individual families or to villages of "tillers" that could not be sold, as prescribed by Article 27 of the 1917 Mexican Constitution.

ÉMEUTE. French term for riot, but this translation is far too simple to express the complexity of the sentiments and passions that lead to the action and its organization. In England the term "riot" was rarely employed during most riotous centuries; mutiny, commotion, turbulence served instead. *Émeute* and emotion have the same cognate.

ENCLOSURE. The action of surrounding land with a fence or hedge, the means of conversion from common land to private property. Juridically, accomplished by acts of Parliament, and actually measured out by the surveyor's chain, or "devil's guts" (slang). Considered by some the original sin of capitalism, a view challenged by Federici, who argues that the enclosure of land was preceded by that of the body, particularly the uterus.

ENCUENTRO. A term in Spanish referring to any meeting. It has been increasingly used by activists in the anti-globalization movement in Europe and North America who have taken the Zapatistas as their political reference point to refer to their international gatherings.

ESTOVERS. "Necessaries allowed by law" would be the translation from Norman French. *OED* says it refers to wood that a tenant is "privileged" to take from his landlord's estate so far as it is necessary for repairing his house, hedges, implements, etc. Under **boot** *OED* has "the right of a tenant to take timber, &c., for repairs, firing, and other necessary purposes." Ambrose Bierce in *The Devil's Dictionary* reminds us that the dictionary is "a malevolent literary device for cramping the growth of a language and making it hard and inelastic."

EYRE. An itinerant court, such as the forest eyre.

FELLOWSHIP. Participation, sharing, companionship are the key notions that the *OED* backs up with quotes from Wycliff, Coverdale, Milton, and Swift. The *OED* says "something in common" and quotes Caxton's *Aesop* offering as a pearl of class etiquette, "The poor ought not to hold fellowship with the mighty."

FENCE. A barrier, wall, hedge, railing, palisade, along the boundary of a park, field, yard, or any place from which intruders are to be excluded. Its etymology belongs with that of "defense." A belligerent action disguised as landscape or architecture, as with the Berlin Wall, the wall around Israel, or fence between the United States and Mexico.

FIREBOTE. The fuel granted by the landlord to the tenant, or the right of the tenant to take firewood from off the landlord's estate. Cf.

gasoline prices in Venezuela, or Nigerian oil taking, to find suitable mod. amps.

FOLK-MOTE. A general assembly of people, compared to a soviet, convention, powwow, or other deliberative gathering of people.

FOREST. Based on medieval Latin term meaning "the outside woods," i.e., unenclosed; a woodland district set apart for hunting and having special laws.

FRANKPLEDGE. A Norman mistranslation of an Anglo or Saxon term meaning an assembly of every inhabitant of a tithing. Eight hundred years later it was the bee in the bonnet of Granville Sharp, searching for a sweet resting place in India, France, and Africa.

FREEMAN. Mark Twain called the expression a sarcasm. Also an open gate to rhetoric that formerly all students were required to walk through: "Had you rather Caesar were living and die all slaves, than that Caesar were dead, to live all free men?" asked Brutus, wiping the still wet blood from the blade. A pedantic means employed by English history professors of crushing any remaining ideals among their students who might have thought there was more to the term than the meaning now foisted upon them of property relations.

FUEROS. These are Spanish equivalents to the medieval charters of England. The term originates in the Latin for forum, an open space, a meeting place, a market, and tribunal. It acknowledges rights rather than grants privileges. Used by militarists and corporativists to bypass legislation.

HABEAS CORPUS. "you should have the body" (Latin). A writ requiring a person named to be brought before a judge; requiring the body of a person restrained of liberty to be brought to court in order that the lawfulness of the restraint may be investigated and determined. Once rather grandly considered indispensable, now become increasingly passé.

A HAND. A person employed by another in any manual work; a worker. A mid-seventeenth-century contribution to the semantics of alienation. The First International referred to "workers of the hand and the brain."

HANGUM TUUM. A hanging; humorous parody of judicial Latin, always expressed in the second person. As a euphemism it belongs to the general class of payments vice pays to virtue; also to a subclass in which the judicial class accepts backtalk as long as it is expressed in a foreign tongue.

HAUBERK. Defensive armor made of chain mail at first to protect neck and shoulders, which evolved gownlike in the course of time and fashion to knee length.

HERBAGE. Herbaceous growth or vegetation; pasture, as distinct from the ground on which the grass grows.

HOUSEBOTE. "The right of a tenant to take wood to repair a house from a landlord's estate." Public housing is the mod. amp.

INSPEXIMUS. A charter in which the grantor avouches to have inspected an earlier charter that he recites and confirms. Latin for "we have inspected," the first words the king uses in confirmation of the charters.

JUNGLE. Derived from the Hindi word for waste or desert, uncultivated ground of "bewildering complexity" *(OED)*. In America a camp for tramps and hoboes.

JURY. A company of persons sworn to render a verdict or give a true answer to questions of fact, of law, or of mixed fact and law. Generally brow-beaten by judges, flattered by lawyers, and ill-paid by employers.

LEVELLERS. The activity of leveling those fences or digging up those hedges that privatized property, an activity that led to a political party under Charles I determined to level differences in rank or status.

LOPS AND TOPS. Cuttings or trimmings of superfluous growth from a tree.

MORAL ECONOMY. Whereas moral theology, moral law, and moral psychology will be found in *OED,* moral economy will not, yet at the end of the twentieth century it expressed a widespread, nonideological alternative to the commodity economy of laissez-faire and devil-take-the-hindmost.

OPEN FIELD. Unenclosed, undivided (hence, champion) arable land. A method of village farming by strips whose loss was lamented. Oliver Goldsmith or John Clare sang its praises. Survived into mid-twentieth century in Laxton parish, Northamptonshire.

PAN-AFRICAN. Pertaining to persons of African birth and descent (and therefore to all human beings, according to contemporary physical anthropology). A political movement of Caribbean and African anticolonial activists in the first half of the twentieth century.

PANNAGE. The feeding of swine in the forest; the right of pasturing pigs in the woods; pig's food or meat called mast, consisting of acorns, nuts, and the like. Thomas Spence edited a communist newspaper in the 1790s entitled *Pig's Meat* "to promote among the laboring part of mankind proper ideas of their situation, of their importance, and of their rights." It is thus historically one of the roots of modern Communist theory. In the cold war George Orwell in *Animal Farm* inverted the relation and made the pigs the privatizers.

PEER. Another term, like freeman, undergoing democratization over the centuries. It still retains its meaning as a member of the British nobility; a second modern meaning, and still subject to legal contention, is used in jury selection as a person of equal status, income, or ethnicity with the defendant in a trial.

PLOUGHBOTE. The wood that the tenant had a right to cut for making and repairing plows. Vehicle repair = mod. amp.

POLLARD. A tree that has been cut back or polled at some height above the ground, for the purpose of producing at that point young branches inaccessible to grazing animals.

PRIMITIVE COMMUNISM. At one time with Lewis Henry Morgan a term to describe clearly the simple technology and classless property relations of the Seneca people and later adopted by Frederick Engels and Karl Marx. Ideologically motivated opponents turned it into an academic put-down often with racialist overtones.

PRIVATIZATION. The policy or process of making private, as opposed to public, a commercial enterprise free of government control or regulation. The relinguishing of what belonged to all to the enjoyment , of a few and called enterprise. Iain Boal shows that in origin the word was related to "deprivation."

RUNDALE. Irish land tenure. Joint occupancy of land kept in small strips. It is also a verb, as land may be rundaled through different farms.

RUNRIG. A form of Scottish land tenure, and the act of making it, as in "lands were runrigged"; a ridge lying among others.

SATYAGRAHA. The philosophy of nonviolent resistance as propounded by Mohandas Gandhi. A Hindu word combining two others meaning truth + force. Martin Luther King Jr. rendered it as silent force or soul force. John Goines, *Concise Dictionary of Indian Philosophy: Sanskrit Terms Defined in English* (1989) gives two meanings for *satya,* absolute truthfulness and the golden age, one putting it in the future, the other in the mythic past.

SCOTALE. A forced contribution levied at an ale or festival where ale was drunk at the invitation of the lord of the manor or a forester. Stubbs in *Constitutional History* says "the nature of this exaction is very obscure. It was however levied by the sheriff for his own emolument." Merrie Englande?

SCUTAGE. A tax paid in lieu of military service; hence a means of avoiding war by the rich.

SIDEWALK. Path running parallel to the main road, the latter for wheeled vehicles and the former for pedestrians. Considered by Jane Jacobs to be the essence of urban civilization. Subject to intense political negotiation, foot by foot and inch by inch, at election time, during picketing and demonstrations.

SNAP WOOD. An 1813 *View of Agriculture in Hampshire* stated, "a claim . . . of taking what is called snap-wood, that is, all fallen branches or such as can be snapped off by hand."

STATUTE. Law or decree made by sovereign authority; an enactment made by legislature expressed in formal document; sometimes a modifier of something recognized by statute, such as a statute fair or annual gathering held in certain towns or villages for hiring agricultural servants.

STINT. A limitation or restriction; customary portion; allotted amount of cattle permitted to each portion of land. Cf. **drifts.**

SUBSISTENCE. This word has fallen from the metaphysical heights of Plato, where it referred to both all physical substance and the reality of the soul, to its medieval and modern meaning of means of support or livelihood, down to the minimum amount of food to sustain life; that which keeps body and soul together.

TURBARY. Land where turf or peat may be dug for fuel; the right to cut such peat or fuel, a right called barbarian by privatizers. Public fuel allotment = mod. amp.

USUFRUCT. Temporary possession, or use, of the advantages of another person's property.

VILLEIN. (The preferred spelling in a virtuous age.) A class of serfs or peasant occupiers, bondsmen who, according to the followers of Kett's Rebellion in 1549, were Christ's blood set free.

WASTE. Ravaged, injured uninhabited or wild (rhetorical). In legal use, a piece of land not in any individual's occupation but lying in common.

FURTHER READING

A goal of this book is to obtain new readers for old texts—primary sources—because they have been helpful in past emergencies. Robert Crowley, Hugh Latimore, John Lilburne, Gerrard Winstanley, Thomas Spence, Thomas Paine, Karl Marx, and William Morris are among these, and citations to them are found in the chapters of the book.

STARTING POINTS

Midnight Notes, *Auroras of the Zapatistas: Local and Global Struggles of the Fourth World War* (New York: Autonomedia, 2001) is a collective response from the United States to the Mexican insurgence. Maria Mies and Veronika Bennholdt-Thomsen, *The Subsistence Perspective: Beyond the Globalised Economy,* trans. Patrick Camiller, Marie Mies, and Gerd Wieh (New York: Zed Books, 1999) suggests a new world in the shell of the old. Eddie Yuen, Daniel Burton Rose, and George Katsiaficas, eds., *The Battle of Seattle: The New Challenge to Capitalist Globalization* (New York: Soft Skull Press, 2001), another collective effort, begins the story. Iain Boal et al., *Afflicted Powers: Capital and Spectacle in a New Age of War* (London: Verso, 2005), is a collectively written, analytic jere-miad. David McNally, *Another World Is Possible: Globalization and Anti-Capitalism* (Winnipeg: Arbeiter Ring, 2002) summarizes the anti-globalization movement. Other possible worlds must be constituted from contradictory forces, and C. Douglas Lummis, *Radical Democracy* (Ithaca: Cornell University Press, 1996), helps to explain how this may happen.

Christopher Hill, "The Norman Yoke," reprinted in his *Puritanism and Revolution* (New York: Schocken Books, 1958) is a marvelous study that parallels this one. C. George Caffentzis, "The Scottish Origin of 'Civilization,'" in *Enduring Western Civilization: The Construction of the Concept of Western Civilization and Its "Others,"* ed. Silvia Federici (Westport: Praeger, 1995) shows the ideological weakness of the stages theory of history and explains how privatization passes as civilization.

MEDIEVAL TIMES

Max Beer in *Social Struggles in the Middle Ages,* trans. H. J. Stenning (Boston: Small, Maynard, 1924) wrote "the metamorphosis of communal law into private property law . . . form the essence of the history of the middle ages." In legal history this theme is developed more in Victorian scholarship as in F. W. Maitland, *The Constitutional History of England* (Cambridge: Cambridge University Press, 1926); or William Stubbs, *The Constitutional History of England,* vol. 2 (Oxford: Clarendon Press, 1894) than subsequently until it was reprised and its gender aspect made clear in Silvia Federici, *Caliban and the Witch: Women, The Body, and Primitive Accumulation* (New York: Autonomedia, 2004). Anne Pallister, *Magna Carta: The Heritage of Liberty* (Oxford: Clarendon Press, 1971) is the clearest short introduction to the great charter, J. C. Holt, *Magna Carta,* 2nd ed. (Cambridge: Cambridge University Press, 1992) is the authoritative scholarly treatment; and William Sharp McKechnie, *Magna Carta: A Commentary on the Great Charter of King John* (Glasgow: J. Macklehose and Sons, 1914) remains the most practical for exegesis.

THE COUNTRYSIDE

Richard Mabey, *Flora Britannica* (London: Chatto and Windus, 1996) is an indispensable book for the naturalist and historian alike, being modest, thorough, and beautifully produced. Gareth Lovell Jones and Richard Mabey, *The Wildwood: In Search of Britain's Ancient Forests* (London: Aurum Press, 1993). Oliver Rackham, *The History of the Countryside* (London: J. M. Dent, 1986), is fascinating, essential, and scientific. J. C. Holt, *Robin Hood* (New York: Thames and Hudson, 1982) is both readable and reliable. C. S. and C. S. Orwin, *The Open Field* (Oxford: Oxford University Press, 1938) is the classic, hands-on study of surviving pre-enclosure agriculture. Raymond Williams, *The Country and the City* (New York: Oxford University Press, 1973) surveys with characteristic intelligence how the discipline of English literature treats the subject.

THE ENGLISH REVOLUTION

R. H. Tawney, *The Agrarian Problem in the Sixteenth-Century* (London: Longmans, 1912), is a grand and confident study of primitive accumulation. A companion study giving the urban side to the ruthless expropriation in the countryside is the hard-boiled crime studies in A. V. Judges, ed., *The Elizabethan Underworld: A Collection of Tudor and Early Stuart Tracts and Ballads* (London: Routledge, 1930). John U. Nef, *Industry and Government in France and England, 1540–1640* (Ithaca: Cornell University Press, 1957), is a short, clear comparative study; and Buchanan Sharp, *In Contempt of All Authority: Rural Artisans and Riot in the West of England, 1586–1660* (Berkeley: University of California Press, 1980) locates the forest disturbances in the economic structure. Pauline Gregg, *Free-born John: A Biography of John Lilburne* (London: George Harrap, 1961), describes this hero of democracy, and A. S. P. Woodhouse, ed., *Puritanism and Liberty* (Chicago: University of Chicago Press, 1951) assembles its primary sources.

ENGLISH SOCIAL HISTORY

Of the four late twentieth-century English schools of social history—Ruskin, Birmingham, Cambridge, and Warwick—this study has inevitably developed from that of Warwick with constitutionalism added. J. M. Neeson, *Commoners: Common Right, Enclosure and Social Change in England, 1700–1820* (New York: Cambridge University Press, 1993), written with a scholar's care and passion, should be the first book consulted. Two works of many from E. P. Thompson, "The Moral Economy of the English Crowd," in his *Customs in Common* (London: Merlin, 1991) and *The Making of the English Working Class* (New York: Vintage Books, 1963) remain classics. Robert Malcolmson and Stephanos Mastoris, *The English Pig: A History* (London: Hambledon, 2001), is a gem with several facets. Steve Hindle, " 'Not by bread only?' Common Right, Parish Relief, and Endowed Charity in a Forest Economy, c. 1600–1800," in *The Poor in England, 1700–1850: An Economy of Makeshifts,* ed. Steven King and Alannah Tomkins (Manchester: Manchester University Press, 2003). See also Steve Hindle, *The State and Social Change in Early Modern England, c. 1550–1640* (New York: St. Martin's, 2000); it is excellent. Chris Fisher, *Custom, Work and Market Capitalism: The Forest of Dean Colliers, 1788–1888* (London: Croom Helm, 1981) is brilliant, neat, and local. Peter Linebaugh, *The London Hanged,* 2nd ed. (London: Verso, 2003), describes the criminalization of commoning.

Bob Bushaway, *By Rite* (London: Junction Books, 1982) is a helpful survey of generations of folklore and social history of the British commoners. Peter King, "Customary Rights and Women's Earnings: The Importance of Gleaning to the Rural Labouring Poor," *Economic History Review,* 2nd s, 44, no. 3 (1991); and Jane Humphries, "Enclosures, Common Rights, and Women: The Proletarianization of Families in the Late Eighteenth and Early Nineteenth Centuries," *Journal of Economic History* 50, no. 1 (March 1990) help to give historical depth to the association of women with the commons.

THE ATLANTIC

E. P. Thompson, *Whigs and Hunters: The Origin of the Waltham Black Act* (New York: Pantheon, 1975) can be read with Marcus Rediker, *Villains of All Nations: Atlantic Pirates in the Golden Age* (Boston: Beacon Press, 2004). While Olaudah Equiano's autobiography has been well served with a modern edition, it is one of the peculiarities of English scholarship that there is no modern biography of Granville Sharp, although Peter Fryer, *Staying Power: The History of Black People in Britain* (London: Pluto, 1984) and Adam Hochschild, *Bury the Chains: Prophets and Rebels in the Fight to Free an Empire's Slaves* (Boston: Houghton Mifflin, 2005) are both essential for clear thinking on the abolitionist. Peter Linebaugh and Marcus Rediker, *The Many-Headed Hydra* (Beacon: Boston, 2000) provide an Atlantic history "from below." Thomas Clarkson, *History of the Rise, Progress, and Accomplishment of the Abolition of the African Slave Trade by the British Parliament* (London: Longman, Hurst, Rees, and Orme, 1808) helped to move a nation, while David Roediger, *The Wages of Whiteness: Race and the Making of the American Working Class* (New York: Verso, 1991) caused an important discussion. Carl Becker, *The Declaration of Independence* (New York: Knopf, 1942) writes of the philosophy of the declaration that it was "good old English doctrine," a view not much followed in Pauline Maier, *Scripture: Making of the Declaration of Independence* (New York: Knopf, 1997). James A. Epstein, *Radical Expression: Political Language, Ritual, and Symbol in England, 1790–1850* (New York: Oxford University Press, 1994) is the best of its kind.

INDIA

Vandana Shiva, *Staying Alive: Women, Ecology, and Development* (London: Zed, 1989) helped to start an international debate; and Arundhati Roy, *The Cost of Living* (New York: Modern Library, 1999), raised an international voice. Mike Davis, *Late Victorian Holocausts: El Niño Famines and the Making of the Third World* (London: Verso, 2001) is erudite, vertiginous, and makes essential and complementary reading with Madhav Gadgil and Ramachandra Guha, *This Fissured Land: An Ecological History of India* (Berkeley: University of California Press, 1993) which avoids the famines. Ajay Skaria, *Hybrid Histories: Forests, Frontiers and Wildness in Western India* (Delhi: Oxford University Press, 1999) and Sumit Sarkar, "Primitive Rebellion and Modern Nationalism: A Note on Forest Satyagraha in the Non-Cooperation and Civil Disobedience Movements," in his *Critique of Colonial India* (Calcutta: Papyrus, 1985) have been crucial. Ross A. Slotten, *The Heretic in Darwin's Court: The Life of Alfred Russel Wallace* (New York: Columbia University Press, 2004) raises the problem of the relation between evolution and commoning.

AMERICA

There are some special books written for the general reader that bring together many of the themes of this book. John Hanson Mitchell, *Trespassing: An Inquiry into the Private Ownership of Land* (Reading, MA: Perseus Books, 1998) is one of these. Daniel Worster, *Rivers of Empire: Water, Aridity, and the Growth of the American West* (New York: Pantheon Books, 1985); Rebecca Solnit, *River of Shadows: Eadweard Muybridge and the Technological Wild West* (New York: Viking, 2003); and Karl Jacoby, *Crimes Against Nature: Squatters, Poachers, Thieves and the Hidden History of American Conservatism* (Berkeley: University of California Press, 2001) tell important stories of commoning and ecology. Urban lineaments of commoning can be found in Jane Jacobs, *The Death and Life of Great American Cities* (New York: Random House, 1961).

On the Supreme Court: Robert G. McCloskey, *The American Supreme Court* (Chicago: University of Chicago Press, 1960); Eric Foner, *Reconstruction: America's Unfinished Revolution, 1863–1877* (New York: Harper and Row, 1988); Bernard Schwartz, *A History of the Supreme Court* (NY: Oxford University Press, 1993); Joyce Kornbluh, ed., *Rebel Voices: An I.W.W. Anthology* (Ann Arbor: University of Michigan Press, 1964); and David Montgomery, *Workers' Control in America* (New

York: Cambridge University Press, 1979) are foundational. Saul Alinsky, *John L. Lewis: An Unauthorized Biography* (New York, 1949); Paul Avrich, *Sacco and Vanzetti: The Anarchist Background* (Princeton: Princeton University Press, 1991); and Christopher Tomlins, *The State and the Unions: Labor Relations, Law, and the Organized Labor Movement in America, 1880–1960* (New York: Cambridge University Press, 1985) are good books.

The third volume of the autobiography of Roxanne Dunbar-Ortiz called *Blood on the Border: A Memoir of the Contra War* (Cambridge, MA: South End Press, 2005) expresses the continuity of the struggle for indigenous rights in the twentieth century. See also her *Roots of Resistance: Land Tenure in New Mexico, 1680–1980* (Los Angeles: American Indian Studies Center, UCLA, 1980). Philip J. Deloria, *Playing Indian* (New Haven: Yale University Press, 1998) explains the representations.

In African American history three books have been especially helpful, namely, Julie Saville, *The Work of Reconstruction: From Slave to Wage Laborer in South Carolina, 1860–1870* (New York: Cambridge University Press, 1994); Penny Von Eschen, *Race against Empire: Black Americans and Anticolonialism, 1937–1957* (Ithaca: Cornell University Press, 1997); and Barbara Ransby, *Ella Baker and the Black Freedom Movement: A Radical Democratic Vision* (Chapel Hill: University of North Carolina Press, 2003).

Linda K. Kerber, *No Constitutional Right to Be Ladies: Women and the Obligations of Citizenship* (New York: Hill and Wang, 1998) and Linda Gordon, *Pitied but not Entitled: Single Mothers and the History of Welfare 1890–1935* (New York: Free Press, 1994) are indispensable introductions to American women's history.

MISCELLANEOUS

Lord Eversley, *Commons, Forests, and Footpaths,* rev. ed. (New York: Cassell, 1910) domesticates, as it were, the Victorian struggle for the commons. Susanna Hecht and Alexander Cockburn, *The Fate of the Forest: Developers, Destroyers and Defenders of the Amazon* (London:

Verso, 1989), anticipates subsequent themes. Petr Kropotkin, *The Great French Revolution,* trans. N. F. Dryhurst (1909; New York: Schocken Books, 1971), is a justly celebrated narrative unafraid of communism or the commons. Albert Boime, *Art and the French Commune: Imagining Paris after War and Revolution* (Princeton: Princeton University Press, 1995) looks at the crimes underneath the impressions of the Impressionists. Henry Miller, *The Air-Conditioned Nightmare* (1945; New York: New Directions, 1970) is seminal. Walter Carruthers Sellar and Robert Julian Yeatman, *1066 and All That: A Memorable History of England* (New York: E. P. Dutton, 1931) is full of laughs; and Mary Poovey, *A History of the Modern Fact* (Chicago: University of Chicago Press, 1998) is full of pondering: in their different ways they explore the relation between "expertise" and the enclosure of the mind.

INDEX

Page references in italics refer to illustrations

Text: 11/15 Granjon
Compositor: Binghamton Valley Composition
Indexer: Roberta Engleman
Printer and Binder: Maple-Vail Manufacturing Group